RELIGION AND

SUSTAINABILITY

宝库山精选：宗教与可持续性

Digital editions
Religion and Sustainability is available through most major ebook and database services (please check with them for pricing).

For information, contact:
Berkshire Publishing Group LLC
122 Castle Street
Great Barrington, Massachusetts 01230-1506, USA
www.berkshirepublishing.com
Printed in the United States of America

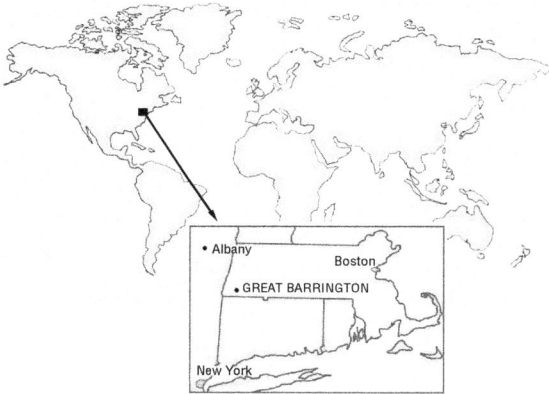

Library of Congress Cataloging-in-Publication Data

Religion and sustainability / editor Willis Jenkins; assistant editor Whitney Bauman. — 1
    pages cm
Includes bibliographical references and index.
    ISBN 978-1-61472-956-3 (pbk. : alk. paper) — ISBN 978-1-61472-928-0 (hardcover : alk. paper) —
    ISBN 978-1-61472-957-0 (ebook)
    1. Human ecology—Religious aspects.   2. Religions.   I. Jenkins, Willis.
    BL65.E36R447 2016
    201'.77—dc23   2016042338

BERKSHIRE 宝库山

Essentials

RELIGION AND SUSTAINABILITY

宝库山精选：宗教与可持续性

Editor Willis Jenkins, *Assistant Editor* Whitney Bauman

BERKSHIRE
A global point of reference

About *Religion and Sustainability*

Bringing together in one volume Berkshire Publishing's network of environmental scholars, religion scholars, environmental ethicists, and naturalists, *Religion and Sustainability* explores the ties between humans and their environment across a wide range of perspectives: from Buddhism, Bahá'í, Hinduism, and Daoism to Christianity, Judaism, and Islam, as well as those of indigenous traditions around the world. The volume examines major theories in philosophy and environmental ethics, such as the concepts of deep ecology, theocentrism versus anthropocentrism (i.e., is God or humankind the center of the world), and the occasionally conflicting (but often harmonious) roles of science and religion in relation to the world's environment. Other articles outline the various goals of sustainability: ecological integrity, economic health, human dignity, and social justice.

THE **BERKSHIRE** *Essentials* SERIES

Berkshire Sustainability Essentials, distilled from the *Berkshire Encyclopedia of Sustainability*, take a global approach to environmental law, energy, business strategies and management, industrial ecology, and religion, among other topics.

- Business Strategies and Management for Sustainability
- Energy Industries and Sustainability
- Finance and Investment for Sustainability
- Ecosystem Services for Sustainability
- Environmental Law and Sustainability
- Finance and Investment for Sustainability
- Industrial Ecology and Sustainability

Distilled for
the classroom
from Berkshire's
award-winning
encyclopedias

BERKSHIRE ESSENTIALS from the *Berkshire Encyclopedia of China* and the *Berkshire Encyclopedia of World History, 2nd Edition* also available.

Contents

Core Concepts & Practices

Indigenous Traditions

World Religions & Spiritual Movements

About Berkshire Essentials

For more than a decade, Berkshire Publishing has collaborated with a worldwide network of scholars and editors to produce award-winning academic resources on popular subjects for a discerning audience. The "Berkshire Essentials" series are collections of concentrated content, inspired by requests from teachers, curriculum planners, and professors who praise the encyclopedic approach of Berkshire's reference works, but who still crave single volumes for course use.

Each Essentials series draws from Berkshire publications on a big topic—world history, Chinese studies, and environmental sustainability, for instance—to provide thematic volumes that can be purchased alone, in any combination, or as a set. Teachers will find the insightful articles indispensable for stimulating classroom discussion or independent study. Students, professionals, and general readers all will find the articles invaluable when exploring a line of research or an abiding interest.

These affordable books are available in paperback as well as ebook formats for convenient reading on mobile devices.

Preface: Writing about the Divine with Gendered Language

Referring to God is always a perilous linguistic activity—some monotheistic traditions in fact make that peril a key point. In a volume covering many vocabularies of the divine, mundane functions of language—like pronouns—can carry unwanted ideological baggage. They can make it seem like God is a man, *one English-speaking man* no less, which can raise objections for all sorts of reasons. In interfaith context, our language can lead us not only into gender trouble but number trouble.

Some scholars still use masculine pronouns as the default neutral, but for many readers that can make it seem as if the writing is emphasizing a masculine image of God. Other scholars might alternate between masculine pronouns in one paragraph and feminine ones in the next. Some even experiment with "hir" and "ze" as hybrids of his/her and she/he. In our view such contrivances start to trip up the reader, but they do show that talk about the divine stresses language, especially when cultural systems are under criticism for their complicity in sexism. Acknowledging what can be called a sexist patrimony (!) of language, many scholars use feminine pronouns as the default, in order to interrupt the dominant gendered images they produce. We may not have any gender-appropriate language for God.

So in this volume we have encouraged authors to avoid using pronouns altogether. The effect can be clunky, for example, in a sentence like "God's got the whole world in God's hands," but one can take theological consolation in that it *should* be a little awkward to try to talk about the divine.

Beyond that encouragement, however, we have let the authors' prose stand as it appears, assuming that they are representing their tradition or subject with their language use. The divine in a tradition may be plural, immanent, transcendent, nonpersonal, specifically male, specifically female, androgynous, or any combination of those. Authors use the names and pronouns they think most appropriate to their topic or tradition.

WILLIS JENKINS
Editor, The Spirit of Sustainability

Introduction: World Religions and Ecology

The complexity and depth of sustainability challenges require familiarity with the religious, spiritual, and moral inheritances that shape how cultures interpret and respond to their problems. This compact collection of articles by leading scholars helps readers identify and begin to explore the moral dimensions of sustainability, introducing key concepts, major traditions, and significant practices. Thinking about sustainability involves paradoxical depths: merely prudential questions about sustaining conditions for a decent human survival raise foundational questions about what is worth sustaining and why. Answering those questions involves the many different worlds through which we interpret humanity's purposes on Earth. We inhabit many moral worlds; can we learn to inhabit one shared planet?

This convenient reader explores the ties between humans and their environment across a wide range of perspectives: from Hinduism, Buddhism, and Daoism to Judaism, Christianity, and Islam, as well as those of indigenous traditions around the world. The volume introduces concepts such as deep ecology and fundamentalism and practices like pilgrimage and meditation; it explains the tensions between theocentrism, ecocentrism, and anthropocentrism (i.e., where lies the moral center of the world?); and it treats questions about the various roles for science and religion in shaping humanity's inhabitation of the planet.

A number of articles charge us with examining received notions of sustainability, or ask us to consider how sustainability challenges received notions of other social goals. The root concept of sustainability refers to the ability of an activity to endure without undermining the conditions on which it depends. A related series of ecological and social problems—like biodiversity loss, demographic instability, toxic pollution, and climate change—indicate that the human endeavor may be undermining the conditions of its own endurance. Even a modest prudence suggests that we ask why, and what must be done to change things.

Sustainability is not deployed in this volume as a defined principle, then; it represents a series of questions, asking cultures to consider the prospects for the survival of the human species, and raising issues about the value of nonhuman life forms, the goals of economies, the form of humanity's presence on Earth, and the kind of futures we want to make possible. As we begin to consider what we should sustain, we are eventually forced to reflect on what sustains us. On what do human cultures and economies depend? How do human and ecological systems relate? What are the conditions for the human spirit? Ethical frameworks and religious traditions can help foster civic debate about problems that call into question the trajectory of our economic, political, and technological systems.

Confronting those questions requires not only ecological thinking but practical deliberations over such issues as the economic common good amid global poverty, a stable international peace in the face of nuclear weapons, public health despite new anthropogenic risks, and social justice in fairness to future generations. Not only must we know how religious and spiritual traditions think about their environments, or how nature provokes spirituality, but how we can meet the integrative, comprehensive challenges of sustainability with the civic and moral resources available to us.

It should also be noted that volume 1 of the *Berkshire Encyclopedia of Sustainability*, from which this selection comes, is a more comprehensive resource, and many topics included in this reader are expanded on in other volumes of the *Encyclopedia of Sustainability*. The editors hope, however, that this compact collection of essential topics will provide much food for thought and lay a foundation for future exploration.

WILLIS JENKINS
Associate Professor of Religion, Ethics, and Environment
University of Virginia

Core Concepts
& Practices

God

The Western perception of God's transcendence has implications for human action in promoting a sustainable world. Faith that God will sustain the Earth may limit human will to advance sustainability; conviction that all value exists in God may lead to a devaluation of creation; and attempts to know the world as God does, without self-interest, may result in an uncritical approach to future planning.

In most Western religions and for many Western philosophers, God is typically understood to be the transcendent reality that exists in relationship to the created order as being "other." These religions (and most of these philosophers) have traditionally represented the main issue of concern vis-à-vis God to be humanity's relationship with the divine, with the rest of the cosmos playing a decidedly secondary role.

The two sentences above point to some difficulties and contradictions. As seen from the first sentence, it is very hard, if not impossible, to define "God" without reference to what God is understood to stand for or against, and without mentioning that to which God is supposed to relate. Thus one decisive characteristic of God is that God, being wholly other and not "here" in some locally constraining way, is *not creation*. Yet God is also understood to have some relationship with creation, typically one of governance over it. As for the second sentence, the priority of the God–humanity relationship means that, in general, persons have tended to want to organize their existence around God, perhaps downplaying the importance of their relationship to the rest of the cosmos.

The concept of God's transcendence poses some complications for practicing sustainability ethics. On one hand, God's existence above and apart from the material world may bolster the ambitions of those who purport to have a "God's eye view" of the nature of reality, a view that is legitimated by its radical escape from parochial perspectives. In this way conceptions of God often function to reinforce our confidence in our apprehension of reality. Perhaps this is necessary for genuine objectivity, and insofar as we seek a knowledge untainted by narrow self-interest, it is well and good. But at times a provisional understanding of the world (e.g., its meaning, significance, and direction) may be elevated to an ultimate view. The self then sprints to facilitate the unfolding of the world and its future, drawing exuberant confidence from its ability to know the world as a transcendent (and omniscient) God knows the self. When confronted with questions about sustainability, this confidence may uncritically hasten provisional plans and pridefully exalt one's ability to advance history. Epistemologically, then, "God" may symbolize both the human intellect's most noble ambitions and one of its most dangerous predilections.

On the other hand, God's transcendence can also produce in believers a sense that the true value of the created order is wholly derivative from elsewhere, and thus has no genuine value in itself. In short, that is, all real value exists "altogether elsewhere," namely, in God. Those who come to believe this may well be tempted toward a thoroughgoing instrumentalization of the world, in which everything in the world is valuable only insofar as it is of use for us and our own projects, projects which may be decidedly "otherworldly" in their aims. So God can provoke in us a hyperactive structural hostility to the givens of nature and creation.

Alternatively, such believers may be tempted toward an attitude of quietist escapism from the world, whereby all worldly things are seen merely as impediments to our true end, which is fundamentally elsewhere. Since, on this view, God as creator and governor is master of creation, the narrative of history should feature God as the prime actor and agent. When confronted with questions of sustainability, one's relatively diminutive capacity to act should not be inordinately elevated. God will direct the course of history, sustaining the world until it comes to its close. When one meets the intermediate questions of sustainability, the most fitting response may be for one to wait for God's answer, thus perhaps too hastily surrendering the capacities to sustain that one may have. Ethically, then, "God" may present deep and profound challenges to any moral system of sustainability.

For all this, however, God is not simply a difficulty to be overcome. Indeed, the basic concerns about sustainability have come to grip many believers who affirm a transcendent deity. To strengthen and broaden these convictions, "God" should probably be understood in a way that implies divine responsibility for the world without also implying exclusive (i.e., humanity-paralyzing) agency for directing the course and setting the end of history.

Many other theological avenues may provide one understanding of God sufficient to elicit the need to take up sustainability questions, as well as the responsibility necessary to answer them well. But for many, the understanding of a transcendent God will be a temptation toward provisional answers or will dull the need to provide any answer at all.

Charles MATHEWES
Chad WAYNER
University of Virginia

FURTHER READING

Bouma-Prediger, Steven. (1995). *The greening of theology: The ecological models of Rosemary Radford Ruether, Joseph Sittler, and Jürgen Moltmann*. American Academy of Religion Academy Series. Atlanta: Scholars Press.
Jenkins, Willis. (2008). *Ecologies of grace*. New York: Oxford University Press.
McFague, Sallie. (1987). *Models of God: Theology for an ecological, nuclear age*. Philadelphia: Fortress Press.
Tanner, Kathryn. (2006). *God and creation in Christian theology*. Philadelphia: Fortress Press.

Sacrament

Early definitions of sacrament *and understandings of the immanence of the Creator expressed awareness of the presence of divinity in the natural world. Although Western Christianity later restricted the term to church-administered ritual, some Christians have returned to the view that all creation can be a natural sacrament. With traditions from other faiths and secular humanism, this spiritual consciousness promotes concrete conservation practices and Earth's sustainability.*

Sacrament, a concept with Christian origins, has broad contemporary significance for addressing issues of community well-being and environmental sustainability. In the Christian tradition, developing understandings and ritual expressions of distinct types of sacraments have had a significant impact on the ways that Christians relate to God, their Earth home, and each other. Over millennia, biblical understandings of divine encounters and of rituals that remember and renew them have led to diverse types of evolving sacramental consciousness. In the twenty-first century, sacraments have come to include, for some, not only church-based and clergy-led rituals: Earth, too is a sacrament when viewed as the original and still primary place of contact and communion with the sacred. Both natural and ecclesial sacraments then, can offer significant resources for spirituality to contribute to sustainability. This new understanding, important for Christian faith and for Earth's well-being, complements perspectives from other faith traditions and developing ideas from secular humanists. A shared ideology among these groups could catalyze collaborative conservation efforts, and significantly promote planetary sustainability.

Early Definitions

In Christian doctrine, the term *sacrament* has come, over millennia, to mean a religious ritual celebrated in a sacred structure rather than a transcendent experience in pristine nature. Theologically the earliest description of a sacrament was that of Augustine of Hippo (354–430), who had a strong sense of the presence of God in creation. Augustine defined sacraments as visible expressions of invisible grace, an understanding that allowed for a virtually limitless number and variety of mediations and experiences of the sacred in creation. The Latin Christian Church soon diminished Augustine's sacramental largesse and limited sacraments to seven church-defined and -administered rituals (baptism, confirmation, penance, holy communion, matrimony, holy orders, and anointing of the sick); Protestant reformers reduced these to baptism and communion. In Eastern Christianity, the celebration of the Divine Liturgy always retained a profound sense of the unity of religious ritual and divine creation, influenced by the thought of the monk, mystic, and martyr Maximus the Confessor (c. 580–662). Maximus described an ongoing dialogue of the divine Logos (Word) with the Logoi, the creating words of the divine that remain within each part of creation. Maximus described creation as a cloak worn by the creating Word (this imagery would be complemented in the twentieth century by Sallie McFague's metaphor of creation as the "body of God") and as the context and revelation of divine immanence.

Western Christianity's departure from Augustine's definition of sacrament stimulated a significant shift in understanding: no longer were both nature and

ritual regarded as bases for experiences of God. Personal sacred moments in nature, mediated by creation, were no longer regarded as sacramental experiences. These experiences were limited to community and individual participation in rituals, usually in a church building and mediated by clergy or their representatives. "Sacred space" now ordinarily meant the area of a building that people constructed and clergy consecrated, supplanting creation as the sacred place revelatory of and consecrated by divine presence.

Western Christianity briefly recovered the idea of creation as a sacrament in the thought of Hildegard of Bingen (1098–1179) and Francis of Assisi (1181/1182–1226). In words reflective of Maximus, Hildegard, a musician, pharmacologist, poet, writer, and mystic, described God in her *Book of Divine Works* as a fiery power who kindled every spark of life and permeated everything in creation; people, through faith, can see God in creation and creatures. The itinerant monk and mystic Francis of Assisi, in his *Canticle of Creation*, celebrated inanimate creation in words and animate creation in music; he called upon all creation to praise God, in a poetic recognition of creation's sacramental revelation of God.

Creation as Sacrament

Biblical teachings and Christian theology eventually provided the bases for recovery of an earlier sacramental creation consciousness. Recognition of revelatory (but not sacramental) aspects of creation was noted in the *Catechism of the Catholic Church* (1997), which teaches that God speaks to people through visible creation. The *Catechism*, however, restricts sacraments to specific efficacious signs of grace instituted by Jesus and ritually administered by the Church. The U.S. Catholic bishops had gone further than this previously, in *Renewing the Earth* (1991), when they stated that people encounter the Creator in nature, and perceive a "sacramental universe," which presents visible signs of God's presence; this experience can stimulate people to care for their Earth home. Contemporary Catholic theologians express complementary ideas: Thomas Berry in *The Dream of the Earth* (1988) sees the natural world as a primary revelation of divine presence, and declares that species extinction is destructive of modes of that presence. Rosemary Ruether declares in *Gaia and God* (1992) that ecology informs ethics and spirituality that all things are interrelated and that species extinction is analogous to tearing out a page of the book of life. John Hart in *Sacramental Commons* (2006) states that the sacramental universe is localized in the *sacramental commons*, in which

revelatory places and moments enable people to experience the Spirit's presence, and to enhance their relationship with divine being and their concern for and commitment to conservation and community.

The renewed understanding that all creation can be a sacrament has profound theoretical and practical implications. In Earth as sacramental commons, spirituality and sustainability are integrated. As a natural sacrament, creation can be revelatory of God, a sign and symbol of divine immanence, and a visible expression of invisible divine solicitude when it is not polluted, when it is responsibly shared and used, and when it supports the evolving community of life in its Earth habitat. The elements of the ritual sacraments—bread; juice or wine—require pure, environmentally sustainable natural sacraments: organic wheat and grapes grown in clean soil with pure water. A consciousness of natural sacrament promotes sustainable conservation of sacramental Earth for present and future generations.

Biotic and abiotic sustainability in local and integrated planetary ecosystems has a greater likelihood of realization where similar perspectives are promoted by theists from diverse traditions and by secular humanists. Among theists, creation stories and other narratives about the presence of divine being or of a sacred Mother Earth contribute to planetary respect. Among secular humanists, the biologist Edward O. Wilson writes and speaks about saving "the creation," thereby sharing a term previously used primarily in biblical and other ancient religious traditions.

While "sacrament" is a specifically Christian term, then, the appreciation it expresses for creation's intrinsic value, the gratitude it implies for creation's instrumental value, and its profession of the presence of a creating Spirit are all complemented in some form by the understandings of others. The result is a shared regard for natural beauty, for all biota, and for human community; a recognition of all life's interrelated and interdependent need for Earth's natural goods ("resources"); promotion of ecojustice; and a renewed spiritual (however it is defined) sensibility. The growth of these values will promote the well-being of the human community, sustainably protect Earth's species, and conservatively use Earth's natural goods and places to create, overall, a sustainable Earth community.

John HART
Boston University

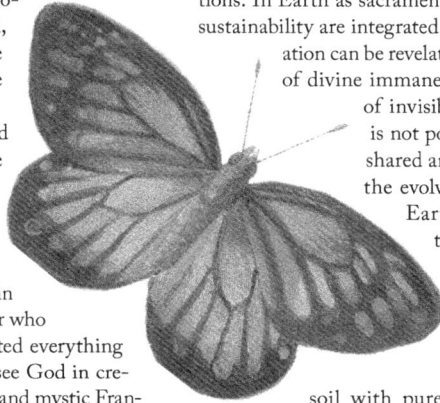

FURTHER READING

Armstrong, Regis J., OFM Cap.; Hellmann, J. A. Wayne, OFM Conv.; & Short, William J., OFM. (1999). *Francis of Assisi: The Saint.* Vol. 1 of *Francis of Assisi: Early Documents.* New York: New City Press.

Berry, Thomas M. (1988). *The dream of the earth.* San Francisco: Sierra Club Books.

Fortini, Arnaldo. (1981). *Francis of Assisi* (Helen Moak, Trans.). New York: Crossroad.

Hart, John. (2006). *Sacramental commons: Christian ecological ethics.* Lanham, MD: Rowman & Littlefield.

Hildegard of Bingen. (1987). *Hildegard of Bingen's book of divine works* (Matthew Fox, Ed.). Santa Fe, NM: Bear.

Louth, Andrew. (1996). *Maximus the Confessor.* London: Routledge.

Maximus. (1985). *Maximus confessor: Selected writings.* In George C. Berthold (Trans.), *Classics of Western Spirituality.* New York: Paulist Press.

McFague, Sallie. (1993). *The body of God: An ecological theology.* Minneapolis: Fortress Press.

Ruether, Rosemary Radford. (1992). *Gaia and God.* San Francisco: Harper.

U.S. Catholic Bishops. (1991). *Renewing the earth: An invitation to reflection and action on environment in light of Catholic social teaching.* Washington, DC: United States Catholic Conference.

U.S. Catholic Bishops. (1994). *Catechism of the Catholic Church.* Washington, DC: United States Catholic Conference.

Wilson, Edward O. (2006). *The creation: An appeal to save life on earth.* New York: Norton.

THE PATRON SAINT OF ECOLOGY'S "CANTICLE OF CREATION"

St. Francis of Assisi, born Francis Bernardone (1181/82–1226), is honored by the Catholic Church as the patron saint of animals and ecology; one of his most famous sermons was delivered to a flock of birds. A movement is afoot amongst Christians to bring back the celebration of nature as one of the sacraments. The following is St. Francis's "Canticle of Creation," sometimes referred to as the "Canticle of Brother Sun."

Most High, all-powerful, and all-good Lord,
> Praise, glory, honor,
> and all blessing
> are yours.

To you alone, Most High, they belong,
> although no one is worthy
> to say your name.

Praised be my Lord with all your creatures,
> especially my lord Brother Sun,
> through whom you give us day and light.

Beautiful he shines with great splendor:
> Most High, he bears your likeness.

Praised be my Lord, by Sister Moon and Stars:
> in the heavens you made them bright
> and precious and beautiful.

Praised be my Lord, by Brother Wind,
> and air and cloud
> and calm and all weather
> through which you sustain
> your creatures.

Praised be my Lord, by Sister Water,
> who is so helpful and humble
> and precious and pure.

Praised be my Lord, by Brother Fire,
> through whom you brighten the night:
> who is beautiful and playful
> and sinuous and strong.

Praised be my Lord, by our Sister Mother Earth,
> who sustains us and guides us,
> and provides varied fruits
> with colorful flowers and herbs.

Praised and
> blessed be you, my Lord,
> and gratitude and service be given to you
> with great humility.

Source: Francis of Assisi. (2006[1225]). Canticle of creation. In John Hart, *Sacramental Commons: Christian Ecological Ethics*, pp. 28–29. Lanham, MD: Rowman & Littlefield.

Sacred Texts

The impulse toward sustainable practices sometimes arises as a reaction to sacred texts, especially in religious communities where writings are the essential guideposts for belief and action.

Sacred texts are authoritative religious writings; in some religions, this might include thousands of individual texts. Writings such as the Bhagavad Gita and the Quran are called to mind when one thinks of sacred texts. Although these are paradigmatic examples, they do not show fully the diversity of what might be categorized as a "sacred text." These texts arouse devotion, aid in ritual activity, define beliefs, and enunciate moral codes. Some are assumed to be revealed by a god or divine messenger. Other texts are attributed to entirely human origins without any claim to supernatural revelation.

Interpreting Sacred Texts

When analyzing how sacred texts inform sustainability, it is important to recognize variations between and within religions. Classics of ecological literature (e.g., Gary Snyder's poetry) might serve as spiritual texts for certain new religious communities. More conservative branches of the "world religions," on the other hand, tend to look exclusively to a limited set of orthodox texts for guidance.

Once a sacred text is identified as authoritative, the question of hermeneutics (the interpretation of texts) emerges. One's hermeneutical approach helps to show how contemporary issues are related to sacred writings. "Sustainability" is a modern idea, whereas many sacred texts are hundreds or even thousands of years old. As a result, most sacred texts do not directly address the contemporary concept of sustainability. Because of this, some religious believers assert that environmentalism has no relevance to their spiritual identity, or that it must be expressed as subordinate to a traditional belief system. On the other hand, different adherents from these religions argue that scriptures strongly recommend sustainability. In each of these cases, religious communities are making significant choices on how to interpret their religious texts.

Sustainability in Sacred Texts

Assuming that sacred texts in fact are related to sustainability, what are some examples of how sacred texts can further discussions on the subject?

One way that sacred texts influence our understanding of sustainability is through the overarching worldview they present. For example, in Daoism, texts such as the *I Ching* propound a holism that emphasizes "action in inaction," or *wu wei*. Scholars see this holism and its emphasis on interdependence as similar to contemporary ecological perspectives. Hindu and Buddhist texts often stress *ahimsa*, or "non-harm" and reverence to all beings. *Ahimsa* might include the need for sustainability as essential. The theocentrism of some Christian, Islamic, and Jewish texts can be interpreted as mandating sustainable care as God's chosen stewards.

Sacred texts also present stories that enrich our understanding of the meaning of the world. For example, narratives might characterize the right relationship between creation, the sacred, and humanity. It is common for religions to emphasize the need for a cosmic harmony between humanity, the divine, and nature. The Rig Veda (one of the sacred texts of Hinduism) explores the interconnection between the divinity and the entire material world. This might imply the need to care for the divine through proper relationships with the world. Similarly, some (but not all) religions share creation stories in the pages of sacred books.

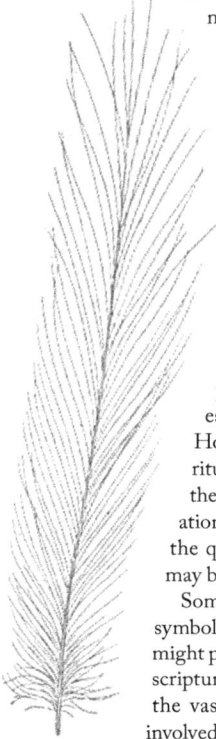

Creation narratives explain the origination, ordering, and purpose of the world. For many Jews, Christians, and Muslims, scripture argues that creation belongs to God. Narratives express the position of humans within God's ordered world, as is the case with the book of Genesis, which identifies humans as stewards of creation. Taken on the whole, religious texts might be ambivalent. Some texts show humans separated from and above nature; for example, humans are commanded to multiply and "subdue the earth" in Genesis. In contrast, groups such as the Hopi and other indigenous religions ritually pass on stories that emphasize the interconnection of the whole of creation (although this example brings up the question of whether oral narratives may be considered "texts").

Some interpret relevant metaphors and symbols as a way to show how sacred texts might promote sustainable practices. Many scriptures were written, for instance, when the vast majority of the population was involved in farming and lived "close to the land." The collapse of local stocks of resources through overuse, natural devastation, or neglect was calamitous. Therefore, religious texts sometimes use metaphors from farming, rural life, and resource gathering, and thereby point out specific responsibilities that humans have toward the land and animals in their care. For example, Jewish and Christian scriptures outline a Sabbath day for all of creation, including the land. Restrictions on harvesting and management are also aimed at just and equitable distribution of the farm fields and other lands. Similarly, some Muslims interpret the words of the Prophet Muhammad as advocating restrictions on the use of certain lands for the benefit of the whole community.

Challenges

Not all religious communities find justification for sustainable practices within their sacred texts, which leads to a problem: what is the relevance of these texts in light of contemporary environmental issues? A related question is, since many sacred texts have ritual and doctrinal uses, how might the use of sacred texts promote or hinder sustainability? The interpretation of sacred texts potentially holds great power in directing sustainability initiatives within many religious traditions, but only if guided by hermeneutical principles that focus on how sacred texts promote more or less "sustainable" attitudes and actions toward the rest of the natural world.

Forrest CLINGERMAN
Ohio Northern University

FURTHER READING

Chapple, Christopher K., & Tucker, Mary Evelyn. (Eds.). (2000). *Hinduism and ecology: The intersection of earth, sky, and water*. Cambridge, MA: Harvard University Press.

Cohen, Jeremy. (1989). *"Be fertile and increase, fill the earth and master it": The ancient and medieval career of a biblical text*. Ithaca, NY: Cornell University Press.

Habel, Norman C. (Ed.). (2000). *Readings from the perspective of the Earth* (*The Earth Bible Vol. 1*). Cleveland, OH: Pilgrim Press.

Kaza, Stephanie, & Kraft, Kenneth. (Eds.). (2000). *Dharma rain: Sources of Buddhist environmentalism*. Boston: Shambhala.

Miller, James; Wang, Richard G.; & Davis, Ned. (2001). What ecological themes are found in Daoist texts? In N. J. Girardot, James Miller, & Liu Xiaogan (Eds.), *Daoism and ecology: Ways within a cosmic landscape* (pp. 149–153). Cambridge, MA: Harvard University Press.

Özdemir, İbrahim. (2003). Toward an understanding of environmental ethics from a Qur'anic perspective. In Richard C. Foltz, Frederick M. Denny, & Azizan Baharuddin (Eds.), *Islam and ecology: A bestowed trust* (pp. 3–37). Cambridge, MA: Harvard University Press

Santmire, H. Paul. (1985). *The travail of nature: The ambiguous ecological promise of Christian theology*. Philadelphia: Fortress Press.

Suzuki, David, & Knudtson, Peter. (Eds.). (1993). *Wisdom of the elders: Sacred native stories of nature*. New York: Bantam Books.

Anthropocentrism

Controversies over sustainability often involve debate over whether and how anthropocentrism (human-centeredness) is appropriate. There are three major kinds of anthropocentric concepts: interest-based, epistemological, and cosomological. Each may be used differently for envisioning or debating the ethical obligations of sustainability.

Anthropocentrism means human-centeredness (from *anthropos* and *centrum*, a mixed Greek-Latin etymology). For many critics, ecological destruction traces to an anthropocentric moral logic—a failure to respect or care beyond the human world. Alternative views involve non-anthropocentric antonyms, like biocentrism, ecocentrism, or theocentrism. Others think that sustainability rather depends on an expanded, long-term or otherwise more satisfactory anthropocentrism.

Understanding debates over sustainability requires recognizing the various and sometimes conflicting conceptual uses of anthropocentrism. There are three major ways of understanding the claim that humanity lies at the center of the moral universe. Each can generate some kind of sustainability ethic, and each can resist nonanthropocentric alternatives.

Interest Anthropocentrism

First, in its most common sense, anthropocentrism designates ethical approaches that privilege human interests over the interests of nonhumans, including other organisms, other species, nature in general, and/or God. This may mean that *only* human interests count, or that among human and other-than-human interests, human interests are always the priority. The former view simply does not admit other-than-human interests as morally important; the latter view admits them but assigns them less significance than human interests.

Either claim can support an ethic of sustainability, perhaps even one with relatively strong commitments to ecological protection. It all depends on what counts as a genuine human interest. The botanist William H. Murdy writes that "our current ecological problems do not stem from an anthropocentric attitude per se, but from one too narrowly conceived" (Murdy 1975, 1172). From an ecological and long-term perspective, Murdy claims, a proper view of human interests must include protecting some degree of ecological integrity. This is sometimes called "weak anthropocentrism" to distinguish it from more exploitative views (see Bryan Norton's 2005 study *Sustainability: A Philosophy of Adaptive Ecosystem Management*). But the adjective "weak" misleads; this view might more accurately be described as a broadened or deepened sense of what objective human interests include.

Human interests, of course, extend beyond the minimum conditions for keeping the species alive; they are concerned with protecting the social, economic, and political conditions that sustain important cultural values. Valuing human dignity, for example, requires sustaining requisite environmental health, political freedom, and economic welfare. Valuing the experience of wilderness could justify preservationist environmental policies. A full account of human interest might therefore lead to measures protecting natural beauty, beloved animals, or symbolic landscapes; to precautions avoiding risks to cultural achievements; or maintenance of biodiversity for the sake of ongoing scientific exploration. Some even argue that human virtue, spirituality, or faith depends on intimate relations with the natural world, which makes sustaining the possibility of caring for the Earth a

fundamental human interest (see John O'Neill's 1993 work *Ecology, Policy, and Politics: Human Well-Being and the Natural World*).

In each case, an anthropocentric ethic of sustainability involves putting *indirect* value on sustaining other-than-human creatures or ecological processes by *directly* valuing the ongoing realization of human interests. Some account of the character and context of human interest then determines what sustainability means (see Norton 2005).

Epistemological Anthropocentrism

In a second major kind of conceptual use, anthropocentrism refers to the claim that moral values always originate in human subjects. Or, in other words, moral values are anthropogenic: They are generated from human experience. This is an epistemological anthropocentrism because it claims that the values of other-than-human entities never come from beyond the human world, or at least that humans have no way of knowing any such values. Values come not from nature or from God, but from valuing human subjects.

The nonanthropocentric alternative to this view would be a realist claim that some other-than-human entities generate value for themselves and that we can recognize the claim this value makes on our moral regard for them. The environmental ethicist Holmes Rolston argues for this kind of epistemological nonanthropocentrism, claiming that all living organisms generate value as they defend the natural goods of their kind. An ethicist like J. Baird Callicott takes the anthropocentric side, arguing that humans can and should take into account the interests of nonhuman organisms and systems, but that the moral values at stake in doing so are entirely a cultural product, made from human sentiment.

Observe, then, that an ethical view may refuse anthropocentrism in the first sense while accepting it in the second sense. For example, one might value all sentient life equally (nonanthropocentric in the first sense), while admitting that one's notions about the value of sentience arise from human experience (anthropocentric in the second sense). Or a sustainability ethic might make biodiversity a more important objective than any competing human interests (nonanthropocentric in the first sense), while justifying that commitment with cultural notions about the goods of diversity (anthropocentric in the second sense).

Cosmological Anthropocentrism

In its third major use, anthropocentrism refers to a cosmological view that the human is the symbolic center for understanding Earth's history and future. In this hermeneutic (interpretive) use the human figure shapes how we make sense of the Earth, evolutionary history, or the cosmos. Any view supposing that humanity marks the apex of evolution is anthropocentric in this third sense. A view may also suppose that some human quality, if not the species itself, represents the ultimate end of nature. Perhaps humanity's subjective consciousness, however imperfect, reveals the teleological trajectory of nonhuman processes. In that case, the evolutionary Earth tends toward self-conscious complexity, currently represented in the human. Humanity might then have a very small ecological role in the story of the universe and yet provide a crucial interpretive key for making Earth's past and future into an intelligible narrative.

This third use also characterizes some religious worldviews. It is found, for example, in the Eastern Orthodox Christian view of the human as a "microcosm" of creation and creation as a "macrocosm" of the human. Here humanity's liturgical capacity to gather all creatures together in creative praise provides the image of the Earth's unity and center. A nonanthropocentric alternative would include a Gaian view, in which the self-regulatory capacities of the living organism provide the paradigm for interpreting the Earth. Any other view in which some process, logic, or randomness unrelated to humanity provides the intelligible key for making sense of the universe would also be nonanthropocentric in this third sense.

Debates over sustainability sometimes confuse these three different uses of anthropocentrism, so it is important to discriminate carefully how the concept works in various contexts.

Willis JENKINS
Yale Divinity School

FURTHER READING

Callicott, J. Baird. (1999). *Beyond the land ethic: More essays in environmental philosophy*. New York: SUNY Press.

Murdy, William H. (1975). Anthropocentrism: A modern view. *Science*, 187, 4182: 1168–1172.

Norton, Bryan. (2005). *Sustainability: A philosophy of adaptive ecosystem management*. Chicago: University of Chicago Press.

O'Neill, John. (1993). *Ecology, policy, and politics: Human well-being and the natural world*. London: Routledge.

Rolston, Holmes, III. (1994). *Conserving natural value*. New York: Columbia University Press.

Ecocentrism

Ecocentrism refers to an ethical perspective that privileges the integrity, health, or functioning of ecological systems. It usually stands in contrast to anthropocentric (human-centered) perspectives. Biocentrism represents another nonanthropocentric perspective, but it differs from ecocentrism in that it focuses on life or the life community rather than ecological systems.

Like anthropocentrism, the concept of ecocentrism functions in several different ways. It can refer to a principle or hierarchy of value, as in an argument that asserts ecological integrity as the most important moral good or that considers ecological systems as the bearer of ultimate value. In contrast, a second, weaker ecocentric argument may hold that ecological systems bear significance as the most basic context for human thought and action, or for the realization of transcendent goods (such as beauty or complexity). Those human or transcendent goods might have greater value, but because they depend on ecological systems, those systems accrue a final or genetic value of their own. In that case, ecocentrism refers to a contextual framework for ethics.

In a third way, ecocentric arguments may ask humans to imaginatively occupy a nonhuman perspective as they consider some course of action. In this way, ecocentrism functions to consider a policy, problem, or situation from the perspective of another species or the Earth itself, or as a moment in an unfolding evolutionary narrative. In this third way, the ecocentric component may form one aspect of a broader ethical system.

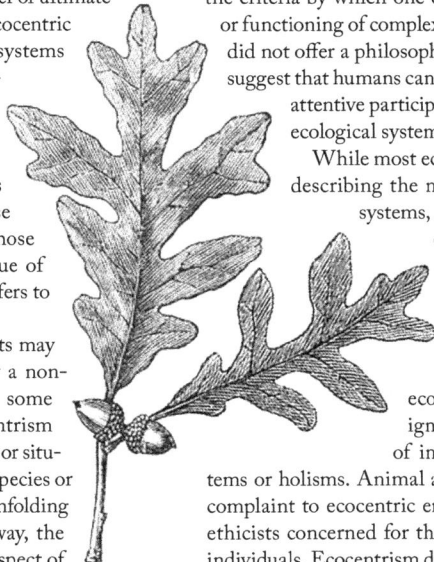

The author and environmentalist Aldo Leopold's "land ethic" is perhaps the greatest contribution to the formation of the ecocentric approach to ethics. Asking readers to include all the members and systems of the land in their sense of moral community, Leopold's *Sand County Almanac, and Sketches Here and There* includes all of the above functions: Sometimes he presents ecological systems and their creatures as bearing their own value, sometimes as valuable because of higher moral goods (beauty, integrity, and stability), and sometimes he asks readers to "think like a mountain." One of the great challenges to an ecocentric perspective is justifying nonanthropocentric knowledge, or the criteria by which one can assess the integrity, health, or functioning of complex evolutionary systems. Leopold did not offer a philosophical justification but seemed to suggest that humans can come into this wisdom through attentive participation in biotic communities and ecological systems.

While most ecocentric ethics usually focus on describing the moral importance of ecological systems, they must also resolve apparent conflicts between protecting or enhancing ecological systems and other moral values. Those who place moral value on individuals, whether human or nonhuman, worry that ecocentric approaches can lead to ignoring or suppressing the rights of individuals for the sake of systems or holisms. Animal advocates have pressed just this complaint to ecocentric environmental ethicists, as have ethicists concerned for the rights and dignity of human individuals. Ecocentrism does not necessarily suspend concern for individuals; animal rights and human rights may fit within an ecocentric approach so long as their protection accords with the healthy functioning of ecological systems.

Ecocentric perspectives may also be opposed by those who argue for a theocentric approach. A theocentric approach privileges the purposes, values, relations, or commands of God, as these are known by some religious traditions. Theocentric ethicists may worry that an ecocentric perspective places ultimate moral value on something other than God or divine law.

The same tension holds true for the relation between anthropocentric and theocentric approaches and is usually resolved by arguing that God's purposes align with the true purposes of humanity. Of course, ecocentric and theocentric perspectives could also converge in that way, as the Christian ethicist James Gustafson argues. Gustafson's *Ethics from a Theocentric Perspective* proposes that humans should relate to all things as they relate to God, which in Gustafson's system means that humans must respect ecological systems apart from any service they have for human benefit. When theocentric and ecocentric perspectives converge like that, it may produce moral attitudes of awe or reverence.

An ethicist might arrive at reverence from an ecocentric starting point as well. The environmental philosopher Holmes Rolston argues that an ecocentric ethic eventually leads one to reverence since it considers nature as a generative matrix of diverse values and as an unfolding evolutionary story. So perceived, nature teaches humans about their own marvelous contingency and complexity. As presented by the environmentalist Joanna Macy (1995), an ecocentric ethic may then begin to reconstruct anthropology, as it depicts selfhood according to its participation in the ecological systems upon which it depends.

Willis JENKINS
Yale Divinity School

Whitney BAUMAN
Florida International University

FURTHER READING

Callicott, J. Baird. (1999). *Beyond the land ethic: More essays in environmental philosophy.* Albany: State University of New York Press.

Gustafson, James. (1981). *Ethics from a theocentric perspective: Vol. 1. Theology and ethics.* Chicago: University of Chicago Press.

Leopold, Aldo. (1949). *A Sand County almanac, and sketches here and there.* New York: Oxford University Press.

Macy, Joanna. (1995). The ecological self: Postmodern ground for right action. In Mary Heather MacKinnon & Moni McIntyre (Eds.), *Readings in ecology and feminist theology* (pp. 259–269). Kansas City, MO: Sheed & Ward.

Rolston, Holmes, III. (2004). Caring for nature: From fact to value, from respect to reverence. *Zygon 39*(2), 277–302.

THINKING LIKE A MOUNTAIN

The pioneering U.S. environmentalist and writer Aldo Leopold (1887–1948) was perhaps the greatest contributor to the formation of the ecocentric, as opposed to the anthropocentric, approach to ethics. His 1949 book Sand County Almanac, and Sketches Here and There, *published posthumously and, on its fiftieth anniversay seemingly timeless in its message, begins with a rich depiction of life on his "farmed-out" land in central Wisconsin, expands to cover the natural beauty and rhythms of other locales, and culminates with a challenge for readers: to embrace his land ethic—or, as he writes elsewhere in the book, to "think like a mountain."*

The land ethic . . . enlarges the boundaries of the community to include soils, waters, plants, and animals, or collectively: the land.

This sounds simple: do we not already sing our love for and obligation to the land of the free and the home of the brave? Yes, but just what and whom do we love? Certainly not the soil, which we are sending helter-skelter downriver. Certainly not the waters, which we assume have no function except to turn turbines, float barges, and carry off sewage. Certainly not the plants, of which we exterminate whole communities without batting an eye. Certainly not the animals, of which we have already extirpated many of the largest and most beautiful species. A land ethic of course cannot prevent the alteration, management, and use of these 'resources,' but it does affirm their right to continued existence, and, at least in spots, their continued existence in a natural state.

In short, a land ethic changes the role of *Homo sapiens* from conqueror of the land-community to plain member and citizen of it. It implies respect for his fellow-members, and also respect for the community as such.

Source: Aldo Leopold. (1949). *A Sand County Almanac, and Sketches Here and There*, p. 204. New York: Oxford University Press.

Theocentrism

By positing that God is the center of all value, theocentrism sees the human and nonhuman equally, thus avoiding challenges to sustainability, such as anthropocentrism, arising in other approaches. But theocentrism can also be said to dismiss sustainability by asserting that God wants us to use whatever resources we find, even to the point of exhausting them, because God will provide other resources if necessary.

Theocentrism identifies God (Greek: *theos*) as the central basis for ethical value, existence, and/or knowledge. Thus, theocentric approaches to sustainability affirm that God is the foundation for any value and meaning that humans find in nature. Some advocates consider God to be the only thing to have true value, insofar as the entirety of creation belongs to God. All other entities have a relative value through their relationship to the divine.

As a concept, theocentrism often is compared with other positions that attempt to find the location of meaning or worth in nature. Some approaches define value in terms of a total system of the environment or all life (i.e., ecocentrism and biocentrism), while others concentrate on the human species or individuals (i.e., anthropocentrism and egocentrism). Although these other approaches are used in both religious and nonreligious contexts, theocentrism is explicitly religious in its outlook and often includes a critique of secular reasoning with regard to the environment. Often found in monotheistic religions (particularly within Christianity), theocentrism emphasizes theological and spiritual justifications as the basis for environmental ethics. For example, the Genesis narrative of creation repeatedly explains that "God saw that [what was created] was good." For Christians and Jews, this expression of value by God means that love for God leads to a respect for creation (humans and nonhumans alike).

One of the strengths of theocentric positions is that they offer a way beyond certain dichotomies sometimes found in discussions about sustainability. For example, by classifying all value as dependent upon theological concerns, theocentrism bypasses some controversies over the relationship between human culture and nonhuman nature. Theocentrism emphasizes the closeness of humanity with the rest of creation, rather than focusing on the differences. Likewise, theocentrism attempts to overcome the dilemma between present use and future needs. Because God is defined as both eternal and the center of value, theocentric approaches see God as an intermediary through which to balance the worth of humans and nature in the past, present, and future. Evaluations of future needs versus the current use of resources are dependent on how the divine has ordered or created the cosmos. Yet such benefits highlight the potential difficulties of theocentrism. Of greatest concern is the possibility of overemphasizing the spiritual at the expense of the physical world. Unless God somehow is anchored to the material world, theocentrism can result in a view that downplays the value of the material world in favor of the spiritual. In this case, God is conceptualized as creating the world simply for human and divine use. Sustainability can be dismissed by asserting that God wants us to use whatever resources we find, even to the point of exhausting them, because God will provide other resources if necessary.

Forrest CLINGERMAN
Ohio Northern University

FURTHER READING

Hoffman, Andrew J., & Sandelands, Lloyd E. (2005). Getting right with nature: Anthropocentrism, ecocentrism, and theocentrism. *Organization & Environment, 18*, 141–162.

Northcott, Michael S. (1996). The flowering of ecotheology. In Michael S. Northcott (Ed.), *The environment and Christian ethics* (pp. 124–163). Cambridge, U.K.: Cambridge University Press.

Fundamentalism

Fundamentalists adhere to foundational truth that is often grounded in literalist interpretations of sacred texts. Some religious fundamentalists may oppose environmentalism because it challenges God's supremacy or God's plan for the Earth, or because worldly care detracts from faith. Some combine anti-environmentalism with support for free-market capitalism. There are, however, fundamentalist groups whose cultural practices reflect ecological and social sustainability.

Fundamentalism is a term loaded with connotations, but it is basically used to describe groups that demand a strict adherence to a basic set of principles and are to some degree aggressive in their defense. The term is usually used in reference to religious groups, but sometimes it may describe nonreligious groups or social movements. There is no definitive type of fundamentalism that can be applied to all of the various manifestations of twentieth-century religious movements that respond to modernization (or the incursion of certain forms of Westernization), secularization (or the declining influence of religion and religious truth claims), and religious pluralism—all of which challenge the validity and hold of traditional religious forms in a wide variety of faiths. Fundamentalists see or perceive a threat to their way of life and their claims of foundational truth, which are often grounded in literalist or rigid readings of sacred texts or practices. Fundamentalist stances can be related to conservative or orthodox beliefs but exceed them both in the intensity or rigidity.

Because fundamentalist groups focus on defending the past and achieving a triumphant future, they often do not address contemporary concerns for sustainability, and they may be opposed to such movements. Because of the centrality of non-negotiable truth claims in their belief structures, fundamentalists are often less interested in any kind of interfaith or ecumenical cooperative work with those judged more liberal in their faith or with those who have allegiance to other ideologies. Since many religious efforts toward sustainability embrace interfaith efforts, fundamentalists within the Abrahamic, sacred-text-based religions—Judaism, Islam, and Christianity—are far less likely to be involved in such efforts.

Whereas fundamentalist groups reject some aspects of modernity and modernization, they are not entirely anti-modern, and they may adeptly use technological, financial, and political instruments of modernity. Their critique of the modern embrace of science and natural knowledge over religious revealed knowledge pertains to sustainability. Ironically, in their critique of modernization—its disenchantment of the world and resulting spiritual alienation, the dominance of an often destructive technological orientation, and the erasure of particularity—along with a nostalgia for a lost or threatened way of life, religious fundamentalists can appear to have common cause with what might be termed "green fundamentalism."

Great political differences color the relations between religious fundamentalists and religious environmentalists on many issues such as the family, the place of women, the role of the religion in the state, the economic system, or the truth claims of science and the need for environmental concern. Significant differences among religious fundamentalists in general in the rejection or embrace of the global economic market may also affect these views. Indeed, many Christian fundamentalists find more of a common cause with what might be termed a certain "market fundamentalism," in which neoclassical ways of organizing the economy are seen as almost sacred practices that cannot be changed in the face of the planetary demand for a more sustainable economy.

Yet even within any one religious tradition in any given locale, it is often hard to discern who might be termed fundamentalist, other than those who claim the term. For example, in Judaism, some would assert that the ultra-orthodox (Haredi) and the Lubavitch-Chabad Chassidim could be viewed as fundamentalist (although the attitude toward scripture is not the same as Christian literalism) and that many Orthodox Jews have fundamentalist views about science. But this becomes less clear in Israel, where the Heschel Center for Environmental Learning and Leadership works with "the ultra-religious, religious and secular" and where there is growing environmental concern within the Chabad. Similarly, what part of the spectrum of conservative Christianity in the United States is fundamentalist versus evangelical? The general public and media tend to confuse these terms; even scholars differ, and many scholars consider fundamentalism to be a subset of evangelicalism. Christian fundamentalists tend, however, to be more literal in their reading of scripture and more inclined toward a premillennial dispensational theology (the belief that Jesus will return before his one-thousand-year reign).

Like fundamentalists, most evangelicals tend to be political and social conservatives. Those referred to as the Christian Right in the United States are more fundamentalist than evangelical and often are not members of evangelical associations such as the National Association of Evangelicals (NAE). Although there has been a surge of interest and commitment to a variety of environmental issues among evangelicals, this is harder to find within the world of Christian fundamentalism, and what is there often aims to counter the influence of "green evangelicalism" and its embrace by high profile evangelical leaders such as the Reverends Joel Hunter, Tri Robinson, or Richard Cizik, the former vice president of governmental affairs for the National Association of Evangelicals.

Fundamentalist Views on Environmentalism and Evolution

Examples of Christian fundamentalist interest in environmental issues illustrate another viewpoint. One of the earliest fundamentalist/evangelical Christian voices on the environment was Francis Schaeffer, whose prescient voice was very influential on green evangelicals through his 1970 book *Pollution and the Death of Man*. Perhaps the most well-known Christian fundamentalist to champion an environmental cause is Pat Robertson with his 2006 "conversion" to accepting the reality of global warming, but that was not necessarily an embrace of larger sustainability issues. Other significant indicators of a shift within some sectors of the U.S. Christian fundamentalist world are the recent statements by leading Southern Baptists (but not the Southern

Baptist Convention) on the need to respond to global climate change, and the nascent greening of the Salvation Army (which may or may not be considered fundamentalist). Still, Christian fundamentalism strongly tends toward anti-environmental positions, sometimes vehemently so, and for a variety of reasons.

Religious fundamentalists may be wary of environmentalism as a new paganism or as a competing religion. In more fundamentalist Christian circles, it may even be associated with the Antichrist and a one-world government (as indicated by treaties such as Kyoto and other international governmental environmental efforts), all of which may be taken as signs of the end-times. Other reasons for the frequent anti-environmental stance of fundamentalists include the perception that the central task of most religious fundamentalists is the advancement and protection of the faith, from which too much care for this world, or for worldly things, detracts. Christian fundamentalists intensify this with an otherworldly focus, which can range from a primary regard for the rewards of salvation and the afterlife and/or heaven (and thus a disregard for this world) to a theology of imminent eschatology, or the end of this world and the return of Christ. If this world is going to end soon, then there is often no perceived need for environmental concern and, in fact, the environmental deterioration of the planet fits into some dramatic interpretations of the last book of the Christian scriptures, Revelation. Such views may be supported by a hard (as opposed to soft) interpretation of dominion in the book of Genesis. In this reading, the bounty and resources of the Earth were put here by God for human thriving and to help humans "be fruitful and multiply." To question either population growth or resource consumption out of concern for the sustainability of the planet, then, would doubt God's will and commands.

Furthermore, within the Abrahamic religions, the wide scientific conversation regarding evolution is seen by some as a direct challenge to the literalist readings of Genesis and of a creator God who directs all Earthly processes. Whereas this is especially true within Christianity, the embrace of creationism has a similar effect within Orthodox Judaism, especially within the ultra-Orthodox, where a major split has developed over whether the world is several thousands of years old rather than millions or billions of years old. Within Islam, for example, some parts of the Gulen movement in Turkey embrace creationism and work with creationists in the United States.

Views of the age of the Earth and how it came into being relate to fundamentalist understandings of the omnipotence of God and the uniqueness of humanity. To worry about something like the sustainability of the oceans or global warming may doubt that God is in charge and that God will right things according to a grand plan. Further, from a fundamentalist perspective, science often is accused of viewing humans as another animal (as opposed to being distinct from the rest of creation and in the image of God) by pointing out the biological similarities with other species and the biological underpinnings of our thoughts and actions (Acton 2007, 22). Due to these tensions with science, however, there is vehement opposition by some to the scientific consensus on global warming. It is, however, worth noting that fundamentalists do not reject all science, and often go out of their way to promote science that is seen to agree with their worldview, such as in their dispute with climate change science. (The "Global Warming Petition" of the Oregon Institute for Science and Medicine [www.oism.org/pproject], lists thousands of scientists who challenge climate change science, but who are often in unrelated fields or medicine or engineering, are high school biology teachers, or use fraudulent names.)

Religious Fundamentalism and Capitalism

Contrary to what one might expect from movements that respond to modernization, another central motivation of opposition to environmentalism within fundamentalist (and more moderate) Christians comes not from explicit religious and theological doctrines, but from their implicit belief in the supremacy of free-market capitalism, often viewed as a system that rewards those who are blessed by God. Critics point out that this "health and wealth" Gospel is seen by many to promote consumerism. For these religious and economic conservatives, anything that is seen to thwart the workings of the invisible hand of the market, as most regulation concerned with sustainability is viewed, is a threat (Acton 2007, 60 and 71–110). This view is also embraced by many Jews, such as the influential Rabbi Daniel Lapin, whose group, the American Alliance of Jews & Christians, lists "Environmental Stewardship Consistent with Free Markets and Property Rights" as one of its priorities on its website (www.rabbidaniellapin.com).

The Acton Institute for the Study of Religion and Liberty, and the related Interfaith Council on Environmental Stewardship (ICES), now the Cornwall Alliance, are prominent examples of the well funded, religiously based, free-market-oriented, counter-environmentalist "green" movement. These groups particularly take aim at the "green" evangelicals that make the headlines, such as the aforementioned Richard Cizik. They have clear ties with the "Wise Use" movement and its anti-environmental regulation agenda, as well as with well-known fundamentalist U.S. Christian-right activists such as James Dobson of Focus on the Family (FOF) and Donald Holdel, a past president of FOF who was secretary of energy and then secretary of the interior under former president Ronald

Reagan. Holdel is listed as one of the environment advisers of the "Effective Stewardship" video curriculum produced and distributed by Acton and the Cornwall Alliance. Publications and activist campaigns of these groups demonstrate the connection between a firm belief in free-market capitalism and a critical or dismissive stance toward many key sustainability issues: for instance, the booklet that accompanies the Effective Stewardship curriculum asserts that "the world is not experiencing overpopulation or destructive, manmade global warming or rampant species loss" (Acton 2007, 100). A central figure for these groups is E. Calvin Beisner, listed as the national spokesman for the Cornwall Alliance and author of *Where Garden Meets Wilderness: Evangelical Entry into the Environmental Debate*, which criticizes well-known green evangelicals such as Calvin DeWitt and the Evangelical Environmental Network. Among documents Beisner has written for the Cornwall Alliance that challenge key green evangelical documents is "The Cornwall Declaration" (2007) written in response to "The Evangelical Declaration on the Care of Creation." The Cornwall Declaration, sent to 37,000 religious leaders, affirms private property ownership and market economies, while the Evangelical Declaration (2000) promotes "lifestyle choices that express humility, forbearance, self-restraint, and frugality" and "godly, just, and sustainable choices." Another example of the contrast between the two groups is seen in an "open letter" to the signers of the Evangelical Climate Initiative's "Call to Action," arguing "against the extent, the significance, and perhaps the existence of the much touted scientific consensus on catastrophic, human-induced global warming" (An open letter 2009). In addition to being skeptical of anthropogenic climate change, the open letter also demonstrates the complex logic related to their clear allegiance to free-market capitalism: "we believe it is far wiser to promote economic growth, partly through keeping energy inexpensive, than to fight against potential global warming and thus slow economic growth. And there is a side benefit, too: wealthier societies are better able and more willing to spend to protect and improve the natural environment than poorer societies. Our policy, therefore, is better not only for humanity but also for the rest of the planet" (An open letter 2009). This quote illustrates how any "market fundamentalism" can hinder efforts to achieve sustainability or even to begin to understand what a sustainable economic system might look like.

Fundamentalist Groups and Sustainable Living

Skepticism and opposition to the idea that human actions create potentially disastrous climate change, as in the "We Get It" campaign's concern to protect the poor from environmental policies that "further oppress the poor" and prevent them from fulfilling "their God-given potential as producers and stewards" (The WeGetIt.org Declaration [n.d.]), are rallying points for more conservative Christian environmentalism. There is, however, a broader spectrum of conservative Christian sustainability activity that refrains from involvement in the heated debate over climate change. Many point to some Amish and Mennonites as examples of more sustainable living, although few would term them fundamentalists. Organizations that explicitly link addressing poverty and furthering sustainability around the globe include Floresta, which aims to educate, assist, and develop programs to combat the problems caused by deforestation in third world countries that have been, and Target Earth International, whose mission is to serve the Earth and serve the Poor." Both organizations work in the Caribbean and Central America. Within ultra-Orthodox and Orthodox Judaism, Rabbi Natan Slifkin, creator of the concept and organization Zoo Torah, develops programs to show conservative Jews in Israel the importance of all animals. (Slifkin's books were banned in 2005 by a coalition of about twenty prominent Haredi rabbis in Israel and the United States because he suggested that the Talmud needed to be read in light of scientific evidence over the age of the Earth.) There is growing concern for sustainability within the more moderate segments of Jewish Orthodoxy.

Many local Christian environmental movements in the developing world would fit much of the theological profile of fundamentalism such as the Association of African Earthkeeping Churches in Zimbabwe, whose members are primarily Zionists and Apostles, and the Baptist Brackenhurst Environmental Program in Kenya. Both of these organizations have worked to plant millions of trees and to establish more sustainable agricultural practices, while the Khanya Programme in South Africa emphasizes permaculture techniques. Although this article has focused on many of the U.S.-based, politically activist Christian fundamentalists who are the most ardent in opposing environmentalism and sustainability, there are many in the broad spectrum of fundamentalist belief across the globe who neither care for nor militate against sustainability. Others work on local sustainability issues but remain silent in the global debate. And many use cultural practices that are already far more sustainable than those of the United States.

Laurel D. KEARNS
Drew Theological School and University

FURTHER READINGS

Acton Institute. (2007). *Environmental stewardship in the Judeo-Christian tradition.* Grand Rapids, MI: Acton Institute.

An open letter to the signers of climate change: An evangelical call to action and others concerned about global warming. (2009). Retrieved June 2, 2009, from http://www.cornwallalliance.org/docs/an-open-letter-to-the-signers-of-climate-change-an-evangelical-call-to-action-and-others-concerned-about-global-warming.pdf

Beisner, E. Calvin. (1997). *Where garden meets wilderness: Evangelical entry into the environmental debate.* Acton Institute for the Study of Religion and Liberty. Grand Rapids, MI: W. B. Eerdmans.

Bliese, John R. E. (2002). *The greening of conservative America.* Boulder, CO: Westview End Press.

Beisner, E. Calvin. (2006, July 27). A call to truth, prudence, and the protection of the poor. Retrieved April 26, 2009, from http://erlc.com/article/a-call-to-truth-prudence-and-protection/

The Cornwall Declaration on Environmental Stewardship. (2007). In *Environmental stewardship in the Judeo-Christian Tradition* (pp. 7–11). Grand Rapids, MI: Acton Institute. (Also retrieved June 4, 2009, from http://www.cornwallalliance.org/articles/read/call-to-truth/)

Climate change: An evangelical call to action. (n.d.). Retrieved July 13, 2009, from http://christiansandclimate.org/learn/call-to-action/

Cromartie, Michael & Derr, Thomas Sieger. (1995) *Creation at risk? Religion, science, and environmentalism.* Wilmington, DE: ISI Books.

Daneel, Marthinus L. (2001). *African Earthkeepers: Wholistic interfaith mission.* Maryknoll, NY: Orbis Books.

Evangelical declaration on the care of Creation. (2000). In R. J. Berry (Ed.), *The Care of Creation: Focusing Concern and Action* (pp. 17–22). Downer's Grove, IL: Intervarsity Press. (Also retrieved June 4, 2009, from http://www.creationcare.org/resources/declaration.php)

Kearns, Laurel & Keller, Catherine. (Eds.). (2007). *EcoSpirit: Religions and philosophies for the Earth.* New York: Fordham Press.

Martin, Marty & Appleby, R. Scott. (Eds.). (1993–2004) *The fundamentalism project* (Vols. 1–5). Chicago: University of Chicago Press.

Peterson, Anna L. (2005). *Seeds of the kingdom: Utopian communities in the Americas.* New York: Oxford University Press.

Schaefer, Francis A. (1970). *Pollution and the death of man: The Christian view of ecology.* London: Hodder & Stoughton.

Slifkin, Natan. (2006). *The challenge of creation: Judaism's encounter with science, cosmology and evolution.* Brooklyn, NY: Yashar Books.

The WeGetIt.org Declaration. (n.d.). Retrieved June 4, 2009, from www.wegetit.org/declaration

Wright, Richard T. (1995, June). Tearing down the green: Environmental backlash in the Evangelical sub-culture. *Perspectives on Science and the Christian Faith 47,* 80–91. Retrieved June 4, 2009, from, http://www.asa3.org/aSA/PSCF/1995/PSCF6-95Wright.html

Eschatology

Doctrines regarding eschatology—beliefs about the "end-times"—have been accused of denigrating the Earth in preference for a future paradise. In actuality, however, eschatological texts and traditions are more complex than this accusation would suggest and have provided inspiration for both the support and the subversion of sustainability.

The term "eschatology" (from the Greek *eschata*, meaning "last things") refers to religious and philosophical doctrines concerning the ultimate fate of the cosmos and the collective destiny of humanity. Although speculation concerning the interim fate of individual souls after death may be included within an eschatological doctrine, it is the corporate destiny of the world that forms eschatology's primary theme.

Origins in Holy Texts

While most religions contain some speculation about the future of the cosmos, in many cases, these are "relative" eschatologies only, since no ultimate end of history is envisioned but only the relative end of one cosmic cycle followed by an endless repetition of successive cycles. In both Hinduism and Buddhism, for instance, cosmic epochs of growth and decay are said to come to a temporary end when the universe is annihilated. This annihilation is followed by a rebirth in which the epochal cycles of growth and decay begin again. In contrast, the Abrahamic religions (Judaism, Christianity, and Islam) present history as a linear progression in which the current age will come to a final end or edge (*eschaton*) beyond which something fundamentally new will occur.

Within Judaism, eschatological texts do not appear before the Second Temple period (536 BCE–70 CE). Biblical texts written during the First Temple period (1006–587 BCE) make no mention of an "end-time" and say very little about an afterlife. Heaven, within these texts, is the exclusive abode of God and His angelic retinue, not a reward for the righteous (Psalms 115:16). Two possible exceptions to human exclusion from heaven exist: Enoch, who is ambiguously "taken" by God (Genesis 5:24), and Elijah, who is unambiguously lifted up to heaven in a whirlwind (2 Kings 2:11). These exceptions, however, are not presented as models that can be emulated by others. On the contrary, the rest of humanity is said to share a common home after death (Job 3:11–19). Most frequently, this home is located in Sheol, a place beneath the ground, which is pictured as dark, gloomy, and disordered but not as a location of distinctive punishment (Genesis 3:19; Psalms 6:5; Job 10:20–22). Instead, reward and punishment are meted out during life and are connected with such embodied concerns as long life, possession of property, and successful procreation. Time upon Earth is presented as precious, and humanity is encouraged to enjoy and appreciate our brief sojourn upon the planet, for each of us has a limited span of days before we vanish (Job 14; Psalms 90:10–17).

During the Second Temple period, Israelites came under first Persian and then Hellenistic imperial influences. Persian Zoroastrianism envisioned an eschatological battle between cosmic forces of good and evil, ending in a planetary conflagration and a physical resurrection of the dead upon a transformed Earth. Greek Platonism rejected notions of resurrected flesh and instead insisted on the

immortality of the soul within the heavens. Over time, both of these ideas—separately and in various combinations—entered Jewish thought, perhaps because continuing foreign domination and domestic disappointments required the deferral of covenantal promises to a future date. Despite deferral to the end-time, however, these promises continued to be envisioned largely in Earthly terms, with their final fulfillment providing not only a renewal of the Jewish nation but also the material blessings of verdant pastures, abundant harvests, clean water teeming with fish, and justice between all people and among all creatures (Isaiah 11:3–9; Ezekiel 34:14, 27; 47:7–12).

Jesus' teachings on the Kingdom of God are consonant with other Jewish eschatological beliefs of the day, with perhaps a greater emphasis on the inauguration of the Kingdom within the present and its consummation in the immediate future. This sense of immediacy was reinforced when followers experienced their crucified Messiah as having been resurrected and raised to the right hand of God. This experience was interpreted by them as a signal that the *eschaton*, with its anticipated resurrection of the dead, had arrived—an arrival that they expected to be accompanied by a Second Coming (Parousia), the establishment of God's reign on Earth, a judgment on the living and the dead, an abolition of unjust social and political systems, and a renewal of the planet and its life-giving resources. As generations passed and the Parousia failed to occur, Christians changed their emphasis from an embodied resurrection upon a transformed Earth to a spiritual reward within heaven.

Islamic eschatology differs in specific details from Jewish and Christian variations, but there are broad similarities between the three arising out of cross-cultural fertilization during Islam's formative period. Similarities include an end-time appearance of a messianic figure, the resurrection of the dead, a final judgment, and the universal reign of God. In the Quran, eschatological fulfillment is pictured in physical but not in Earth-bound terms. The final reward is said to take place within an eternal Garden (al-Jannah) "the extensiveness of which is as the extensiveness of the heaven and the earth" (Surah 57:21). In the Garden, all the pleasures of Earth will be intensified and perfected, including cooling shade, flowing rivers, magnificent mansions, fine clothing and jewelry, banquets of fruit, fowl, and wine, and "pure" spouses of great beauty (Surah 18:30–31; 44:51–56; 56:1–38).

Modern Interpretations

In the current era, scholars have linked eschatological expectations with the ecological crisis. The historian Lynn White Jr., for instance, contended that "What people do about their ecology . . . is deeply conditioned by [religious] beliefs about our nature and destiny" (White 1968, 84). Whether our "destiny" is believed to be upon an Earthly paradise or within a heavenly paradise, Earth in its present form is devalued and rendered replaceable. This critique has sparked interest in recovering ecological wisdom within religious traditions. To date, however, sustained analysis of the specific eschatology-ecology connection has occurred predominantly within Christianity, perhaps because White identified Christian eschatology as the context within which the world-altering capabilities of modern science and technology arose. While many of the details of Christian analysis are inapplicable to other eschatological traditions, general assertions concerning the goodness of creation and the need for current human response in the face of future possibilities do occur elsewhere.

Within Christianity, attempts to negate ecologically destructive interpretations of eschatological doctrines have focused particularly on Jesus' conception of the Kingdom of God and on the Revelation of John (the final book of the New Testament). When analyzed using an ecological hermeneutic, Jesus' words and ministry can be seen to point toward a Kingdom characterized by natural verdancy, divine imminence, and human-divine-nonhuman reciprocity. For example, Jesus begins his ministry in the wilderness and repeatedly seeks divine connection, spiritual wisdom, and emotional comfort there (Matt. 4:1; Mark 6:31–32, 46; 9:2; Luke 9:28). He prays for God's reign to come to Earth and associates that reign with such mundane concerns as an adequate food supply and relief from indebtedness (Matt. 6:10–12). He assures his followers that God cares for both human and nonhuman creatures (Matt. 6:26a, 28b–29; 10:29; Luke 12:6, 24, 27); increases nature's abundance and restores its depleted resources (Matt. 14:16–21; Luke 5:4–6); uncovers the divine presence within corporeal matter (Mark 14:22–24); calls for peace between all creatures (Mark 4:37–39; 6:48–51; Luke 10:5); and reveals that his message is good news for the entirety of creation (Mark 16:15).

The Revelation of John provides a similar model of a just and relational future. Written within a generation of

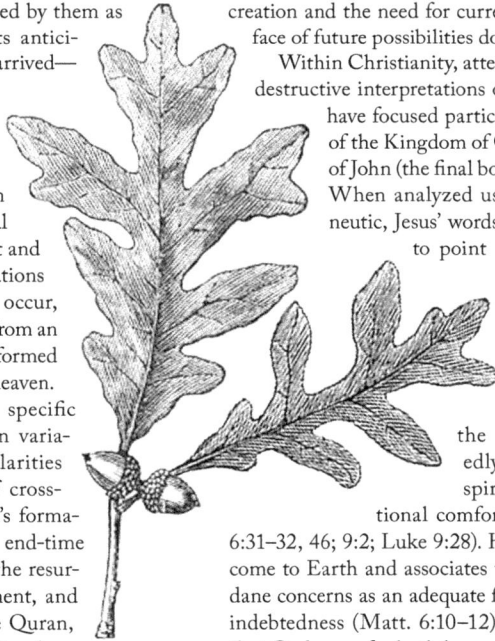

Rome's destruction of the Second Jerusalem Temple, the book juxtaposes the "already" of oppressive political and economic systems with the "not yet" of an equitable society. Imperialism and economic greed are portrayed as bringing about war, slavery, and hunger for the masses while preserving luxury items for the wealthy (Rev. 6:6; 18). The text predicts that these injustices will result in the pollution of fresh water, the decimation of ocean life, and the destruction of previously fertile land (8:7–11). These ecological catastrophes are portrayed as the result of human choices, not as the inalterable will of God, when the text proclaims that a time will come "for destroying those who destroy the earth" (11:18). In contrast to the toxicity of this "old" way, a "new" way is anticipated—coming into existence only after the establishment of human-nature collaboration and cooperation (12:6, 14, 16). Revelation ends with a hopeful vision of God making a home on Earth (21:2–3) and of redemption and renewal bringing about a fertile planet where even urban centers abound in green-space and are replete with life-giving waters (22:1–2).

Antonia GORMAN
Humane Society of the
United States

FURTHER READING

Cragg, Kenneth. (Ed. and Trans). (1991). *Readings in the Qur'ān*. London: Collins Religious Publishing.

Keller, Catherine. (1996). *Apocalypse now and then: A feminist guide to the end of the world*. Boston: Beacon Press.

Maier, Harry O. (2002). There's a new world coming! Reading the Apocalypse in the shadow of the Canadian Rockies. In Norman C. Habel & Vicky Balabanski (Eds.), *The Earth story in the New Testament: The Earth Bible, Vol. 5* (pp. 166–179). Cleveland, OH: The Pilgrim Press.

Rossing, Barbara R. (2002). Alas for Earth! Lament and resistance in Revelation 12. In Norman C. Habel & Vicky Balabanski (Eds.), *The Earth story in the New Testament: The Earth Bible, Vol. 5* (pp. 180–192). Cleveland, OH: The Pilgrim Press.

Rossing, Barbara R. (2000). River of life in God's New Jerusalem: An eschatological vision for Earth's future. In Dieter T. Hessel & Rosemary Radford Ruether (Eds.), *Christianity and ecology: Seeking the well-being of Earth and humans* (pp. 205–224). Cambridge, MA: Harvard University Press.

Rowland, Christopher. (1982). *The open heaven: A study of Apocalyptic in Judaism and early Christianity*. New York: Crossroad.

Segal, Alan F. (2004). *Life after death: A history of the afterlife in Western religion*. New York: Doubleday.

Werblowsky, R. J. Zwi. (1987). Eschatology: Asian religions. In Mircea Eliade (Ed.), *The encyclopedia of religion* (p. 149). New York: MacMillan.

White, Lynn, Jr. (1968). *Machina ex deo: Essays in the dynamism of Western culture*. Cambridge: The Massachusetts Institute of Technology Press.

Wright, J. Edward. (2000). *The early history of heaven*. New York: Oxford University Press.

Ecology, Deep

First used in 1973 by Norwegian philosopher Arne Naess, the term "deep ecology" refers to a fundamental shift in values, in contrast to the "shallow ecology" of policy reform. Naess pointed the way for people with divergent worldviews to be able to agree on principles leading to concrete environmental activism, but critics of the movement charge that by favoring nature over society its ability to bring about true sustainability is compromised.

Deep ecology is one of the most important contemporary approaches to environmental philosophy. The term was first used in print in the 1973 article "The Shallow and the Deep, Long-Range Ecology Movement" by Arne Naess (1912–2009), a Norwegian philosopher. For Naess, the "shallow ecology" of resource conservation and policy reform was insufficient to deal with our deep-seated environmental problems. What is needed for true sustainability is a fundamental change in the way we conceive of and value the natural world, a change that at least implicitly involves religious values and assumptions. As such, deep ecology is radical in its critique and idealist in its emphasis on worldview rather than social structures.

Meanings and Characteristics

The relationship between deep ecology, sustainability, and spirituality is quite complex, in part because of the various meanings and associations of the terms. There have been, for instance, at least five primary ways the term "deep ecology" has been used. The first is a profound inquiry into the beliefs and values concerning nonhuman nature and our ontological and ethical relationship

to it. No specific views are detailed in this inclusive definition; any thoroughgoing questioning into nature and the human relationship to it would be considered deep ecology. Because of the fundamental character of the questioning, spiritual ideas and values would usually be involved. A second, similarly inclusive meaning derives from the assumption that any such deep questioning will result in one form or another of a philosophy that affirms the profound value of nature, our intimate relationship with it, and our responsibility to it. In some ways, these philosophies can be quite different, such as ecofeminism and social ecology, but whatever the specific goals and practices identified, the ideal is a far more sustainable way of living with nature.

The third meaning of deep ecology is far more pragmatic: a platform of eight principles first articulated by Naess and George Sessions in 1984 (Devall and Sessions 1985). The principles include the intrinsic value of nature and the value of biodiversity; a recognition of the ongoing ruination of the planet; the need to reduce human exploitation of nature; a call for major changes in policy and a decrease in human population; an appreciation of quality of life over material standard of living; and the responsibility to embody these principles by working for personal and social change. The focus on sustainability here is obvious, but the spiritual dimension is implicit in the fact that Naess formulated the platform in part as a way for people with divergent worldviews and spiritual values related to nature to come to agreement on principles that will lead to action. Naess illustrated this with the "apron" diagram, in which a diversity of religious ideas and

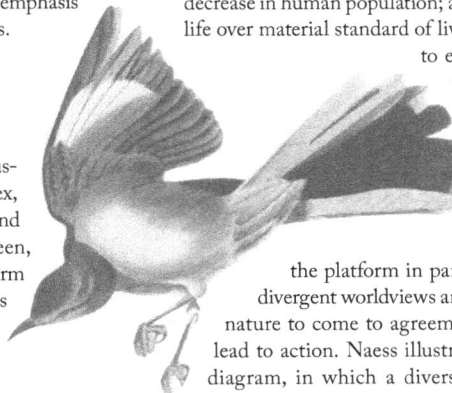

intuitions at the top can logically support the deep ecology platform, and the platform can logically lead to divergent lifestyles, policies, and actions.

The fourth meaning of deep ecology, probably the most common, is a nature-affirming worldview (called "ecosophy" by Naess) with specific qualities: (1) a holistic view of nature as an interrelated system; (2) the equal intrinsic value of all of nature, often termed "biocentric egalitarianism"; (3) a rejection of anthropocentrism, the human-centeredness that focuses value and attention on humans to the detriment of nature; (4) an affirmation that humans are fully a part of nature with no "ontological divide" or essential difference dividing humans from the natural world; (5) an identification of the individual with the larger natural world, with the person not an autonomous individual but rather a "self-in-Self," a distinct individual who is also fully integrated into the whole of nature, which is our greater Self; and (6) an intuitive communion with nature rather than rational ethical obligations resulting in a spontaneous sense of care for the planet's suffering ("I am the rainforest defending itself," said the deep ecologist John Seed [Devall and Sessions, 1985]). Such ecosophies usually diverge from other approaches such as ecofeminism and social ecology in key points (i.e., that lead, unfortunately, to sectarian squabbles).

Deep ecology sometimes refers to the on-the-ground movement to enact deep ecology principles and values, providing a fifth meaning for the term. Here the focus is on a radically different lifestyle (sometimes in the form of primitivism) or on radical environmental activism—both based on the third and fourth meanings noted in the paragraph above. In this instance, the most famous example is the Earth First! organization. Their goal is not only sustainability or preservation but also the return to a state that existed before humans massively degraded the environment. Usually an Earth-based spirituality informs this movement.

Interest in spiritual attitudes toward nature in other cultures has been a common characteristic of deep ecology, particularly in the last two meanings of ecosophy and radical activism. Buddhist, Daoist, and Native American cultures have been a source of insight into the "new/old" view of nature—suggesting that, while deep ecology is new in terms of Western thought, it draws on long held views in non-Western cultures.

Another key characteristic of deep ecology is its focus on wilderness. Because anthropocentrism is the principal source of human degradation of the natural world, the ideal is often seen as pristine nature untrammeled by human manipulation. Many deep ecologists have considered personal experience of wilderness to be a spiritual encounter that leads to self-in-Self realization through the biocentric identification with nature. The protection of wilderness has also been emphasized by deep ecology, echoing the preservationism of the naturalist John Muir (1838–1914).

Deep Ecology and Sustainability

Given its acute interest in wilderness, deep ecology is profoundly interested in sustainability. But the term *sustainability* is also complex, and to make the analysis of the relationship between deep ecology and sustainability more precise, several distinctions can be made. First, some forms of sustainability are reductive and exploitive, such as a forestry practice that creates a one-crop tree farm where all other vegetation is killed by herbicides until the trees are clear-cut and replanted. Other forms of sustainability are ecological, seeking to conform to nature's processes and complexities and constraints. Deep ecology clearly supports the latter definition of ecological sustainability and offers a comprehensive critique both of the worldview and of the effects of exploitive sustainability.

Second, sustainability can be anthropocentric or biocentric. Most policies aimed at sustainability are focused on the goal of conserving resources for future human generations. Deep ecology rejects such a perspective, calling for the biocentric sustainability of the entire community of life.

A third distinction concerns the range of focus. Sustainability can be limited to environmental issues, dealing only with the preserving the nonhuman natural world. On the other hand, it can be ecosocial, involving social and economic dimensions as well as environmental ones. This "triple bottom line" approach (environmental, social, and economic) is increasingly common, particularly in sustainable development policies, in part because it includes attention to human well-being.

Criticisms

Some deep ecologists might object to this ecosocial perspective because they are worried about slipping into anthropocentrism. However, the ecosocial notion of sustainability can justifiably be used to critique deep ecology. As ecofeminists

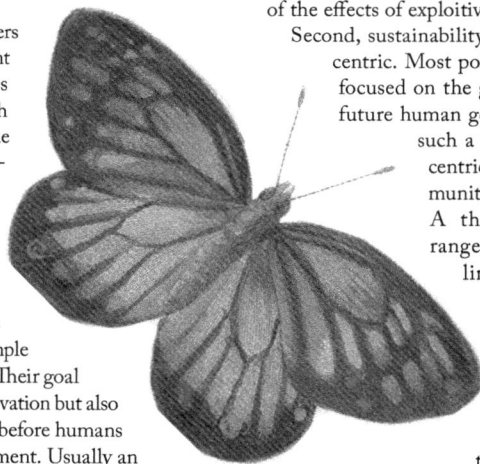

and social ecologists have argued, at least some versions of deep ecology reveal a multifaceted neglect of human society, crippling its ability to bring about true sustainability. One criticism censures deep ecology's emphasis on worldview as the source of the problem (anthropocentrism) and the ideal (an ecosophy). In this view, environmental problems involve the social dimension in various and essential ways. Some critics would argue, for instance, that political and economic structures, such as industrial capitalism and the nation-state, are principal agents of environmental pillage. Other causes of ecological devastation, some have claimed, are social ideologies (e.g., associating women with nature and devaluing both, or upholding an authoritarian social hierarchy) that enable the exploitation of both people and nature.

As such, critics contend, simply developing an ecocentric worldview and preserving wilderness ignores gross social injustice and will not halt the pillage of the planet. We need political and economic analysis, and we need a change in social ideology and social structures. Such a critique of deep ecology conforms to the ecosocial approach to sustainability, which includes social and economic dimensions as well as environmental.

Other criticisms of deep ecology are more philosophical or psychological. While deep ecology affirms that there is no ontological divide between humans and the rest of nature, it has tended to emphasize human degradation of the environment so much that humans can seem to be inevitably destructive, with no proper place in nature. Thus the responding emphasis on wilderness preservation emerges. Sustainability, however, calls for the sustainable use of the natural world and implies our interactive relationship with it. Deep ecology has praised hunter–gatherer cultures as a model for a sustainable society, but critics reject that ideal as inadequate for a world of over six billion people.

In addition, deep ecology's ideal of self-realization, of the identification with nature and loss of the individual ego, has been criticized by ecofeminists as a masculine ambition of psychological aggrandizement of the world. Similarly, some have argued that such a holistic ideal denies the reality and value of individuals, their relationships, and the community of different selves. Both of these limitations, it could be argued, are contrary to true sustainability.

Synthesis with Other Approaches

At this point it is useful to apply another distinction, between conventional deep ecology and critical deep ecology. *Conventional* deep ecology refers to the views and values that do not respond to the valid criticisms that have been made. It holds to the original principles without significant open-minded engagement with other views. *Critical* deep ecology, on the other hand, refers to a philosophy that adheres to the basic perspective of the philosophy while learning from and interacting with the substantial criticisms that have been made. There are perspectives (e.g., critical Marxism and critical utopianism) that remain within these traditions while at the same time reappraising certain aspects in light of new ideas or divergent views. Critical deep ecology joins self-criticism with the insights of social ecology, ecofeminism, and Christian stewardship.

The distinction between conventional deep ecology and critical deep ecology is certainly not absolute, but, rather, it marks a continuum upon which to locate different versions of deep ecology. The main point is that deep ecology need not be limited to the form that is so often criticized. By learning from other approaches, deep ecology can become even more significant to the notion of sustainability. A number of thinkers have shown how the basic perspective of deep ecology can be enriched by association with other views. Gary Snyder (b. 1930), author of *Turtle Island* and *Practice of the Wild*, for instance, is often heralded as a key deep ecology thinker. But he has always been intensely interested in social issues and has combined his radical environmental philosophy with anarchism. Snyder has criticized preservationists for attempting to freeze specific areas as pristine, in effect treating them like a commodity. Roger S. Gottlieb, who has written and edited a number of books on religion and the environment, has argued for the possibility of a reconciliation of spiritual deep ecology and leftist politics. The social ecologist John Clark has called for a dialectical engagement between deep ecology and social ecology, claiming that deep ecologists can support a social ecological perspective. In addition, it is also possible to show that deep ecology's holism can be articulated as relational rather than monistic, and thus in harmony with ecofeminism's insights about relationality. That is, while deep ecology stresses the unity of the natural world and the importance of thinking in terms of the whole of nature, it does not necessarily deny the distinctness of individuals or the reality and importance of relationships, as some have claimed.

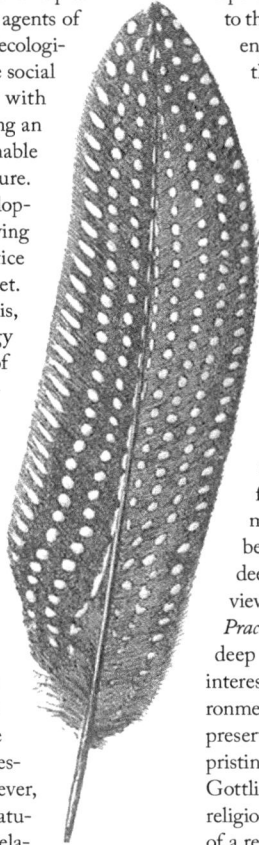

A critical approach to deep ecology makes the methodology more sustainable in two senses. First, the inculcation of social concerns makes it resonant with the ecosocial version of sustainability, and second such a change can help make deep ecology remain a vibrant and enduring approach to environmental philosophy.

As a global community progresses toward a sustainable future, the work of researchers and philosophers in the field of deep ecology will provide an important foundation for the synthesis of environmental, social, and economic debates.

David Landis BARNHILL
University of Wisconsin, Oshkosh

FURTHER READING

Barnhill, David Landis. (2001). Relational holism: Huayan Buddhism and deep ecology. In David Landis Barnhill & Roger S. Gottlieb (Eds.), *Deep ecology and world religions* (pp. 77–106). Albany: State University of New York Press.

Barnhill, David Landis, & Gottlieb, Roger. S. (Eds.). (2001). *Deep ecology and world religion: New essays on sacred ground*. Albany: State University of New York Press.

Clark, John P. (1996). How wide is deep ecology? *Inquiry 39*, 189–201.

Clark, John P. (1998). A social ecology. In Michael Zimmerstein et al. (Eds.), *Environmental Philosophy: From Animal Rights to Radical Ecology* (2nd ed.) (pp. 416–440). Prentice-Hall.

Devall, Bill, & Sessions, George. (1985). *Deep ecology: Living as if nature mattered*. Salt Lake City, UT: Peregrine Smith.

Drengson, Alan, & Inoue, Yuichi. (Eds.). (1995). *The deep ecology movement: An introductory anthology*. Berkeley, CA: North Atlantic Books.

Fox, Warwick. (1990). *Toward a transpersonal ecology: Developing new foundations for environmentalism*. Boston: Shambhala.

Gottlieb, Roger S. (1995). Deep ecology and the left. *Capitalism, Nature, and Society, 6*(3), 1–20.

Gottlieb, Roger S. (1995). Reply to critics. *Capitalism, Nature, and Society, 6*(3), 41–45.

Katz, Eric; Light, Andrew; & Rothenberg, David. (Eds.). (2000). *Beneath the surface: Critical essays in the philosophy of deep ecology*. Cambridge, MA: M.I.T. Press.

Naess, Arne. (1973). The shallow and the deep, long-range ecology movement. A summary. *Inquiry, 16*, 95–100.

Naess, Arne. (1989). *Ecology, community and lifestyle: Outline of an ecosophy* (D. Rothenberg, Trans. and Ed.). Cambridge, U.K.: Cambridge University Press.

Sessions, George, (Ed.). (1995). *Deep ecology for the 21st century*. Boston: Shambhala.

Snyder, Gary. (1990). *The practice of the wild*. San Francisco: North Point Press.

Snyder, Gary. (1974). *Turtle Island*. New York: New Directions Press.

Gaia

The name Gaia, Earth goddess of the Greeks, refers today to the scientific theory first proposed and developed by James Lovelock in the 1970s. It views the Earth as a superorganism—a single, dynamic, self-regulating system. To sustain this self-regulation we must stop using and depleting natural resources as if they exist solely for human use.

The English scientist James Lovelock (b. 1919) first developed Gaia theory, the theory that the Earth is a self-regulating superorganism in which life is intricately entwined with everything else on the surface of the Earth, in the 1970s. Despite criticism from scientific colleagues Lovelock has continued to use the name Gaia for his theory because it conveys the image of a living Earth. According to the Greek creation myth *Theogony*—related and compiled by the eighth-century BCE poet Hesiod—Gaia, the primal Earth goddess, brought forth the world out of Chaos. Alone she gave birth, first to Uranos (the Sky) so that he might cover and surround her and provide a home for the "blessed gods." Then she brought forth the Mountains and Pontos (the Sea). Although Earth goddesses abound in creation myths of numerous cultures as diverse as the Sumerian and Maori, Gaia's name has become the ubiquitous symbol of Earth as a living, divine body. Some, however, see Gaia as a pagan cult and enemy of Christianity (especially those defensive of the view that monotheism has set humans apart from nature and stripped nature of its sacredness). Others, notably Al Gore in his book *Earth in the Balance*, see a return to the spiritual sense of our place in nature (and a panreligious perspective) as an integral part of our global civilization's responsibility for the Earth.

Gaia Theory

With the growth of climate change awareness, Gaia is now a recognized scientific term, a theory based on the concept of Earth as a superorganism composed of all life tightly entwined with the air, the oceans, and the surface rocks. James Lovelock developed Gaia theory to describe how and why, as life appeared on the planet and grew abundant, its evolution and the Earth's evolution merged into a single dynamic system. At the suggestion of his friend and neighbor William Golding, author of *Lord of the Flies,* Lovelock named the system *Gaia* after the primordial cosmic goddess of Greek myth.

Gaia theory describes how Earth's ability to sustain life results from the following properties of living organisms, three of them being intrinsic and one extrinsic. First, all organisms alter their environment by taking in free energy and excreting high-entropy waste products in order to maintain a low level of internal entropy. (Entropy is the technical term for energy still existing but unavailable for work purposes.) Second, organisms grow and multiply, thus providing an intrinsic positive feedback to life (the more life there is, the more life it can beget). Third, for each environmental variable there is a maximum level or range for the growth of a particular organism. The important extrinsic (fourth) factor is that organisms both alter and are constrained by their environments.

Together these factors ensure feedback between life and its environment, such that organic life is sustained through a dynamic disequilibrium between its component parts. Therefore changes within organisms and in organisms' relationships with the environment are built into the system. The properties that make the system sustainable alter and constrain the environment of each organism—to the point where any organism may lose the ability to sustain

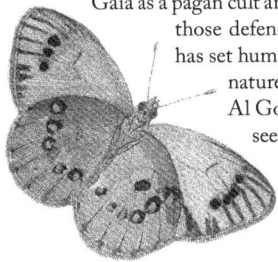

life and become extinct. That being so, accounts of sustainability based on use of global environmental resources must presuppose that what is sustainable at one period in Earth's history is not so forever.

The greatest value of Gaia theory in regard to sustainability is its insistence that we focus on our essential status as organic members of the entire community of life on Earth. This view offers a comprehensive interpretive framework for thinking through the challenges of sustainability by considering human life as part of a single, self-regulating system comprising physical, chemical, biological, and human components. So it follows that the ability of the planet to sustain human life is constrained by the functioning of common environmental resources, climatic variables, and the limits of the ecosystem. A primary Gaian insight is that as an emergent phenomenon, human life is neither external to nor independent of the planetary system's self-regulatory whole and cannot be analyzed reductively by separating it or by cutting it off from the processes or the flow of evolution. Gaia theory's cohesive approach to sustainability embodies goals that pertain to all aspects of the planetary system, not just human life alone.

Implications of Gaian Insight

Adhering to Gaian views of Earth as a single self-regulating system means renouncing our species' claim to absolute privilege regarding use of the Earth's material resources. The very factors that make such resources sustainable for any species constrain their use: overuse or abuse lead to extinctions. Practically, this means that we cannot assume that the Earth and its resources evolved and now exist solely for human use and benefit. The effects of such claims to human exceptionalism are now evident in the reduction of biodiversity and the shrinkage of the Earth's resources through our exploitation, over-industrialization, and technologization. The scale of this exploitation far outstrips that of natural resource replacement or disposal. The Gaian vision of human interaction with the environment—and of human rights constrained by those of our planetary partners—finds far-reaching implications of this imbalance for both ecological integrity and social justice.

Such implications are of particular concern to four classes of people singled out in the proceedings from the 1992 United Nations Conference on Environment and Development as being most at risk from environmental degradation, most vulnerable to its effects, and most powerless to do anything about them: women, children, indigenous peoples, and the poor. Yet the dominant free-market model of development and continuing growth presupposes that the resources needed to sustain such a model are and will be available. Relying on science, technology, and the spread and improvement of education, we expect to pass on a better, more prosperous global situation than the one we inherited. The presupposition behind this expectation is that the global biophysical environment will sustain such growth. In the light of Gaia theory, that expectation is itself unsustainable.

As a religious moral focus rather than a scientific term, Gaia offers a vision of the world and a possibility of speaking about it as a sacred totality. That means that supporters of the Gaian vision see human participation in the system as ultimately sustained by the power of the whole: human life cannot be separated from our understanding of the whole of existence. Therefore, those who relate to Gaia as sacred consider it a religious duty to sustain all aspects of her life.

Anne PRIMAVESI
University of London

Further Reading

Lovelock, James. (1991). *Gaia, the practical science of planetary medicine.* London: Gaia Books.

Lovelock, James. (1995). *Gaia: A new look at life on Earth* (rev. ed.). Oxford, U.K.: Oxford University Press.

Lovelock, James. (1995). *The ages of Gaia: A biography of our living Earth* (2nd ed.). Oxford, U.K.: Oxford University Press.

Lovelock, James. (2003, December 18). The living earth. *Nature, 426,* 769–770.

Lovelock, James, (2009). *The vanishing face of Gaia.* London: Allen Lane.

Primavesi, Anne. (2000). *Sacred Gaia: Holistic theology and earth system science.* London: Routledge.

Primavesi, Anne. (2009). *Gaia and climate change: A theology of gift events.* London: Routledge.

United Nations Conference on Environment and Development, 1992. (1997, May 23). Retrieved May 26, 2009, from http://www.un.org/geninfo/bp/enviro.html

Virtues and Vices

Virtues (such as compassion and moderation) are defined as cultivated cognitive-emotional habits that allow people to respond fittingly in diverse situations. By contrast, vices (such as wanton neglect and greed) are cultivated ways of being and acting that lead to harm, including injustice and environmental damage. The cultivation of virtues plays a role in all indigenous and world religions and is essential for a sustainable lifestyle.

As a species, human beings have evolved with a remarkable ability to live in and move between quite diverse natural and social environments. This adaptability is biologically supported by malleable patterns of cognitive and emotional processing, also called habits. Cognitive-emotional habits that allow people to respond fittingly in varying situations are commonly known as virtues (for example, respect, courage, compassion, and moderation). What counts as fitting in any particular context depends on culturally articulated visions of the good life. These normative visions usually involve a balance of personal and communal well-being. When people calibrate their cognitive-emotional habits to socially and ecologically inclusive visions of flourishing, their virtues tend to undergird sustainable lifestyles.

Still inchoate in children, virtues are perfected through experience. Once established, they produce reliable patterns of thought and action that can last a lifetime. For example, people who respect their bioregions are inclined to notice natural rhythms, other inhabitants, and their interactions. Such people are more likely than others to spot harmful changes and to take protective measures when necessary. Early warnings about climate change thus came from Inuit, whose deep respect for their Arctic regions—to them, respect for the *inuat* or spiritual owners of the universe—allowed them to notice a warming trend

through changes in the ice well before mainstream climate science confirmed it.

Virtues, Religions, and Sustainability

Being group animals, people typically cultivate virtues in sociocultural contexts. There they find not only mentoring and peer feedback, but also institutionalized rules of thumb and models of personal and communal well-being that help them to fine-tune their cognitive-emotional habits. Often, such sociocultural anchors of the good life are embedded in religious myths and rituals.

Virtues play a role in all indigenous and world religions. For example, all religious traditions encourage their practitioners to cultivate compassion and moderation, but each tradition uniquely interprets what is involved in cultivating compassion and moderation through its own universe of stories, practices, and role models. Comparing virtues across religious traditions therefore involves seeing "similarities within differences and differences within similarities" (Yearley 1990, 1). Many religious beliefs and practices encourage people to cultivate virtues with alertness to the needs of the entire community of planetary life, both present and future. Typical religion-supported "sustainability virtues" are wonder, humility, sensitivity, attentiveness, caution, creativity, courage, frugality, diligence, perseverance, gratitude, generosity, respect, care, compassion, patience, justice, forgiveness, moderation, forbearance, hope, and wisdom. By encouraging people to cultivate such traditional virtues with alertness to the needs of planetary life, religions foster an indispensable aspect of sustainability: *personal* attunement to the boundary conditions of life's flourishing, which include ecological integrity, economic health, human dignity, and social justice.

Vices, Religions, and Sustainability

When people deliberately cultivate cognitive-emotional habits that prevent or undermine inclusive flourishing, their ways of being and acting are commonly referred to as vices. People tend to adopt and perfect such habits to serve limited ends, such as personal wealth. Vices often emerge from extreme behaviors that are unresponsive to feedback, such as overconsumption, excess aggression, or wanton neglect. As a result, vices typically carry harm in their wake, including social injustice and environmental damage.

Religions have a reputation for denouncing vices as personal sins. Resulting from a lack of reverence, sins represent a sickness of mind, emotion, and body that above all requires spiritual healing. Increasingly, the world's religions explicitly call for such spiritual healing as an antidote to persistent violations of the boundary conditions for complex life on Earth.

As fallible human institutions, however, religions can also reinforce the cultivation of vices among their followers. The link between religion and vice became a matter of heated debate in 1967, when the UCLA historian Lynn White Jr. published "The Historical Roots of Our Ecologic Crisis." In this article, White traces modern environmental problems to Christian support for an exploitative attitude toward nature, which replaced the humility fostered by pre-Christian pantheism. The debates stirred by White's article have encouraged many religious practitioners to engage in critical reflection on the ambiguous records of their traditions. In looking for spiritual healing and ways to cultivate sustainability virtues, religious practitioners increasingly find support in interreligious dialogue and cooperation.

At the same time, religious practitioners may also disagree on the sorts of behavior that typify vices. Consumerist behavior, for example, can be variously interpreted as an expression of vice or as justified. Many Roman Catholics view consumerist behavior as a sign of greed. According to Church tradition, greed is one of the deadly sins through which a person foregoes salvation. The Roman Catholic Church encourages its members to cultivate the opposite virtues of simplicity and generosity, which attune them to the Creator and to the needs of all created life. By contrast, many Pentecostal Christians in developing countries view consumerist behavior as an earned right. Following a so-called prosperity gospel, they believe that personal wealth is a sign of a divine reward ethic. Meanwhile, they trust divine providence to deal with its sustainability impacts.

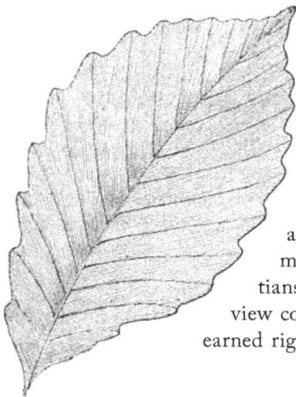

Although religious institutions and movements historically have not always fostered sustainable personal habits, nowadays most aim to do so. The transformation of human cognitive-emotional habits from harmful to ecologically and socially fitting is a necessary, even though by itself an insufficient, condition for realizing the goals of sustainability. In most regions of the world (secularized pockets being the exception), religious involvement is also a necessary condition for such changes of deeply engrained habit.

Virtues and Sustainability in Philosophical Ethics

Virtues and vices function as key concepts in several ancient schools of philosophy, including classical Hindu, Buddhist, Confucian, Platonic, Aristotelian, Stoic, and Christian thought. During the later Middle Ages, Aristotelian virtue ethics became prominent in the Middle East and Europe through creative appropriations by Muslim, Jewish, and Christian thinkers (especially Al-Ghazali, Maimonides, and Thomas Aquinas). When eighteenth-century Enlightenment thinkers introduced the concepts of rights and utility, virtue ethics all but disappeared from Western philosophical discourse. Toward the end of the twentieth century, however, academic philosophers regained interest in the cultivation of virtues (also called *aretaic* ethics, from the ancient Greek *arete*, meaning excellence). Today much scholarly effort goes into clarifying and adjusting key concepts in virtue ethics.

Environmental ethics also became a focus of philosophical inquiry in the last quarter of the twentieth century. Discussions in the field initially unfolded along deontological (based on moral obligation) or consequentialist lines, but subsequently broadened to include the *aretaic* line. As a subfield, environmental virtue ethics (EVE) is dedicated to defining sustainable ways of flourishing and to clarifying the general and specific characteristics of matching virtues and opposing vices. While some traditional schools of virtue ethics have been narrowly anthropocentric, perspectives in environmental virtue ethics range from enlightened self-interest to biocentric egalitarianism (Sandler and Cafaro 2005).

Virtues and Social Transformation

Historically, virtue ethics has been associated more with conservatism than with social change. The stability of social systems partially depends on personal qualities like honesty, respect, cooperation, and moderation. Power elites and their intellectuals, who have an interest in the status

quo, therefore tend to encourage or force citizens to cultivate such character traits. When a social system is unjust, however, mandatory cultivation of civic virtues has little to do with genuine virtue cultivation, because it will further undermine personal and communal flourishing. A scholarly interpretation of the authoritative virtue catalogues of colonialist, sexist, racist, speciesist, and otherwise elitist social systems therefore warrants a critical perspective.

In unsustainable social contexts, the personal cultivation of genuine virtues may appear radical. Virtue cultivation can play a key role in grassroots resistance. In India, for example, the Hindu virtue of respect for life, expressed in the practice of seed-keeping, has inspired the seed *satyagraha* movement, a successful resistance effort (based on Gandhi's nonviolent practice) against patented seeds, which Monsanto had genetically engineered to be sterile to protect its profits. Similarly, indigenous spiritual attitudes towards nonhuman nature inspire many participants in the so-called alternative globalization movement, which opposes the ruling neoliberal model of globalization on the ground that it is unsustainable.

In the mainstream environmental movement, virtue cultivation initially received less attention as a driver of social change than public pressure, legal reform, and fiscal measures. After several decades of effort, however, these macromeasures are showing their limits. Today mainstream environmental activists and policy makers increasingly recognize the importance of matching personal transformation. The Dalai Lama, Ecumenical Patriarch Bartholomew of the Greek Orthodox Church, Pope Benedict XVI, and other spiritual leaders who inspire the cultivation of sustainability virtues are now widely recognized as key leaders in driving the transformation towards sustainable societies.

Cultivating Virtues

From an operational perspective, the personal cultivation of virtues is a form of value-guided biological conditioning. Through practice and habituation, people are able to develop stable, situation-adjustable patterns of cognitive and emotional processing. Within a certain range of genetic, contextual and biographical possibilities, they can shape these character tools to fit their simultaneously deepening understanding of personal and communal flourishing. For example, the cultivation of generosity typically requires regular practice in giving. Through feedback from others and by observing their own reactions, people learn to adjust the timing, wording, and gestures of giving to the point where their gifts appear truly fitting.

People need social networks, such as families, friends, colleagues, or even virtual communities, in order to cultivate virtues. Although companies have a reputation

for encouraging the cultivation of attitudes that support financial gain at the expense of personal and communal flourishing, they can also provide social matrices for the cultivation of virtues, including sustainability virtues. This typically happens when the pillars of corporate identity—including core values and role models, targets and metrics, rewards and incentives, office rituals and stories, site architecture, process design, and corporate branding—are streamlined to support the goals of sustainability. Like all complex social systems, business matrices for the cultivation of sustainability virtues require several years of growing time.

Practices such as cooking, horticulture, and flute playing are also cradles of character formation. People engaged in such culturally encoded productive activities must nurture and refine the requisite virtues, such as attentiveness and creativity. Musicians, for example, learn to listen closely to their own sounds and adjust them as the music requires. When playing together, musicians also learn to listen and respond to the sounds of others, moderating their personal rhythms and impulses so that they can literally go with the flow. Through regular practice, artistic traits such as attentiveness and creativity can become second nature and support the cultivation of virtues in any other life context.

With the help of the tools of neuroscience (through functional magnetic resonance imaging, for example), existing insights into ways of cultivating virtues can now be further tested, refined, and supplemented. The human ability to trust, for example, plays a key role in sustainability virtues like generosity and hope. Recent research shows that the ability to trust is supported by a rise in the level of oxytocin, a neuroactive hormone best known for its role in labor (Zak 2008). This means that people can enhance their cultivation of trust-based virtues through timely social activities that are known to raise oxytocin levels, such as touching (including massage and dancing), grooming (including hair braiding), and sharing meals. Moreover, because much of the supporting neural circuitry is laid down during early mother-and-child bonding, social structures and policies that protect this bonding process are directly relevant to the cultivation of trust-based sustainability virtues later in life.

The Spirit of Virtue Cultivation

From a spiritual perspective, the personal cultivation of virtues is often described as a process of sanctification. People who seek to perceive signs of grace in their lives tend to be struck by the many internal and external gifts that allow them to grow in virtue. At the same time, they underscore their experience that sanctification also requires purification, which may involve a lifelong struggle. This is especially true for the cultivation of virtues that mold and balance basic drives and emotions, such as courage (overcoming fear), moderation (channeling desires), and humility (inflating pride). As the gathered memory of such deeply personal journeys, most religious traditions recognize that the cultivation of virtues is a process with ups and downs, where growth ultimately occurs not as a product of human engineering but as a gift.

Monastic traditions in particular tend to retain and develop insight into the ways of virtue cultivation. For example, the three vows taken by Benedictine monks support life-long growth in virtue, each in their own way. The vow of *stabilitas* encourages the perseverance needed for dealing with the challenges of personal formation. The vow of *conversio morum* supports growing into a new life-style through daily, small steps. And the vow of *obedientia* supports attentively listening to what it going on and discerning how to respond. Together, these three guidelines have demonstrated their value for virtue cultivation, both inside and outside the monastery, for more than a millennium. Today, they are also showing promise as a spiritual backbone for the cultivation of sustainability virtues among Benedictines, lay Roman Catholics and other people attracted to monastic spirituality. This trend parallels the growing interest in Buddhist ways of practicing mindfulness, *ahimsa* (nonviolence), and compassion in the awareness that these habits engender sustainable ways of living (Thich Nhat Hanh 2008). The ubiquity of virtue cultivation across cultures and religions provides those who seek to develop a global sustainability ethic with a rich spiritual-ethical lingua franca. The Earth Charter—a document prepared by an independent, global commission that presents the principles required for creating a more sustainable twenty-first century—illustrates the accessible appeal of virtue cultivation with its simple yet clear call "to care for the Earth and one another" (Earth Charter 2000, Preamble).

Louke van WENSVEEN
Academia Vitae

FURTHER READING

Earth Charter. (2000). Retrieved April 28, 2009, from http://www.earth-charterinaction.org/invent/images/uploads/echarter_english.pdf

Hursthouse, Rosalind. (2002). *On virtue ethics.* Oxford, U.K.: Oxford University Press.

Newton, Lisa H. (2002). *Ethics and sustainability: Sustainable development and the moral life.* Upper Saddle River, NJ: Prentice Hall.

Sandler, Ronald, & Cafaro, Philip. (Eds.). (2005). *Environmental virtue ethics.* Lanham, MD: Rowman & Littlefield.

Thich Nhat Hanh. (2008). *The world we have. A Buddhist approach to peace and ecology.* Berkeley, CA: Parallax Press.

White, Lynn, Jr. (1967, March 10). The historical roots of our ecologic crisis. *Science, 155,* 1203–1207.

Yearley, Lee H. (1990). *Mencius and Aquinas: Theories of virtue and conceptions of courage.* Albany: State University of New York Press.

Zak, Paul J. (2008, June). The neurobiology of trust. *Scientific American,* 88–95.

Peace

Scholars focus on social, economic, and environmental dimensions when analyzing how to achieve peace, and, with it, the basis for a sustainable existence. Theorists admit all three of these categories contain some valid and essential aspects that would contribute to sustainable peace in spite of their extremely different recommendations.

The sustainability of the environment and the resolution of political conflicts are integrally related. When analyzing how to achieve a sustainable peace, scholars tend to focus on three dimensions of relationships in their analysis: the social dimension, the economic dimension, and the environmental dimension. In their analyses, scholars look at the networks of relationships present in each dimension.

Three Dimensions

The social dimension pertains to our relationships with each other. The economic dimension focuses on the relationships around production. Finally, the environmental dimension examines the relationship of humans to the rest of the biosphere. A sustainable peace is considered to be one in which the configuration of relationships across these three dimensions allows all organisms to live well while not jeopardizing the quality of life of future generations. Conflict can be seen as an indication that something within these three dimensions has deviated from what is required for sustainability.

Although any final verdict on sustainability must await the test of time, we can focus on certain specific indicators that serve as litmus tests for whether a system might be sustainable into the future. These indicators are: biodiversity (environment), true-cost accounting (economic), and social capital and civil society (social).

Biodiversity is defined as the range of noninvasive biological diversity found within an ecosystem. True-cost accounting (or pricing) is when the price of a product in the market reflects the true costs to society and the environment of its production and consumption. High social capital is evidenced by dense, inclusive, and overlapping social networks that contain norms of mutual trust and generalized reciprocity.

Practitioners within the peace studies field analyze these three indicators and develop interventions around the vulnerable dimension(s) to rearrange or develop relationships such that civil society, true-cost accounting, or biodiversity are maintained. Considerable variation, however, exists among peace scholars concerning the most appropriate practices to achieve these sustainable indicators. These variations can be catalogued roughly into three general categories of perspectives: the conservative perspective, the managerial perspective, and the radical perspective (Humphrey 2002).

Three Perspectives

The conservative cluster emphasizes individual-oriented, free-market approaches as the mechanism for ensuring sustainability. Practitioners within this perspective tend to focus on individual education or awareness campaigns and letting the market decide what types of relationships should emerge. For example, contemporary theorists in this paradigm would argue that there is no environmental crisis around oil. Eventually, the high price of petroleum will force new alternatives to arise and, subsequently, new relationships will emerge.

The conservative paradigm views conflict as a temporary phase that occurs during a time of transition between sets of values, whether economic or cultural. Conflict is perceived as a clash between "appropriate" and "inappropriate" cultural values, and generally is only considered relevant when the conflict directly addresses a cause-and-effect relationship. Once citizens with inappropriate values have been reeducated, or the proponents of an inappropriate system have died out, then conflict should disappear. (Interestingly, both individual-oriented environmental education campaigns [such as a recycling campaign] and the political scientist Samuel Huntington's view of the clash of civilizations, in which he predicted that violent conflict would be caused by religious and cultural differences, not the ideological friction among nation-states, would fall within the conservative paradigm.)

The managerial cluster of social theories focuses on the importance of ensuring that individuals and corporations absorb the true consequences of their actions. This paradigm contends that free markets are going to be unsustainable in the long term because individuals and groups constantly will be seeking to capture the positive consequences of their actions while foisting the negative consequences of their actions on to others. Garrett Hardin's "The Tragedy of the Commons" is a good example of this tendency within the commons era of England. Simply put, in a system in which the community absorbs the negative consequences (long term) and the individual gains the positive outcome (in the short term), all individuals will choose short-term gain over long-term stability.

Managerial theorists see conflict emerging from groups that have crossed a tipping point in the amount of negative consequences they can absorb. To avoid this conflict, practitioners in this paradigm advocate creating mechanisms that force organizations and individuals to absorb the full consequences, both negative and positive, of their actions. These might be a set of individual-oriented rewards and punishments, forms of social pressure, or state interventions—laws of coercion, tax breaks of persuasion, or institutions such as the Environmental Protection Agency (EPA) that monitor behavior and can distribute punishments for infractions. Unfortunately, this perspective only really becomes fully engaged after the conflict has risen to the level of expressing itself toward the cause of the negative consequences. The normal cycle of conflict doesn't necessarily point to the root causes in early stages when violence and aggression are more likely pointed at members of the oppressed group or other scapegoat figures.

The social theorists that fall into the radical category are more suspicious of assumptions about the sustainability of democratic capitalism as a system. They would contend that a system that requires the treadmill of production to survive cannot be ultimately sustainable—socially or environmentally. In the social arena, these theorists contend that power inevitably will become concentrated as competition forces individuals or organizations to "cheat" and push the negative consequences on to someone else. These theorists see conflict as inevitable as the environment degrades and forces marginalized individuals to react or as the social systems become more and more power-centralized in an attempt to maintain growth in a competitive environment. Intervention strategies in this category tend to be oriented around zero-growth economics, power decentralization, and the overthrow or elimination of the entire system.

Solutions for the Future

Which cluster of theories are the most appropriate for achieving sustainability has been difficult to verify empirically. Theorists admit that as a result of the highly integrated and extremely complex nature of society and the environment, all three of these categories contain some element of truth in spite of their extremely different recommendations for achieving a sustainable peace. Pragmatic practitioners immersed in the complexity of social interventions tend to draw on a mixture of elements from each of the clusters. For example, pragmatists may recognize the radical paradigm critique concerning the dangers of a growth-orientation in the economy yet also recognize that the capitalist system has generated a level of well-being unheard of in previous epochs. Or they may recognize that free-market pressures are important solutions as advocated by the conservative theorists, yet also recognize that allowing groups and individuals to foist the negative consequences of their actions on to others or the environment is a temptation in society. As such, pragmatists tend to emphasize maintaining a balance between the paradigms of intervention by advocating sustainable growth, balancing the exploitation of resources with the preservation of future potential, and recognizing the importance of individual choice and corporate responsibility while still seeing the necessity of state or social incentives and disincentives to avoid cheating or unsustainable behaviors. Ultimately, what pragmatists focus on in any situation of conflict or social need are questions such as: Is civil society being strengthened? Is true-cost accounting in evidence? And, perhaps most important, is biodiversity being maintained?

Terrence JANTZI
Eastern Mennonite University

Aaron KISHBAUGH
Independent scholar, Singers Glen, Virginia

FURTHER READING

Hardin, Garrett. (1968). The tragedy of the commons. *Science*, 162, 1243–1248.

Humphrey, Craig R.; Lewis, Tammy L.; & Buttel, Frederick H. (2002). *Environment, energy & society: A new synthesis*. Belmont, CA: Wadsworth Books.

Huntington, Samuel. (1997). *The clash of civilizations and the remaking of world order*. London: Simon & Schuster.

Gilligan, James. (2001). *Preventing violence*. New York: Thames & Hudson.

Sacrifice

Traditional models of sacrifice in Western, Confucian, and dharmic religious and ethical thought served to redirect actual violence to something more positive, but post-modern consumer-oriented society has lost the sense that sacrifice can lead to greater good; the violence of selfish greed drives human action. By regaining a sense of sacrifice and consequently conscience, the greater good of environmental and cultural sustainability may be achieved.

The word *sacrifice* refers both to acts of religious ritual and an approach to human action that sets aside immediate benefit for the sake of a greater good. In the past, Jewish and Hellenistic traditions have included bloody offerings in the form of animal sacrifice. In Christianity this has been replaced with the Eucharist, which promotes human conscience and adherence to a moral code. The contemporary challenge presented by the need to develop sustainable lifestyles can draw from the traditions of sacrifice, serving as an inspiration for the development of reasonable patterns for resource management.

Sacrifice has been defined by the theologian Dennis Keenan as "a necessary passage through suffering and/or death (of either oneself or someone else) on the way to a supreme moment of transcendent truth" (2005, 11). Transcendent truth in light of global warming, resource diminishment, and species decimation has been replaced with the "inconvenient truth" that human behavior in quest of the "good life" has become rapacious and destructive. How might the practice of sacrifice move human cultures away from these behaviors and toward the actualization of a sustainable lifestyle?

The word *sacrifice* in the English language means *to make* (Latin *facere*) *sacred* (*sacre*). Throughout world history, this has often entailed killing an animal or a human in the context of religious ritual. Early anthropologists were fascinated with this process, prompting Henri Hubert and Marcel Mauss, in their seminal 1899 book *Sacrifice: Its Nature and Function*, to write that "sacrifice is a religious act which, through the consecration of a victim, modifies the condition of the moral person who accomplishes it" (1964, 13), indicating that sacrifice establishes a change in the one who performs a sacrifice and produces a larger social function. The renowned French sociologist Émile Durkheim postulated that sacrifice served an integral function in the social creation of religion, and hence in human civility.

Traditional Models of Sacrifice

The core story of sacrifice in Western civilization can be gleaned from three sources: the Hebrew Bible; Euripides's play *The Bacchae*, based on the Greek myth involving Dionysus (also called Bacchus), the god of wine and ecstatic release; and the New Testament. In the first narrative, God requests Abraham to sacrifice his first-born son. In the second story female followers of Dionysus (the Bacchae of the title), habitually driven by the god in rituals of worship to kill wild animals and livestock with their bare hands, also, in a moment of frenzy, kill Pentheus, the young king of Thebes, for denying Dionysus's divinity. The third narrative entails the Crucifixion of Jesus.

As the narratives progress, the ramifications of each sacrifice unfold. In the Hebrew Bible story, God orders Abraham to substitute an animal, sparing the life of the son. In the ancient Greek play violence spins out of control, and although the women of Dionysus's cult regret their actions—one member is Pentheus's mother—Pentheus, who has been torn apart, cannot be brought back to life. The death of Jesus gives birth to a theology of atonement, a doctrine that contemplation on the suffering and painful death of Jesus, combined with reflection on and repentance for one's own sins, results in rectification and forgiveness. The story of Abraham indicates a transition from violence to humanistic compassion; *The Bacchae* warns that humans hold the capacity to stray from the rational and fall prey to violent urges; the story of Jesus suggests a framework for learning from the mistakes of others (the Roman soldiers) and altering one's behavior. In accord with Durkheim, all three instances hold a moral imperative for the maintenance of the social order.

According to the historian and philosopher René Girard, violence has played a central role in the history of sacrifice. He suggests that sacrifice, generally of a scapegoat, "serves to protect the entire community from its *own* violence. . . . [T]he elements of dissension scattered throughout the community are drawn to the person of the sacrificial victim and eliminated" (1977, 8). In his study of world history and human civilizations, Girard detects an irrefutable link between religion and violence, stating that the sacrificial act "curtails reciprocal violence and imposes structure on the community" (1977, 317). For Girard, the Christian faith successfully defuses the power and allure of violence. Dennis Keenan comes to a similar conclusion, citing the statement of the French philosopher Emmanuel Levinas: "sacrifice requires being for the other." Keenan notes that sacrifice leads to *agape* (one of several words from ancient Greek conveying various aspects "love"), which he defines as "the sacrifice *of* the sacrifice of one's pathological sinful desire to transgress the Law" (2005, 75)—the selfless love that allows for social stability. By participating in the Christian Eucharist, a ritual that recalls the passion and love of Jesus, one is brought to atonement. By drawing the Christian lesson into oneself through the act of mimesis, seeing one's own sin in light of the larger story of Jesus, violence within oneself can be mitigated. By replacing mimetic desires of violence with imitation of Christ, one becomes rectified.

In a simpler time, this paradigm of defusing tension through religious ritual and the observance of commandments for curbing human excess prevailed throughout much of Europe and those areas of the world subjected to European colonization and Christian conversion. Persons were given a list of commandments, authorities enforced them through the rule of law, and societies were sustained. Similar social norms developed in East Asia with adherence to Confucian propriety and in South Asia with the observance of dharma (Hindu, Buddhist, Jaina, or Sikh). Islam, modeling itself on the Jewish moral code, still considers polity inseparable from religious values; for Muslims, the ultimate act of sacrifice is submitting to the will of God. Even the post-Enlightenment secular world, though proclaiming that its social norms are based solely on reason and natural law, in fact abounds with examples of sacrificial

practices through which society is held in balance. One example is the insistence that one sacrifice one's own selfish needs for the sake of the common good, a foundational principle for civil society.

The birth of scientific method in the seventeenth century and its linkage first with technology, then resource exploitation, and finally with the perfection of marketing has resulted in a voracious new religion referred to by the theologian John Cobb as "economism." With advances in technology, immediate consequences of resource exploitation have become obscured and deferred. Obsession with human comfort with little or no regard for the true cost to the environment has resulted in quintessentially modern forms of idolatry. These include over-concern with one's social status and body image, excessive consumerism, and a desire to postpone one's death at all costs. Cultural cynicism and despair also may be seen as an outgrowth or byproduct of the success of the eighteenth-century European Enlightenment, as well as a breakdown of the traditional moral order. The relativism and malaise of the post-Enlightenment emphasis on the supremacy of the human combined with the use of technologically enhanced weapons such as automatic artillery, mustard gas, and nuclear weaponry resulted in great violence in the nineteenth and twentieth centuries. It also prompted a comfort-driven trivialization of human worth and meaning in the latter part of the twentieth century, extending into the twenty-first century. With the rise of individualism and a loss of a concern for the good of the group, a myopia has emerged eclipsing the efficacy of sacrifice.

In years past, the mimetic violence of ritual sacrifice helped slake blood thirst and establish a stable social order. Sacrifice helped quell hatred. Hatred boils into violent rage leading to murder; organized murder on a larger scale leads to war. The stories of Abraham, Pentheus, and Jesus helped direct human behavior away from senseless killing of other human beings. Although the efficacy of the sacrificial order went into a slow and steady decline with the birth of modernity, its enduring lessons helped prompt a turning away from the overwhelming violence that distinguished the first half of the twentieth century as the most violent period in human history. But only with radical reinterpretation can the stories of Abraham, Pentheus, and Jesus be seen as moral fables for countering human greed. Greed differs from violence. It entails a different, deferred form of destruction. This destruction can be found in exploitation of natural resources, devastation of landscapes and ecosystems, and a colonization of the mind with manufactured notions of products that must be consumed.

Today we suffer from the malaise of greed, stemming from what the Zen Buddhist philosopher David Loy has referred to as the "religion of the market" (1997, 275–290). War still simmers in various parts of the world, though the great destruction of the early to middle twentieth century will most likely (and hopefully) not be repeated. By the overly efficient exploitation of resources, however, human life has been placed in jeopardy by pollution, an autism to the natural world, a consequent lack of acknowledgment of externalities (e.g., waste disposal, deleterious carbon gases), and a lack of political will. The cautionary tales that were learned from Abraham, Pentheus, and Jesus served to provide human beings with means to develop a workable polity, a system that with a few notable exceptions helped tamp down the human tendency toward violence over the long course of history. But making infanticide, passion-driven crimes, and religious and/or political persecution aberrant rather than expected does not construct a view that reaches beyond human concerns. The story of the sacrifice in the Judeo–Greco–Christian–Islamic continuum needs to evolve in the present age into a model that allows for the protection of animals, the protection of women, and the protection of the Earth itself. We need a new model of sacrifice to counter the violence of greed.

Postmodern Thought

Postmodern thinking about sacrifice might benefit from the lessons of other cultures that have been forced to deal with abundance. The American Indians of the Northwest, particularly the Kwakiutl, enjoyed a super-abundant environment that provided untold riches of food, timber, and animal furs. The peoples of this area resolved the unavoidable tension that periodically surfaced in the drama of human life not largely through warfare, but through the potlatch, the bestowal of great riches upon neighboring tribes. Rather than hording things for themselves, the Kwakiutl gifted others, dealing in a profound way with the dark side of human inclination to compete and to provoke conflict. (In a potlatch ceremony, rather than showing one's social standing by accumulating more goods than one's neighbor, families compete to see who can bestow more wealth on others. This stands in stark contrast to the American tradition of "keeping up with the Joneses," with its ever-increasing conspicuous consumption.) For the past several decades, our merchandising machinery has enabled suburbs to sprawl further, car culture to spill over

into Asia, and food to be taken for granted, particularly in the developed world where it requires only a tiny fraction of an individual's income to procure in abundance. Rather than celebrating this surfeit of goods, the consuming public has been consistently exhorted to consume more. Patriotism in America, as some say, has been reduced to shopping.

With the limits to growth upon us, with fuller understanding of the problem of global warming, and with the inevitable adjustments to the costs of fuel and food in evidence, a shift is beginning to take place from an ideology of hording to an appreciation of sacrifice and conservationism as primary values. Sacrifice in its evolving meaning took on a negative connotation in the past thirty years, with little notion that sacrifice might result in an eventual benefit. The first part of the process—as defined in Webster's dictionary, "a giving up, destroying, foregoing of some valued thing" and "a giving up of something for less than its supposed value"—eclipsed an understanding that this process could lead to "something of greater value." The current generation has no recollection of the food rationing and other sacrifices (e.g., foregoing nylon stockings, using margarine instead of butter, etc.) made by Americans during World War II. But a change has begun. Rather than simply plucking items from the grocery store shelf or purchasing automobiles based on style and decadent or high-performance "options," individuals are reintroducing a thoughtful process into their purchases, reengaging the tools of conscience and moral judgment. By examining health effects to one's body as well as becoming cognizant of the horrors of factory farming, people are changing their food choices. By considering the social and physical effects on the human body of long commutes in oversized vehicles, as well as the impact of fossil fuels on global weather patterns, people are beginning to adjust their lifestyle expectations. Two web-based animations have been particularly effective in communicating these concerns in a graphic, easily graspable format: *The Meatrix* on factory farming and *The Story of Stuff* about the underbelly of consumer culture. Sociologists such as Robert Putnam and Juliet Schor have pointed out the loss of human connectivity that has resulted from a purchase-driven culture.

Sustainability seen through the prism of sacrifice suggests that direct human action must be taken to rectify the excesses of the modern era. The violence of Jesus' crucifixion symbolized by the Eucharist prompts the cultivation of human conscience and a move toward rectification and reconciliation.

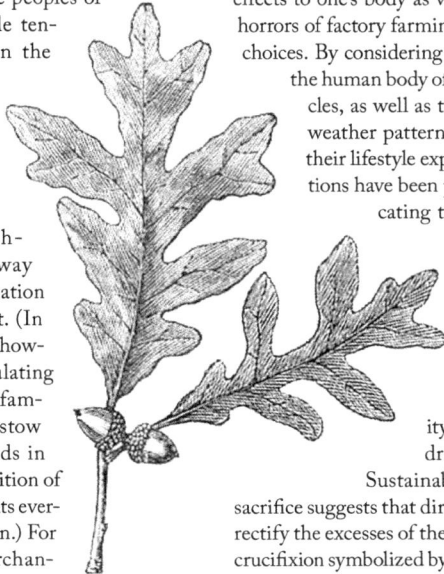

Sacrifice and Sustainability

For the European world and North America, the killing of the goat, Pentheus, and Jesus provided a model of sacrifice that involves giving up an object for the sake of a greater good. In the case of environmental degradation, this greater good would be a cleaner environment within the context of a sustainable economic system. Just as the goat, Pentheus, and Jesus gave up their lives, modern people are being called upon to give up aspects of their lifestyles that cause harm to the environment. This can take many shapes. First, people need to be educated about the deleterious effects that energy consumption has on the planet, leading to pollution and global warming. Second, people need to feel a sense of connectedness with these problems that will spark their moral conscience. Third, the political leaders must take note and provide legislation to correct the harmful excess generated by profligate lifestyles. In the current globalized economy, changes will be required to make a shift from nonrenewable energy sources such as oil to renewable sources such as wind and solar power, from health-damaging foods to healthy, from isolating activities that promote malaise to community-building activities that promote connectivity and well-being. The giving up of bad habits will need to be accompanied with replacement strategies to avoid economic and social upheaval. Redeveloping a healthy sense of sacrifice will be essential for an effective change in energy and economic policies. This sacrificial model calls for a return to conscience, a reflection on the sin of over-consumption, and a resolve to develop a new conscience and abstemiousness.

Rethinking Sacrifice

Thomas Berry (1914–2009), a theologian also known as an "historian of the Earth," has made concrete suggestions for revising the concept of sacrifice through the principles of sustainability. His key ideas offer new approaches for constructive sacrificial action that heighten one's sense of inter-connection with the larger forces of society and the universe. Berry regards the Earth to be the primary vehicle for revelation, the context for all human flourishing, and the only path toward self-knowledge. In *The Great Work* he writes (1999, 52):

> Only Earth became a living planet filled with those innumerable forms of geological structure and biological expression that we observe throughout the natural world. Only Earth held a creative balance between the turbulence and the discipline that are necessary for creativity. . . . The universe [established on Earth] a creative disequilibrium expressed in the curvature of space that was sufficiently closed to establish and abiding order in the universe and

sufficiently open to enable the wild creative process to continue.

For Berry, all Earth expresses the sacrificial process. In order for humans to remain viable, they must go beyond themselves and return to an appreciation of the magnificence of the Earth. All encounters with nature can be seen as sacred and hence instructive, from the stark beauty of the Earth, to the realization of the harm done by human greed and exploitation. In a negative sense, the beauty of the world has been sacrificed not as a gateway toward the transcendent, but solely for the pursuit of market-driven values. In *Religion in the 21st Century* Berry (2009, 177) writes:

> Apparently, during the four centuries since Descartes, we have lost our basic sensitivity for the ever-renewing natural world with its wonder, beauty, and intimacy as well as its local and seasonal nourishment in response to our love and care of the land. We were willing to devastate all these for the illusive abundance offered by an industrial society.

Berry has made several proposals to restore balance to human–Earth relations, including foundational science education, a rejection of the idea of the Earth as primarily natural resource for the unlimited use of humans, an improved legal system that extends protection to ecosystems, and a curbing of the power of commercial-industrial corporations. By "sacrificing" the modern fetishes of technology and consumerism in favor of simpler living, we can return to a world of wonder, and recover in Berry's words, "our communication with the deeper reality of things." Our quest for transcendent truth of necessity must take us on a return journey to planet Earth.

The sacrificial model underlying Berry's approach acknowledges that the microcosm reflects the macrocosm. A small act ripples throughout the larger system, for good or ill. If one person owns a highly efficient automobile, or chooses to ride a bicycle rather than drive, it might be seen as an oddity and dismissed as eccentric. The reverse might also pertain and that person's choice might be admired and imitated by others. One person's sacrifice might be another's poison, or alternatively, a source of inspiration and change. The environmental philosopher Holmes Rolston has stated that the Earth itself is cruciform—the word literally means "arranged or shaped in a cross" but is used by Rolston to reflect that Darwinian natural history echoes classical religious themes of death and regeneration—in that the processes of evolution express a sacrificial modality.

Future Considerations

In order to foster a sustainable economic, political, psychological, and spiritual state of affairs, people need to adopt and participate in new models of sacrifice. Rather than feeling punished by high costs for goods and services, the new sacrificial order might help people return to a sense of immediacy and aliveness. As food becomes more expensive, it becomes more cherished. Similarly, travel, whether for work or pleasure, will require careful consideration not only of cost but of its wider impact on the production of carbon. Personal identity, rather than being tied to the acquisition and manipulation of things, can be measured in terms of one's connectivity with others and with the primary source of revelation, the Earth community. In conclusion, sacrificial wisdom, though differing from one cultural context to another, holds promise as a conceptual and practical resource to inspire people to take the steps necessary for personal, social, and economic sustainability.

Christopher Key CHAPPLE
Loyola Marymount University

An earlier version of portions of this entry appeared in *Worldviews: Global Religions, Culture, and Ecology*, volume 12, issue 2/3 (2008).

FURTHER READING

Bailie, Gil. (1995). *Violence unveiled: Humanity at the crossroads.* New York: Crossroad.
Bell, Catherine M. (1997). *Ritual: Perspectives and dimensions.* New York: Oxford University Press.
Berry, Thomas. (1999). *The great work.* New York: Random House.
Berry, Thomas. (2009). *Religion in the 21st century.* Introduction by Mary Evelyn Tucker. New York: Columbia University Press.
Cobb, John. (1999). *The Earthist challenge to economism: A theological critique of the World Bank.* New York: St. Martin's Press.
Durkheim, Émile. (1915 [1965]). *The elementary forms of religious life.* New York: Free Press.
Girard, Réne. (1977). *Violence and the sacred* (Patrick Gregory, Trans.). Baltimore: Johns Hopkins University Press.
Hubert, Henri, & Mauss, Marcel. (1964). *Sacrifice: Its nature and function* (W. D. Halls, Trans.). Chicago: University of Chicago Press. (Original work published 1899)
Keenan, Dennis King. (2005). *The question of sacrifice.* Bloomington: Indiana University Press.
Leonard, Annie. (n.d.). The story of stuff. Retrieved April 22, 2009, from http://www.storyofstuff.com/
Loy, David R. (1997). The religion of the market. *The Journal of the American Academy of Religion, 65*(2), 275–290.
McKenna, Andrew J. (1991). *Violence and difference: Girard, Derrida, and deconstruction.* Urbana: University of Illinois Press.
Putnam, Robert D. (2000). *Bowling alone: The collapse and revival of American community.* New York: Simon & Schuster.
Schor, Juliet. (2000). *Do Americans shop too much?* Boston: Beacon Press.
Strenski, Ivan. (1997). The social and intellectual origins of Hubert and Mauss's theology of ritual sacrifice. In Dick van der Meij, (Ed.), *India and beyond: Aspects of literature, meaning, ritual and thought* (pp. 511–537). London: Kegan Paul International.
The Meatrix. (n.d.) Retrieved April 22, 2009, from http://www.themeatrix.com/inside/

Sin and Evil

The Abrahamic religions describe deviation from God's being or will as sin. Because these religions conceive God to be morally good, sin is closely and complexly related to evil—unjustified harm to sentient beings. Given their putative impropriety and potentially deleterious effects, individual or societal practices that threaten sustainability may be sinful, evil, or both.

Since human departure from moral, ecological, or religious orders can threaten the Earth's resources and inhabitants, the vocabulary of sin and evil may help to illumine sustainability problems.

Sin

Sin is culpable unrighteousness that violates God's will or otherwise deviates from holiness. While sin is consequently a religious notion, it also damages human lives and the environment, and so overlaps with moral categories. As such, sin naturally implies a morally perfect God that humans may disobey and is thus primarily a concept of Judaism, Christianity, and Islam.

The terms "sin" and "sins" often refer to distinct phenomena. Sin describes a basic lack of trust in God, or may denote a force opposed to God with power over human nature and the world. Sins are discrete, culpable acts, thoughts, and omissions that are contrary to God's will. This distinction does not represent a difference between religion and morality, for sin and sins may equally be failures of faith or virtue, or both.

"Original sin" is a distinctly Christian doctrine asserting that human beings are now born into a state of sin as a consequence of the first human couple's disobedience to God and fall from grace. By interpreting all subsequent people to be culpable for that first sin and to have inherited a tendency to sin because of it, the doctrine supports the Christian contention that human beings cannot extricate themselves from sin or its guilt. Nevertheless, original sin has been challenged as historically implausible (since the alleged penalty for that sin—toil, suffering, and death—is said to have always been part of human experience) and morally problematic (since it involves innate culpability).

By attributing sin to social institutions and practices, the concept of "structural sin" provides a way for Christians to maintain their insistence that human beings sin inevitably and culpably without the problems associated with the doctrine of original sin. Structural sin refers to culpably unrighteous social systems that dispose all who participate in them to further sin. Structural sin thus accounts for the inevitability of human sin since it considers people to be formed by and embedded within unjust economic, political, and cultural arrangements. Unlike original sin, however, structural sin is not innate, for people are born into it rather than with it. Similarly, individuals remain meaningfully culpable in the context of structural sin, for individuals perpetuate unrighteous social systems, and it is their character that these systems shape. Yet identification of structural sin is not a contemporary innovation prompted by recent concern with perceived inadequacies in the doctrine of original sin. Instead structural sin is repeatedly denounced in the scriptures of all three Abrahamic faiths and reflects appreciation for the relational character of human being.

Evil

Evil is serious, unjustified harm of sentient beings. A distinction is often drawn between natural evil (suffering caused by impersonal natural powers) and moral evil (wicked activities of responsible agents and the suffering they produce). This distinction should not be overdrawn: at times, humans may be merely natural agents; conversely, evil caused by natural agents may warrant moral condemnation if moral agents had an obligation to avert it.

Sin and evil are closely and complexly related. All moral evil is sinful, and both sin and evil are diametrically opposed to God and the good. Sin, however, is not always evil (consider cultic impropriety), and no exclusively natural evil is sinful.

Sin and evil pose different theological problems. Sin challenges the prospects for salvation since it ruptures appropriate relations between God and human beings, and apparently precludes the communion with a righteous God that constitutes salvation. The Abrahamic faiths respond by confessing that God both gratuitously forgives human beings—thereby annulling their guilt and rectifying their relationship with God—and also transforms them by amending their tendency to sin—thus enabling human beings to cleave to God.

Evil challenges the plausibility of belief in the Abrahamic God since God must want to eradicate evil if good and must be able to eradicate evil if almighty, yet evil exists. Although denying the existence of evil would dispel this dilemma, the Abrahamic faiths have instead sought to reconcile evil's existence with God's. Recourse to free will may be one way to do so, for if moral goodness depends upon freedom, and freedom entails the possibility of evil, then evil's existence is consistent with God's power and goodness so long as moral goodness is. Any successful theodicy—the attempt to justify the existence of evil by providing a morally sufficient reason why a perfectly good and almighty God would allow it—would also resolve the tension. Such explanations commonly contend that the best possible world includes evil, and hence reconcile evil's existence with God's, but they raise the further question of whether a world with as much evil as ours is plausibly the best possible.

Frederick SIMMONS
Yale Divinity School

FURTHER READING

Augustine. (1984). *City of God* (Henry Bettenson, Trans.). New York: Penguin Classics. (Original work published 412–418)

Farley, Edward. (1990). *Good and evil: Interpreting a human condition.* Minneapolis, MN: Fortress Press.

Gutiérrez, Gustavo. (1988). *A theology of liberation: History, politics, and salvation* (rev. ed.). (Caridad Inda & John Eagleson, Trans.). Maryknoll, NY: Orbis.

Hick, John. (2007). *Evil and the God of Love* (2nd ed.). New York: Palgrave Macmillan.

Niebuhr, Reinhold. (1996). *The nature and destiny of man: A Christian interpretation: Vol. I. Human Nature.* Louisville, KY: Westminster John Knox.

Stewardship

Stewardship and environmental sustainability have been linked since biblical times. Stewardship ideals are accepted and discussed by religious congregations, ecologists, environmental organizations, politicians, and corporations alike. Stewardship incorporates sustainable utilization of natural resources, thoughtful care for the environment, and appropriately sharing the Earth as household, with other humans and other species.

The word "stewardship" comes from the Old English word "stiweard," now spelled "steward," which means someone appointed to manage or supervise a house or a hall. A steward may also be responsible for an estate, landholdings, royal household, or guild. The steward serves someone else: a king, a property owner, an organization, or a community. "Stewardship" can have an explicitly religious context, such as administering or distributing wealth provided by God (Trumble 2002, 3026). Used in a modern environmental context, the term stewardship carries many of its original implications, including service in the interest of others, careful management of natural and fiscal resources, and providing for the safety and comfort of both residents and guests. Stewardship invokes images of the Earth as a household, which we share, not just with other humans but with all living organisms, including wildlife, trees, and even microorganisms.

The connection between stewardship and environmental sustainability is of biblical origin, although the concept has spread widely to the general public and even among politicians. Ironically, the King James Bible or "authorized" version utilizes the word "steward" in the parables of Jesus, but not in any biblical passages describing the creation of the Earth, the Garden of Eden, or direct human care for plants or animals (Staff of Thomas Nelson Bibles, 2002). Environmental stewardship is a modern construction on ancient foundations. In Genesis 43, the Torah describes Joseph's brothers coming to Egypt in the time of famine. Joseph instructs his steward to provide food and to place money in their sacks. The household steward also gives them water, washes their feet, and feeds their donkeys. In the Gospel of Mathew 20, the owner of a vineyard, as a metaphor for God, instructs his steward to pay the faithful laborers. Luke 12:42 distinguishes the faithful and wise steward who provides food for his slaves, whereas Luke 16 commends the shrewd steward who ingratiates himself to his master's debtors by forgiving what they owe. Perhaps most directly applicable to the contemporary Christian context is the Letter of Paul to Titus 1:7, which declares a Christian bishop must be a steward of God, blameless and moderate in behavior, avoiding the temptation of "filthy lucre." Christians apply the concept of stewardship specifically to handling congregational finances, or managing personal finances in a responsible way, which sets aside money for charity or for religious purposes (Staff of Thomas Nelson Bibles, 2002; Coogan, Brettler, Newsom, and Perkins 2007).

Christians have combined the role of a steward as a servant of God with the Genesis passages that describe humans as created in the image of God (1:26), and God placing Adam in the garden "to till and to keep it" (2:15) (Coogan, Brettler, Newsom,

and Perkins 2007). These passages imply humans should be stewards of the Earth, using what God has provided, while serving God's interests. Sound stewardship incorporates care of one's neighbors, preserving the beauty of the Creation, protecting the poor and needy, and treating the Earth as if it belongs to God.

The words "ecology" and "economics" are derived from the Greek word *oikos*, which means "house" or "household." The New Testament makes frequent use of *oikos* to identify families, lineage, ethnicities, or homes, including those that are pious or well managed. Both religious and nonreligious environmentalists have reasoned that the stewardship model suggests astute management of the *oikos*, or the Earth's household, as well as of the resource economics of the Earth (Morrison 1979, 283–284). The ideal steward combines thoughtful decision making, accountability, measured administration, a heart for the common good, and a balanced concern for the ecological, family, and national spheres of interest.

Stewardship and Sustainability

Environmental stewardship is often linked to the concept of sustainability. Although sustainability is discussed in diverse arenas—from the United Nations to the U.S. Congress to businesses to high schools—a universally accepted definition of the word has, thus far, proven elusive. The environmentalist Sharad LèLè (1991, 608) notes "the concept of sustainability originated in the context of renewable resources such as forests or fisheries, and has subsequently been adopted as a broad slogan by the environmental movement." Initially, professional resources managers sought "sustainable" means for harvesting resources that could replenish themselves through regrowth, recharge, or reproduction (such as rangelands, tree plantations, or groundwater), or that, like sunlight or geothermal energy, would outlast the human race. Sustainable environmental management practices should provide food, water, energy, or building materials over not just years but centuries. Ideally, sustainable policies and strategies leave productive farms, fisheries, and aquifers for the use and enjoyment of future generations. The concept of sustainability spread easily to environmentally focused awareness organizations such as Greenpeace and Sierra Club, because the public accepts the importance of maintaining the economic viability of natural resource extraction.

Nonprofit organizations, however, are apparently not the only proponents of sustainability. Although multibillion dollar corporations such as the major oil companies have come under fire from environmental groups, they have responded with their own definitions of sustainability. In the company's 2007 Corporate Citizenship Report, ExxonMobil articulated their policy of striving to "conduct business throughout the world in a manner that is protective of the environment and compatible with the environmental and economic needs of the communities in which we operate." The report described of the corporation's commitment to "improving our environmental performance through scientifically sound and practical solutions with the goal of driving incidents with real environmental impact to zero." Although one might question if ExxonMobil's goal of reducing anthropogenic levels of environmental influences to zero is actually possible, ExxonMobil is one of many resource-based corporations considering whether their current production strategies are sustainable over decades or centuries. The U.S. National Science Foundation (2009) supports research into sustainable engineered systems "that support human well-being and that are also compatible with sustaining natural (environmental) systems. These systems provide ecological services vital for human survival. The long-term viability of natural capital is critical for many areas of human endeavor."

Stewardship is compatible with sustainability, as both call for long-term and well-planned economic administration, and both share the goal of continued provision for the entire Earth household or community. The two concepts are often combined to make a more robust model for environmental action or policy. International Business Machine Corporation (2008) released a "white paper" calling for both sustainable energy production business strategies and corporate commitment to "environmental stewardship," in the belief sustainable growth is consistent with corporate social responsibility. To promote environmental sustainability in the twenty-first century, environmental ethicists have proposed a holistic ecological approach based on three of the main facets of our society and implemented through policy initiatives and environmental legislation that foster economic, social, and environmental stewardship. Thus the success in fostering stewardship and implementing environmental sustainability policy at the national level hinges on the reconciliation of different communities' interests concerning resource use, economic growth, and societal wellbeing (Barrett and Grizzle 1998). It is only by defining environmental sustainability as a conscious synthesis of various parties' desires that the health of the Earth will be able to flourish along with economically motivated interests, and all facets of our society will be able to truly thrive.

Religion and Environmental Stewardship

Evangelical theologians began to publish entire volumes on the general topic of stewardship in the 1950s (Sheldon 1992). In the early 1960s, Arthur Peacocke introduced the term into discussions of the relationship between religion and science, and by the 1970s, stewardship had "become the environmentalist path most often proposed by Protestant Christians seeking to serve God and God's creation" (Fowler 1995, 76). In 1980, the Fellows of Calvin Center for Christian Scholarship published *Earthkeeping: Christian Stewardship of Natural Resources,* edited by the theologian Loren Wilkinson. The volume and its revised edition helped to convey the idea of stewardship as "the exercise of delegated dominion in the service of creation" to students at faith-based colleges and to evangelical congregations (Wilkinson 1980, 308). Douglas John Hall culminated a series of theological projects projecting the steward as an ideal Christian caring for life in a world dominated by death and sin (Hall 1986). Jews, including David Ehrenfeld, a founder of the Society for Conservation Biology, entered the dialogue about the biblical basis for environmental care, as did Roman Catholics, who emphasized the critical link between stewardship and social justice (Ehrenfeld and Bentley 1998; Jegen and Mano 1978).

A key religious theme has been that humans do not own the Earth as property, but the planet belonged to God in perpetuity, and therefore should be managed to reflect God's interests, including care for the poor and sharing with others. Stewardship assumes care and provision for future generations, and for all God's creatures. A proper application of stewardship corrects misinterpretation of biblical passages such as Genesis 1:26, which in some translations instructs humans to "take dominion over the Earth." Both secular and religious stewardship advocates believe stewardship is a duty of all humans, which we have often failed to fulfill. Stewardship celebrates the beauty and wonder in nature, as well as the human dependence on a well-cared-for environment (Fowler 1995; Berry 2006).

Criticisms and Successes

Some environmentalists have criticized the stewardship position as too oriented toward resource use and too complacent concerning current economic strategies for environmental exploitation. As such, it can seem to be a compromise with middle-class values. Christian views of stewardship may also view humanity in separation from their environments by holding that humans play a special role in creation or have a divine call to stewardship, whereas some environmentalists reject the concept that humans are unique, or attempt to overcome dualist views that emphasize human uniqueness (Fowler 1995, 78).

A success of the stewardship model, however, is it widely accepted by moderate to conservative members of biblically based faiths, including Evangelical Christians. It incorporates the issues of family care and economic security, which are of high concern to religious practitioners with a commitment to biblical ethics. Stewardship also can provide an attractive basis for religious environmental ethics that emphasize the ultimate authority of God.

Although stewardship has been a widespread model for environmental care, for more than half a century, sophisticated discourse continues. Robert J. Berry (2006), a geneticist, has assembled an entire volume on the topic of Christian environmental stewardship with commentaries on a variety of environmental issues. Berry's collection covers both the weaknesses of the stewardship model, and provides potential new applications, including sea Sabbaths for stressed fisheries and purification for chemically overloaded agricultural soils. The theologian Michael Northcott (2007) has invoked historic Christian commitment to "careful stewardship," including sharing resources with the poor, simultaneously with sustainable dwellings, food production, and energy economics, as a route to resolving a very current issue: the excessive contribution of wealthy nations to the increasing level of green house gases in the atmosphere. Northcott (2007) presents both concepts as encouraging common citizen to pursue actions likely to curtail impending global climate change. Stewardship has become an important model for appropriate attitudes toward long-term environmental use, care, and respect. Today, it is often in combination with advocacy for sustainability. Stewardship ideals are accepted and discussed by religious congregations, ecologists, environmental organizations, politicians, and corporations alike.

Susan Power BRATTON
Austin COOK-LINDSAY
Baylor University

FURTHER READING

Barrett, Christopher B., & Grizzle, Raymond E. (1999). A holistic approach to sustainability based on pluralistic stewardship. *Environmental Ethics, 21*(1), 23–42.

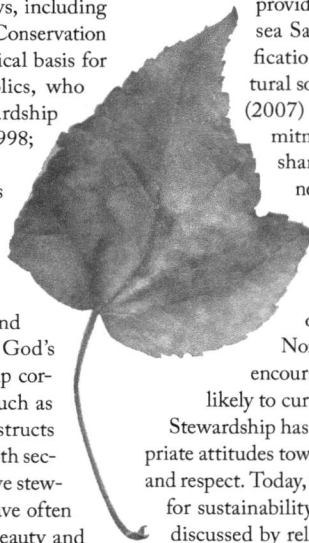

Berry, Robert J. (2006). *Environmental stewardship: Critical perspectives, past and present.* London: Continuum Publishing.

Coogan, Michael D.; Brettler, Mark Z.; Newsom, Carol A.; & Perkins, Pheme. (Eds.). (2007). *New Oxford annotated Bible with the Apocrypha, augmented third edition, New Revised Standard Version.* Oxford, U.K.: Oxford University Press.

Ehrenfeld, David, & Bentley, P. J. (1985). Judaism and the practice of stewardship. *Judaism: A Quarterly Journal of Jewish Life and Thought, 34,* 301–311.

ExxonMobil Corporation. (2007). Corporate citizenship report. (Brochure). Retrieved April 19, 2009, from http://www.exxonmobil.com/Corporate/files/Corporate/community_ccr_2007.pdf

Fowler, Robert Booth. (1995). *The greening of Protestant thought.* Chapel Hill: University of North Carolina Press.

Hall, John Douglas. (1986). *Imaging God: Dominion as stewardship.* New York: Eerdmans/Friendship Press.

International Business Machine Corporation (IBM). (2008). Improving business responsibility through smart energy and environmental policy. Retrieved April 18, 2009, from http://www.935.ibm.com/services/us/cio/energy/assets/ee_feature_offer_wp.pdf

Jegen, M. E., & Manno, B. V. (Eds.). (1978). *The Earth is the Lord's: Essays on stewardship.* New York: Paulist Press.

LèLè, Sharad. (1991). Sustainable development: A critical review. *World Development, 19*(6), 607–621.

Morrison, Clinton. (1979). *An analytical concordance to the Revised Standard Version of the New Testament.* Philadelphia: Westminster Press.

Northcott, Michael. (2007). *A moral climate: The ethics of global warming.* Maryknoll, NY: Orbis Books.

Sheldon, Joseph. (1992). *Rediscovery of Creation: A bibliographic study of the Church's response to the environmental crisis.* American Theological Library Association Bibliography Series, No. 29. Metuchen, NJ: Scarecrow Press.

Staff of Thomas Nelson Bibles. (2002). *Compact Holy Bible King James Version (KJV), containing the Old and New Testaments.* Nashville, TN: Thomas Nelson Publishers.

Trumble, William R. (Ed.). (2002). "Steward" and "Stewardship." *Shorter Oxford English Dictionary, Vol. 2, N–Z, 5th edition.* Oxford, U.K.: Oxford University Press.

U.S. National Science Foundation. (2009). Environmental sustainability (program page). Retrieved April 18, 2009 from http://www.nsf.gov/

Wilkinson, Loren, (Ed.). (1980). *Earthkeeping: Christian stewardship of natural resources.* Grand Rapids, MI: William B. Eerdmans.

Wilkinson, Loren, (Ed.). (1991). *Earthkeeping in the '90s: Stewardship of Creation.* Grand Rapids, MI: William B. Eerdmans.

Pilgrimage

Making a spiritual journey, or pilgrimage, has historically been a ritual for believers of many faiths who find fulfillment in the physical and emotional association with a sacred place. The ideas of connectedness between living beings, the divine, and resources of the ecosystem relate pilgrimage to sustainable ways of living; ironically many religious sites today feel the impact of our ecological footprint.

Pilgrimage is a spiritual journey or quest for fulfillment whose physical destination is often a shrine. The holy place may be a site of local deities, or a place where important events in the history of the religion, the deaths of its martyrs, or the lives of its founders occurred. The English word is derived from the Latin terms *peregrinus*, meaning "wanderer," and *per agrum*, meaning "through the fields." Reverberating through the word is an ancient echo of an intricate relationship between geography and the sacred in motion. In this sense both the concept and the practice of modern pilgrimage can draw attention to sustainable ways of living on Earth and the need to care for the ecosystem: the respect and devotion implicit in pilgrimage can enhance the connection humans feel to the lands they inhabit, the creatures they share them with, and the natural resources that make life possible.

Pilgrimage is common to many indigenous cultures, as well as to the major religions of the world. Jerusalem attracts pilgrims from all of the Abrahamic religions, while Buddhists, Hindus, Jains, and followers of Bön (Tibet's oldest indigenous religion) regard Mount Kailash in the Himalayas as a holy place. Modern Christians, who still have strong ties to the Holy Land, also flock to Roman reliquaries and to Lourdes in France. The largest annual pilgrimage in the world, the hajj, is one of the five pillars (duties) of Islam and requires every Muslim who is capable of traveling to go to Mecca at least once in a lifetime.

Cultural anthropologists in the twentieth century made several attempts to categorize pilgrimage. Victor and Edith Turner regard pilgrimage as a "liminoid" or transitional experience, in which pilgrims leave the established systems of society and form an egalitarian *communitas*, or "a social antistructure," on the road (Turner and Turner 1978, 250–251). John Eade and Michael Sallnow's *Contesting the Sacred* (1991) challenged Turner's concept of *communitas* for being (in part) too idealized and remote. Simon Coleman and John Eade, looking at the "on the road" aspect of a journey, have emphasized the movement involved in pilgrimage processes in various religious traditions, which they portray as "kinetic rituals" (Coleman and Eade 2004).

Turner and Turner (1978, 7) have noted a relationship between pilgrimage and mysticism. "If mysticism is an interior pilgrimage, pilgrimage is an exteriorized mysticism." Such links presuppose cosmologies where the divine is not considered to be distant to nature but immanent and present in landscape, movement, and body. This interconnectedness in nature is an aspect of many indigenous religions whose creation myths derive from an Earth Mother and which today practice sustainable ways of living in the spirit of devotion and respect. Phil Cousineau, the author of *The Art of Pilgrimage: The Seeker's Guide to Making Travel Sacred*, suggests "that we follow our spiritual compass and put the soles of our shoes

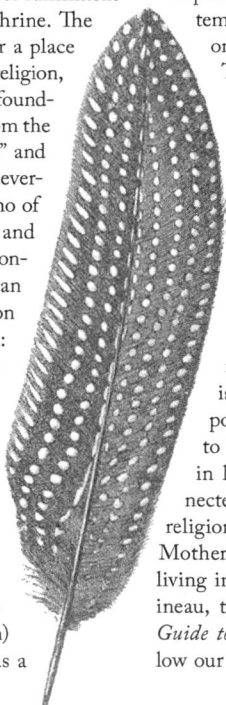

to the soul of the world. It means getting back in touch with our earth, our roots, ourselves" (O'Reilly and O'Reilly 2000, xv).

The positive impact of pilgrimage as it relates to sustainability can be seen in numerous accounts of how such spiritual journeys heighten people's sensitivity to the relation and balance among the human and nonhuman creatures, the divine, and the resources of our ecosystem. While the term *pilgrimage* has adopted an increasingly secular connotation—traveling to pay tribute to a cultural icon, for instance, or calling a popular cultural center a "tourists' Mecca"—the underlying implications of pilgrimage as a quest for fulfillment remain strong. The October 2008 Grace Pilgrimage to the Peace Village of San José de Apartadó, for instance, originated not as a religious-based journey but as a form of social activism in the civil-war-torn areas of Colombia; its focus was

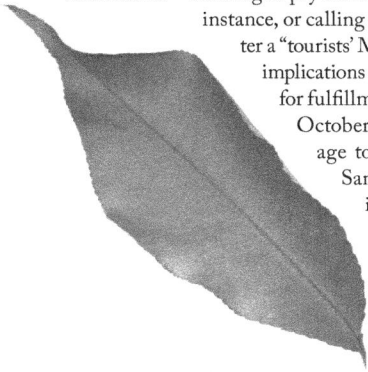

to help villagers work ecologically, technologically, and socially toward a dignified and sustainable future.

The negative impact of pilgrimage—the fact that many religious shrines of the world suffer from traffic, pollution, and the demands of tourism—reminds pilgrims (and enthusiastic tourists alike) that the journey "through the fields" should be made with care, and with an effort to reduce the human ecological footprint on Earth as a whole.

Sigridur GUDMARSDOTTIR
Reykjavik Academy

FURTHER READING

Coleman, Simon, & Eade, John. (Eds.). (2004). *Reframing pilgrimage: Culture in motion*. London: Routledge.

Cousineau, Philip. (2000). *The art of pilgrimage The seeker's guide to making travel sacred*. Newburyport, MA: Red Wheel.

Eade, John, & Sallnow, Michael J. (1991). *Contesting the sacred: The anthropology of pilgrimage*. London and New York: Routledge.

O'Reilly, Sean, & O'Reilly, James. (Eds.). (2000). *Pilgrimage: Adventures of the spirit*. Palo Alto, CA: Travelers' Tales.

Timothy, D. J., & Olsen, Daniel. (Eds.). (2006). *Tourism, religion and spiritual journeys*. London: Routledge.

Turner, Victor, & Turner, Edith. (1978). *Image and pilgrimage in Christian culture: Anthropological perspectives*. New York: Columbia University Press.

Meditation and Prayer

Spirituality is important to the concept of sustainability; it allows humans to observe and embrace the important things in life (as opposed to the material ones). Too often this journey is impeded by inattention; religions can help remove these distractions through prayer and meditation. These acts become forms of listening—ideally, wise and compassionate listening that is essential for sustainability.

The spiritual side of sustainable living is nourished with a sense of being animated and engraced (to be receptive to, and energized by) a healing power greater than oneself: strangers and friends, hills and rivers, stars and galaxies, gods and goddesses. It begins with joy, not anger. In human life, one of the deepest obstacles to receiving such joy is inattention.

The religions of the world offer various correctives to this distractedness. Buddhists typically approach it directly and in psychological terms. They compare our minds to drunken monkeys that are flitting from one branch of a tree to another, such that, for most of us, having a calm and undistracted mind—a mind of presence—is very difficult. We think that we control our thoughts, they say, but in fact our thoughts control us. Accordingly, many Buddhists recommend a daily practice of meditation as one way of developing a calm mind so that we can then bring into our daily activities a less distracted presence. With practice, they say, we can gradually find ourselves more centered and more available to the call of each present moment.

Similarly, some Christians who are influenced by the contemplative traditions within Christianity recommend a daily practice of centering prayer. If we learn to "center down" even for a brief time every morning, say these Christians, we slowly understand that we can live from the immediacy of God's presence in our daily lives. We realize that each present moment is a sacrament of sorts, and

that the very light of God shines through the face of the other people who need our listening ear. Some, such as the Benedictines, go further and say that we meet Christ in the other person, whether stranger or friend, attractive or frightening. The Benedictines are a religious group within Catholic Christianity who highlight listening as a key aspect of the life of discipleship. "When I was hungry you gave me food, and when I was in prison you visited me," says Jesus in the Gospel of Matthew (25:34–36, RSV). "And when I needed someone to talk to," the Benedictines seem to add, "you listened to me."

Here listening refers to the act of being present, of being aware, of being open and available to what is given for experience. Of course, there are many reasons a person might seek to listen. The kind of listening at issue here, the kind that is conducive to sustainability, is best illustrated in what a Buddhist might call wise and compassionate listening. When this listening is directed toward another human being, it is guided not by the aim of conquering or controlling but by the aim of being with that person in a sensitive way, and of responding wisely and compassionately. We might call it attunement or deep listening. It can be the spirit in which people feel attuned not only to one another, but also to plants, animals, and minerals. We might call it ecolistening.

Attunement is not simply a matter of the ears. It can also occur through touch, sight, smell, and sound; it can be guided by intuition, imagination, and reason. When a nurse gently binds the wound of a person who is injured, she is listening with her hands; when a businessman calculates the possible outcomes of a business decision with an eye to helping build a green community, he is listening with his reason. There are many ways to listen and there are many kinds of listeners.

Who is it, then, who should be listened to in an age needful of sustainability. The answer is whoever addresses us. Some people in the modern West would have said that it is humans and only humans who can address us. But most advocates of sustainability recognize that we can be addressed by hills and rivers, trees and stars, cats and dogs. They may not speak to us in languages we learn from childhood or formal schooling, but they present themselves to us to be heard, to be listened to. A primary value of prayer and meditation is to learn to listen and then respond to them.

Of course in many cultural traditions, there is another kind of prayer that is important: namely, prayers in which we ourselves address something greater than ourselves. We may name this something God or the Universe or Ancestors or Amithaba Buddha or Krishna. We may address it with words, our feelings, our rituals, or our dancing. We may seek an active response from this something, or we may be content with the companionship of having been listened to. We may conceive it monotheistically (with a belief in one God), polytheistically (with a belief in many gods), monistically (believing that reality is a unified whole, in which all parts are ascribed to single system, or panentheistically (seeing the whole in God, as opposed to pantheistically, believing that God is the whole). In any instance the very act of addressing can play an important role in sustainable living. It externalizes the depths of human feeling, turning our inner lives inside out, so that we can see who we are and who we seek to become.

Of course the content of the prayer matters, too. If we pray that our enemies be massacred, that the Earth be destroyed, or that people who are "different" be eliminated, our hopes are not consistent with the ethical norms of sustainable living. The better hope is that the content of prayers can contribute to the hope that communities can emerge on Earth in which the will of the Spirit is done on Earth as it is in heaven (to adapt the most remembered prayer of Jesus).

Advocates of sustainability recognize that the Spirit can be conceived in many different ways. Indeed people may not believe in the Spirit and yet still have a sense of spirituality if they have a sense of connection with the Earth and an appreciation of the beauty of life. Healthy agnosticism is among the living options within ecospirituality. But even agnostics can pray. Even agnostics can address the universe in praise, lamentation, and wonder. Their prayers are completed, along with those of monotheists and polytheists, monists and panentheists, when they act on those prayers, helping to add beauty to the world.

Jay McDANIEL
Hendrix College

FURTHER READING

Kaza, Stephanie (Ed.). (2000). *Dharma rain: Sources of Buddhist environmentalism*. Boston: Shambhala.

May, Gerald. (1982). *Will and spirit: A contemplative psychology*. San Francisco: Harper & Row.

McDaniel, Jay B. (2000). *Living from the center: Spirituality in an age of consumerism*. St. Louis, MO: Chalice Press.

Randour, Mary Lou. (2000). *Animal grace: Entering a spiritual relationship with our fellow creatures*. Novato, CA: New World Library.

Thurman, Howard. (2006). *Howard Thurman: Essential writings*. Maryknoll, NY: Orbis Books.

Ware, Kallistos. (1979). *The orthodox way*. Crestwood, NY: St. Vladmir's Seminary Press.

Science, Religion, and Ecology

Science, with its theories of natural selection and equilibrium, and religion, with its biblical descriptions of land forever flowing with "milk and honey," have viewed nature as ever-renewing. Both have prioritized growth and its resulting abundance. As our twenty-first-century environmental crises challenge these concepts, scientists can teach us to sustain the environment while the motivations of biblical stewardship remind us to treasure Earth's biodiversity and celebrate creation.

*L*ife perpetually renewed in the midst of its perpetual perishing: the theme is a common one in both evolutionary natural history and Christian faith. Natural systems have evolved historically and ecosystems have been tested over thousands of years for their dynamic resilience, sometimes remaining stable and at other times undergoing change. As human life evolved, classical monotheism arose with a sense of dwelling in a promised land forever, although biblical writers acknowledged the transience of life. Concern for ecosystem health and integrity have evolved as well. Humans may now stand at a rupture point in history—facing, as some believe, the end of nature. Ecological management, with its scientific focus on preserving nature's resources and developing technologies, continues the concept of biblical stewardship. A critical question is whether to seek sustainable development or a sustainable biosphere.

A Dynamic, Enduring Earth

Both science and religion, in principle and in practice, face concerns about environmental sustainability. Both worldviews encounter an historical dynamism (i.e., forces of change) superimposed on recurring stability. Evolutionary natural history finds natural selection operating over incremental variations across enormous time spans, with the fittest selected to survive. This drives perennial change as species acquire new skills, exploit new niches, and migrate toward shifting environments.

The theory of punctuated equilibrium, in some contrast, interprets the fossil record as evidence for periods of millions of years of relative stasis, punctuated by relatively brief periods of rapid change. Biologists also speak of evolutionary-stable strategies. Natural selection drives changes, but natural selection fails without enough stability in ecosystems to make the mutations selected for dependably reliable for survival over the immediately forthcoming years. Natural systems were often "sustained" in the past for long periods of time. Critics reject such balance of nature in favor of episodic events, open ecological systems, dynamism and change. Disturbances in the orderly succession of ecosystems produce a patchwork landscape. Ecosystems have various kinds of resilience, but if the disturbances become amplified enough, the stability gets swamped by disorder. Equilibrium and non-equilibrium do represent two ends of a spectrum with real ecosystems somewhere in between, and seeing one or the other can depend on the level and scale of analysis. At the levels of population and species diversity, or community composition, ecosystems can show predictable patterns, approaching steady states on restricted ranges. When unusual disturbances come, they can be displaced beyond recovery of their former patterns. Then they settle into new equilibriums.

The processes and products originally in place will, with high probability, have been those for which organisms are naturally selected for their adaptive fits; misfits go extinct and easily disrupted ecosystems collapse and are replaced by more stable ones. Ecosystems get tested over thousands of years for their resilience. As a result, they have both stability and dynamic novelty. Many general characteristics are repeated; many local details vary. Patterns of growth and development are orderly and predictable enough to make ecological science possible. This ecosystemic nature, once flourishing independently and for millennia continuing along with humans, has in the last one hundred years come under increasing jeopardy—variously described as a threat to ecosystem health, integrity, stability, or quality.

Classical monotheism arose with a more fixed account of earth structures and processes, set in place at an initial "start-up" creation, and thereafter ongoing with little change. Facing death, as Jacob is "gathered to my people" he blesses Israel: "The blessings of your father are mighty beyond the blessings of the eternal mountains, the bounties of the everlasting hills" (Genesis 49:26, RSV). Life is an ongoing struggle, and therefore hopes arise for the advent of redemption when the Messiah comes, or, for Christians, comes again. But in the course of Earth history, if Israel keeps the commandments, God says, "then I will let you dwell in this place in the land that I gave of old to your fathers for ever" (Jeremiah 7:7).

The sages and prophets knew the transience of life. Consider "a flower of the field": "the wind passes over it, and it is gone, and its place knows it no more" (Psalm 103:15–16). But they also knew a sustainability and saw, under God, a promised land in which "it might go well with them and with their children for ever" (Deuteronomy 5:29). That certainly sounds like sustainability.

The perpetual cycle of life, which involves renewal in the midst of perishing, is a common theme in both natural evolutionary history and in Christian faith. Both science and religion agree that Earth has long sustained and renewed life, although the classical regeneration of new life out of old on the scale of millennia has expanded to that of billions of years in contemporary science.

Many scientists believe, even in a sustainability crisis, that nature cannot be abolished but nature's ability to sustain life can be irreparably damaged. Nature has not ended and never will. Humans depend on nature for their life support. Humans use nature resourcefully; they may upset and degrade natural systems. But the natural forces can and will return if humans are taken out of the equation. There is always, once, and future nature.

Other more pessimistic scientists believe that humans on Earth are at a rupture point in history. European-Western civilization is self-destructing, spreading and triggering disruptions—climate change and decreasing biodiversity—around the globe. Until now, the technosphere was contained within the biosphere. Hereafter the technosphere will explode these limits. Earth is now in

a post-evolutionary phase, a post-ecological phase. The next millennium is the epoch of the "end of nature." The new epoch is the Anthropocene. That puts us indeed at a hinge point of history. What ought we to do to ensure sustainability?

Stewardship and Management

Scientists turning to environmental policy often appeal for ecosystem management. This is attractive to scientists, who see the need for understanding ecosystems objectively and for developing applied technologies, and also to humanists, who desire benefits for people. The combined ecosystem and/or management policy promises to operate at system-wide levels, presumably to manage for indefinite sustainability of ecosystems and their outputs alike.

"Sound scientific management" connects with the idea of nature as "natural resources" and at least permits a "respect nature" dimension, although the question of "manage for what" is often presumed as human benefits. Christian ethicists note that the secular word "manage" is a stand-in for the earlier theological word "steward." Adam was placed in the garden "to till and keep it" (Genesis 2:15). They may add that "trustee" is a better model than "stewardship," since stewards are managing in the interests of owners, whereas "trustees" are charged with caring for what is put into their trust.

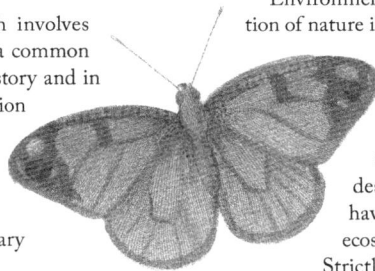

Environmental science can inform the evaluation of nature in subtle ways. Scientists describe the *order, dynamic stability*, and *diversity* in biotic *communities*. They describe *interdependence*, or speak of *health* or *integrity*, perhaps of these communities' *resilience* or *efficiency*. Scientists describe the *adapted fit* that organisms have in their niches. They describe an ecosystem as *flourishing*, as *self-organizing*. Strictly interpreted, these are only descriptive terms; and yet often they are already quasi-evaluative terms. Ecology is rather like medical science, with therapeutic purpose, seeking such flourishing health. Theologians may remark that such terms sound like a secular celebration of the *good earth* described in the Genesis parable of creation, or the *promised land* of Israel.

Religion and science have to be carefully delineated, each in its own domain. Asking about technical ecology in the Bible is a mistake (e.g., the Lotka-Volterra equations dealing with population size and carrying capacity). But ecology is a science at native range. Residents on landscapes live immersed in their local ecology. Within the pragmatic ranges of the sower who sows, waits for the seed to grow, and reaps the harvest, the Hebrews knew their landscape. Abraham and Lot, and later Jacob and Esau, dispersed their flocks and herds because "the land could not support both of them dwelling together" (Genesis 13:2–13, 36:6–8). These nomads were exceeding the carrying capacity, ecologists now say. They knew enough to let land lie fallow in the seventh year for its regeneration.

For sustainability, one needs human ecology, humane ecology, and this requires insight into human nature more so than into wild nature. True, humans cannot know the right way to act if they are ignorant of the causal outcomes in the natural systems they modify. But there must be more. "Hear therefore, O Israel, and be careful to do [these commandments] that it may go well with you, and that you may multiply greatly, as the Lord, the God of your fathers, has promised you, in a land flowing with milk and honey" (Deuteronomy 6:3). It is not the land husbandry or the science, but rather the ethics into which the biblical seers have insight. The deeper claim is that there can be no intelligent human ecology except as people learn to use land justly and charitably. Lands do not flow with milk and honey for all unless and until "justice rolls down like waters" (Amos 5:24).

Limits to Growth

Western religion and Western science have for centuries both joined in pushing back limits. Humans have more genius at this than any other species. We have lived with a deep-seated belief that one should hope for abundance and work toward obtaining it. Christian faith brought "the abundant life"; the DuPont corporation championed "better things for better living though chemistry." One accentuates the spiritual; the other accentuates the material side of life. Still, science and religion joined to get people fed and sheltered, to keep them healthy, and to raise standards of living.

We have built the right to self-development and the right to self-realization into our concept of human rights. Religious activists and missionaries have fought for that as much as economists and development scientists. But now we have begun to realize that such an egalitarian ethic scales everybody up and drives an unsustainable world. When everybody seeks their own good, aided by applied sciences, there is escalating consumption. When everybody seeks everybody else's good, urged by gospel compassion, there is, again, escalating consumption. This brings the worry whether either such development science or such compassionate religion is well equipped to deal with the sorts of global level problems we now face. Global threats require that growth be limited in the name of sustainability.

The four main concerns on the world agenda for the new millennium are these: escalating population, escalating consumption, the increasingly horrific consequences of war, and deteriorating environment. Escalating population and consumption are enabled by science, as is the technology for war, and the spillover is a degraded environment. Religions have fostered population growth, or are ambivalent about it; they have enabled human(e) development with increased consumption; they are often ambivalent about environmental conservation. As a result, population, consumption, and environment are not sustainable on our present course. A World Council of Churches theme, "justice, peace, and the integrity of creation," has focused more attention on conserving population growth and consumption than on saving the environment.

Sustainable Development? Sustainable Biosphere?

The prime model is sustainability, but if one asks what is to be sustained, there are two foci. The favored answer is this: sustainable development. When humans face limits, they need to find growth patterns that can be sustained. Such a duty seems plain and urgent; scientists, developers, social gospel activists, and missionaries can be unanimous about it. Sustainable development is useful just because it is a wide-angle lens, an orienting concept that is at once directed and encompassing, a coalition-level policy that sets aspirations, thresholds, and allows pluralist strategies for their accomplishment.

One needs the best that science can contribute (e.g., genetically modified foods, carbon dioxide monitors, and scientific models and data) and the best that religion can contribute (e.g., agricultural missions, sermons moderating escalating consumerism, etc.).

The underlying conviction is that the trajectory of development is generally right—but the developers in their enthusiasm have hitherto failed to recognize environmental constraints. Scientists can teach us how to sustain the environment, but we will need the motivations of stewardship (and, better yet, trusteeship) to succeed. Economists, who also like to think of themselves as scientists, may remark that a "growth economy" is the only economy theoretically or practically desirable, or even possible. They dislike "no-growth economies," but now accentuate "green economics."

A massive *Millennium Ecosystem Assessment*, sponsored by the United Nations, involving over thirteen hundred experts from almost one hundred

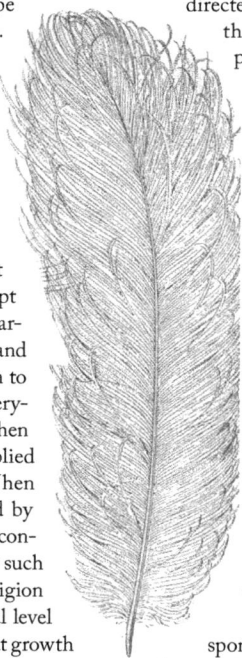

nations, begins this way: "At the heart of this assessment is a stark warning. Human activity is putting such strain on the natural functions of Earth that the ability of the planet's ecosystems to sustain future generations can no longer be taken for granted" (Millennium Ecosystem Assessment 2005, 5).

But there is another possible focus: "sustainable biosphere." Ecologists want to insist that "sustainable" is not so much an economic as an environmental term. The Ecological Society of America claims the following: "Achieving a sustainable biosphere is the single most important task facing humankind today" (Risser, Lubchenco, and Levin 1991). The fundamental flaw in "sustainable development" is that it sees the Earth as a resource only.

The underlying conviction in the sustainable biosphere model is that the current "development" trajectory is generally wrong because it will inevitably overshoot, fed by the aspirations of those who always seek to push back limits. The environment is not some undesirable, unavoidable set of constraints to be subdued and conquered with clever technological fixes. Rather, nature is the matrix of multiple values; many, even most of them are not counted in economic transactions. Nature provides numerous other values (e.g., life support, biodiversity, sense of place) that we wish to sustain. The test of a good Earth is not how much milk and honey can be squeezed out of it to drip into human mouths.

A "sustainable biosphere" model demands that the economy be worked out "within" a quality of life in a quality environment—clean air, water, stable agricultural soils, attractive residential landscapes, forests, mountains, rivers, rural lands, parks, wild lands, wildlife, renewable resources. Decisions about this quality environment will need input from society at large, including its scientists and its peoples of faith. Development is desired, and society must learn to live within the carrying capacity of its landscapes. Even more humans need to treasure Earth's biodiversity, to celebrate creation. Here science and religion complement each other in teaching us how to sustain the home planet, the Earth with promise, the global promised land.

Holmes ROLSTON III
Colorado State University

Further Reading

Attfield, Robin. (2003). Environmental ethics: An overview for the twenty-first century. Cambridge, U.K.: Polity Press.

Burkhardt, Jeffrey. (1989). The morality behind sustainability. *Journal of Agricultural Ethics, 2*, 113–128.

Daly, Herman E., & Cobb, John B., Jr. (1999). *For the common good: Redirecting the economy toward community, the environment, and a sustainable future.* (2nd ed.). Boston: Beacon Press.

Millennium Ecosystem Assessment. (2005). Living beyond our means: Natural assets and human well-being: Statement from the board. Washington, DC: World Resources Institute.

National Commission on the Environment. (1993). *Choosing a sustainable future: The report of the National Commission on the Environment.* Washington, DC: Island Press.

Norton, Bryan G. (2005). *Sustainability: A philosophy of adaptive ecosystem management.* Chicago: University of Chicago Press.

Risser, Paul G.; Lubchenco, Jane; & Levin, Simon A. (1991). Biological research priorities—a sustainable biosphere. *BioScience, 41*, 625–627.

Rolston, Holmes, III. (1996). The Bible and ecology. *Interpretation: Journal of Bible and Theology, 50*, 16–26.

Rolston, Holmes, III. (2003). Justifying sustainable development: A continuing ethical search. *Global Dialogue, 4*(1), 103–113.

Indigenous Traditions

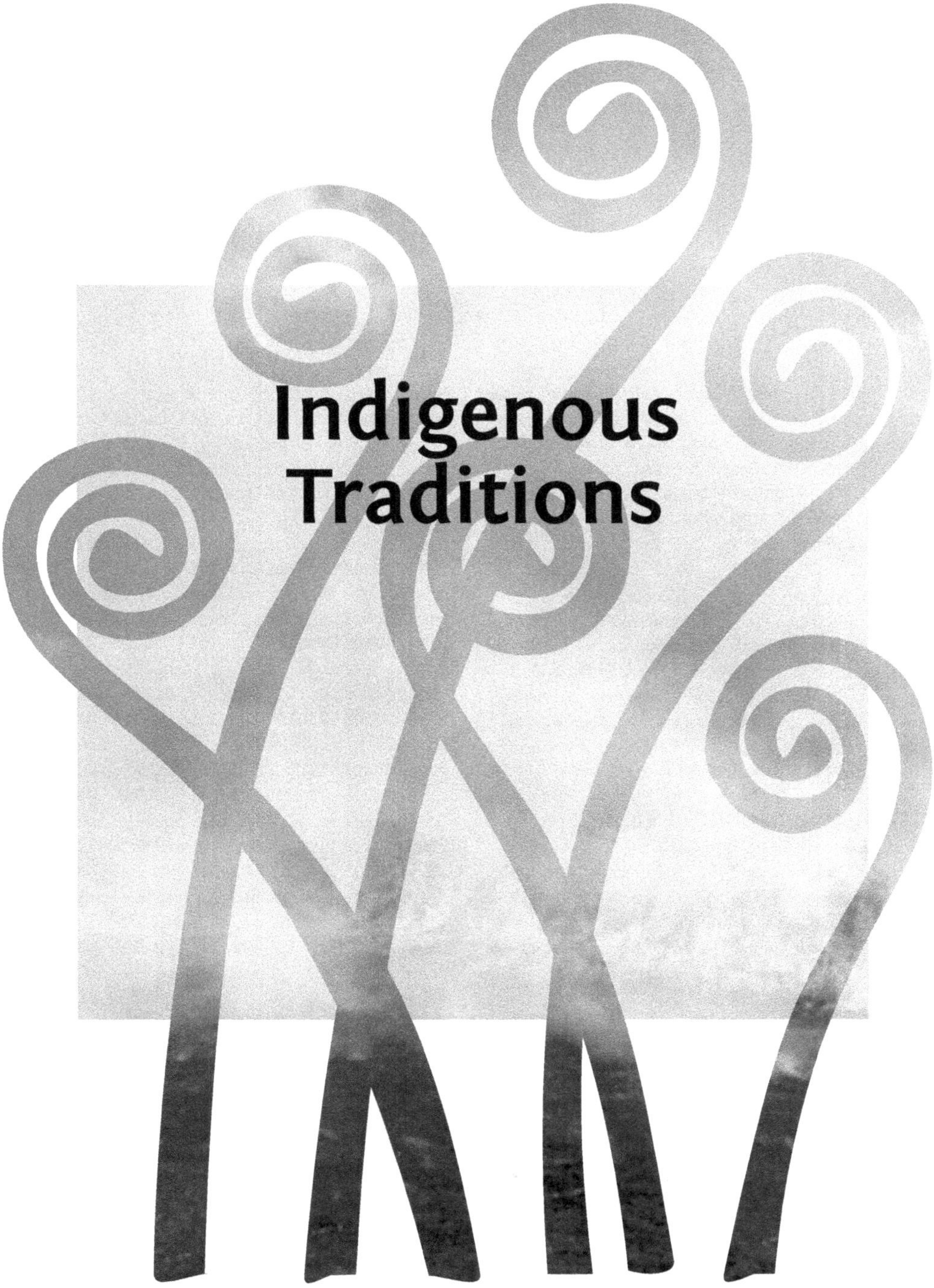

Indigenous Traditions—Africa

African peoples face the challenge of sustaining a unique identity in an increasingly globalized and Westernized society. Their indigenous traditions of proverb, festival, and divination involve values that carry an ethic of respect and celebration for ancestors and the divine from the past to the future, and reflect a general concern for sustaining all life on Earth.

Indigenous religious traditions in Africa universally hold that a life lived in harmony with the environment fosters spiritual and physical health. The question of sustainability as it applies to these traditions and values is twofold: how can indigenous African traditions survive in an increasingly modernized world, and how can these traditions, especially proverb, festival, and divination, help their practitioners face the challenges of sustainable living.

Differences and Shared Values

Due to the expansiveness of the African continent, indigenous religious traditions of Africa are rooted in diverse customs and practices. (While there is no African word equivalent to *religion*, many African terms convey the sense of practice and thought that reflect the meaning of the word in the West.) Most indigenous African traditions, however, share a common reverence for a Supreme Being, and all consider a life lived in harmony with their environment, both social and physical, a key to maintaining spiritual and physical health. Despite considerable differences in the language, the mode of worship, and the ritual used to express the existence and qualities of a Supreme Being, most African indigenous traditions subscribe to a common structure

in their belief system. This belief system is usually divided into major and the minor beliefs. The major beliefs, listed here hierarchically, include beliefs in the Supreme Being and in divinities, spirits, ancestors, and magic and medicine. The minor beliefs, which are essentially derived from the major ones, include, among others, beliefs in morality, life after death, reincarnation, and a last day of judgment.

Indigenous African traditions are characteristically monotheistic. Many casual observers, based on the expansive devotion of Africans to the divinities, have unfortunately labeled the these traditions polytheistic. A deeper examination of the African concept of the Supreme Being contradicts this view. As the religious studies scholar Bolaji Idowu (1973, 23) insists, indigenous traditions in Africa subscribe to a "diffused monotheism," whereby Africans gain access to the Supreme Being through the divinities; the divinities are not ends in themselves. The indigenous African concept of the Supreme Being is therefore not in tandem with the essential nature of polytheism, in which all the gods are "equal" but in which one god is conceded to be the "leader." Indigenous African traditions do not consider the divinities equal in any way to the Supreme Being. In fact, the Supreme Being is their creator, and the divinities are mere representatives or messengers.

Indigenous African traditions pervade every aspect of the everyday lives of their practitioners. Thus, as the religious philosopher John Mbiti (1982, 5) writes, "Africans are notoriously religious." It is therefore quite understandable that, even in contemporary societies, with many Africans following other religions such as Christianity and Islam, Africans still return to the "confines" of their indigenous traditions to find solutions in difficult moments of life, when the "foreign religions" seem to fail them.

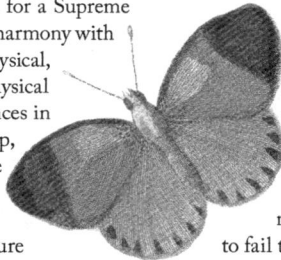

One crucial and common characteristic of these traditions has not only shaped but has actually enhanced the sustainability of indigenous African values and worldviews. Lacking the complement of written scriptural documents afforded other religions such as Christianity, Islam, and Judaism, indigenous African traditions have almost exclusively depended on oral sources to disseminate their vales and views through proverbs, festivals, and divination—dynamic forms of communication that have played vital roles in sustaining the much-cherished African heritage from the past to the present.

Proverbs

African proverbs are highly regarded and existentially employed as "wise sayings." Proverbs, derived from the timeless wisdom of ancestors, are used to drive home points during discussions and to explain figurative contexts for events and situations. In some African traditions there are proverbs about proverbs. The Yoruba people of Nigeria say, "A proverb is a horse that can carry one swiftly to ideas," while the Zulus say, "Without proverbs language would be but a skeleton without flesh, a body without a soul."

Through proverbs Africans express beliefs about the Supreme Being, impart theological and moral teachings, and illustrate the metaphysical dimensions of human existence. There are numerous proverbs on different attributes of the Supreme Being. The Yoruba denote that God is the ultimate custodian of justice by saying, "Leave your fight to Olodumare and look on; he is the defender of the defenseless." The Akan people of Ghana and Côte d'Ivoire express their belief in the omnipresence of God in the proverb that instructs, "If you want to tell it to God, tell it to the wind." But the celebration of proverbs as a means of fostering societal sustainability cannot be undertaken blindly. Proverbs must be approached with discerning minds to ensure that they address the transitory and new challenges of the modern world. This should not, however prevent us from recognizing proverbs as a foundation from the past upon which we can build both the present and the future.

In *The West and the Rest of Us*, Chinweizu, a Nigerian writer and critic of African literature, cautioned against treating ancestral knowledge as "absolute" at a time when Africans are beset by so many societal challenges and the culture itself often discourages adopting new strategies and change—and yet he stressed the importance of maintaining reverence and respect for such wisdom. Chinweizu (1975, 1) included in his book the following version of a well-known passage, attributed by John of Salisbury to Bernard of Chartres, the twelfth-century French philosopher who observed intellectuals of his time relying on the great thinkers of ancient Greece and Rome:

> We are like dwarfs sitting on the shoulders of giants, we see more things and more far off than they did, not because our sight is better, nor because we are taller, but because they raise us up and add to our height by their gigantic loftiness.

This metaphoric saying, a proverb in itself, extends across cultures and eras, but it has a special resonance for indigenous African peoples whose traditions and beliefs have been passed from generation to generation without a formal or scriptural text. In proverbs, concepts of sustainability derive from humbly and patiently listening to the African ancestors and learning from their wisdom, so as to seek guidance not only for the present but for the future. Proverbs have also been extensively used to elevate the relevance of nonhumans in sustainability. For example, many African proverbs use animals as impersonators of humans to teach and pass on the messages of traditional wisdom and the tenacity of purpose in the community. In the forefront of such proverbs are those associated with the cunning of the hare, the mischievous intelligence of the tortoise, the shrewdness of the monkey, and the opportunism of the chameleon.

Festivals

Festivals in African traditional settings are associated with different aspects of communal life. They celebrate milestones such as birth, initiation, marriages, and funerals, and they solemnize community veneration of divinities. John Mbiti points out that festivals create a dynamic for community renewal, unity, and cohesion. Sometimes they serve as the bond that links ancestors (and also the divine) with the living. This bond is central to the survival and sustainability of the community from one generation to the next.

The significance of festivals is demonstrated by the role they play in the day-to-day lives of twenty-first-century African communities and nations. Governments in many African countries have risen to the challenge of not only identifying the values of traditional festivals but actually giving strong support to their celebration as state events. The traditional Intawasa festival in Zimbabwe, for example,

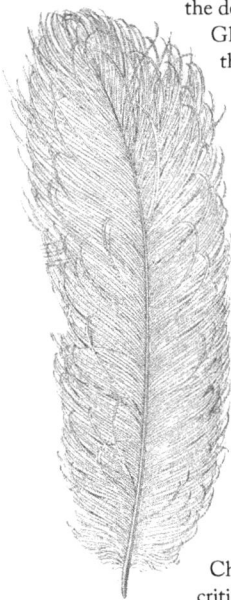

has become an annual national celebration of Zimbabwe's heritage with multidisciplinary offerings of theater, music, literary performance, and dance.

In Swaziland, the traditional Umhlanga festival and Reed Dance is no longer held just to honor the king's mother by gathering reeds to repair her house; it also celebrates the people's belief in "purity" as a moral societal value (a trait symbolized by the fact that young women must remain virgins until they marry). Such purity satisfies a requirement of the gods, through which the people of the land are said to be blessed with prosperity and an abundant harvest for the preservation and continuation of the community. Ironically the focus on puberty, and the festival itself, also calls attention to the fragility of human life in this polygamous country, where the HIV/AIDS epidemic is rampant (with over 40 percent of the population believed to be infected), and the life expectancy, according to the CIA World Factbook (available through www.cia.gov), averages 31.88 years.

In West Africa the Osun Osogbo Festival in Nigeria has become the epitome of traditional festivals, one to which participants flock from all parts of the world. The original festival dated to the early eighteenth century, when the town of Osogbo was founded by a group of hunters. In return for venerating the goddess of the Osun River as the protector and harbinger of fertility, the goddess protected the townspeople from invasion by Fulani warriors. These festivals, like others across Africa, help to sustain national identity by preserving the norms and values of the people, but they also bolster economic sustainability. The Zimbabwean Intawasa festivals, for instance, promote the city of Bulawayo as a tourist destination, create employment, and provide a viable market for artists' wares.

In festivals the dynamics of sustainability surface in the rhythm and the resonance of age-old celebrations in dance, song, and other works of art, all of which bind the present with the past in order to protect the future. This protection is enforced through the Kpalevorgu festival in Ghana, whose degraded forestlands have also been the focus of many promising international partnerships to support sustainable living. Through various festivals celebrated by the Yoruba people of western Africa, groves such as oke-Ibadan, Osun, Olumo, and Orosun have been ritualized and preserved, a practice that increasingly calls attention to their threatened biodiversity.

Divination

Laura Grillo, a researcher who has conducted much fieldwork in urban West African divination, defines *divination* as a technique used to determine the future and make authoritative pronouncement about it. Grillo notes, however, that this definition does not give full credit to the African functional use of divination. For Africans, divination may include prediction but is not by any means limited to it. The practice of divination is essentially considered a diagnosing process to determine the causes of all kinds of life crises, including childbirth, disease, death, economic misfortune, and natural disaster. After the diagnosis, divination prescribes the remedy for the crisis. The ultimate objective—after ensuring favorable dispositions of divine forces, usually through prescribed sacrifice—is to re-engineer a return to well-being of either the individual or the community.

Divination has become central to contemporary African society as a way of implementing sustainability strategies for different sectors of community life or for the environment. Examples of this abound in all parts of Africa. Grillo highlights the use of divination in two urban West African communities: the Dogon people of Mali use divination as a vehicle for bringing about favorable divine responses about the future; the Yoruba people use the process of divination to foster moral uprightness and order in society by assigning individual and communal responsibilities. Nicola Robins, a sustainability strategist, has described the transformation of Sangoma divination in South Africa as it moved from dealing with agro-pastoral related challenges of the traditional community to resolving modern-day challenges on spiritual, social, economic, educational, and even political level, both for the individual and the society.

In the traditional practice of divination, ritual objects have been derived from natural elements, and devotees have always been reminded of their sacredness and the importance of protecting and preserving them. The sacralizing of hills, mountains, forests, and rivers has protected such natural objects from degradation and abuse. Through divination we are able to listen to what is important, determine how to interpret different forms of intuition, and perform sacrifices, not necessarily the physical ones, in order to affect a holistic sustainability of human well-being.

Toward a Sustainable Future

Indigenous African peoples—whose beliefs embrace what Jacob Olupona (2006, 260), a scholar of indigenous African traditions, has called a "reutilization of the environment"—contribute to sustainability through the modern-day practice of their traditions.

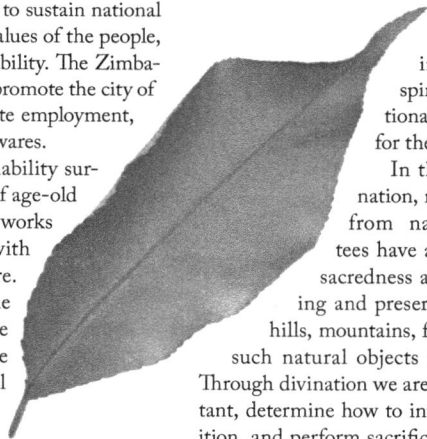

Proverbs, festivals, and divination continue to play central roles in different aspects of fostering economic, ecological, political, moral, social, and spiritual sustainability in the twenty-first-century world. These indigenous traditions can help to ensure the survival of the African identity, and, more importantly, engage in the challenges of propelling the growth and development of the African continent and its people.

Ibigbolade S. ADERIBIGBE
University of Georgia

FURTHER READING

Chinweizu, Onwuchekwa Jemie. (1975). *The West and the rest of us.* London: NOK Publishers.

Dorm-Adzobu, Clement; Ampadu-Agyei, Okkyearne; & Veit, Peter G. (1991). *Religious beliefs and environmental protection: The Malshegu Grove in Northern Ghana.* African Centre for Technology Studies World Resources Institute from the Ground Up Case Study Series 4.

Grillo, Laura. (2005). Trajectories in African ethics. In William Schweiker (Ed.), *Blackwell companion to religious ethics* (pp. 438–448). Oxford, U.K.: Blackwell.

Malunga, Chiku, & Banda, Charles. (2006). *Understanding organizational sustainability through African proverbs: Insights for leaders.* Rugby, U.K.: Practical Action Publishers.

Mbeki, Thabo. (1988). *The African renaissance: South Africa and the world.* Tokyo: UNU Press.

Mbiti, John S. (1988). *Introduction to African religion.* Oxford, U.K.: Heinemann Educational Publishers.

Mbiti, John S. (1994). *African religions and philosophy.* Oxford, U.K.: Heinemann Educational Publishers.

Munoz, Louis J. (2001). *The roots of the West: An introduction to the European cultural tradition.* Ibadan, Nigeria: Book Craft.

Olupona, Jacob. (2006). Religion and ecology in African culture and society. In Rogers S. Gottieb (Ed.), *The Oxford handbook of religion and ecology.* New York: Oxford University Press.

Robins, Nicola. (n.d.). The African spirit of sustainability. Retrieved April 11, 2009, from http://www.enviropaedia.com/topic/default.php?topic_id=258

PROBLEMS WITH CONSERVATION IN AFRICA ... AND SOME SOLUTIONS

Land conservation practices, generally thought of as beneficial, can have a negative impact on those most in need—of either the land's resources or the livelihood they provide. Author Yaa Ntiamoa-Baidu explains the African perspective in this chapter from African Rain Forest Ecology and Conservation: An Interdisciplinary Perspective.

In the Western world, resources conserved are mainly those for which people have no immediate need. In Africa, people are being asked to conserve resources that they depend on for their everyday needs. Protective efforts are purported to be in the interest of the people, but who really benefits from forest and wildlife reserves? Is it the local person who has lost his land to conservation and has neither access to the resources of his land to support his traditional way of life nor access to modern developments to improve his quality of life? Is it the forestry or wildlife officer whose livelihood depends on the maintenance of conservation departments? Is it the government, which requires foreign exchange earnings to provide amenities, most of which is consumed by the city or town dweller? Or is it the Western world, where natural resources have been destroyed in the process of development, and where forest products are required to maintain the overconsumptive way of life, but also where conservation of tropical forest in the interest of global environmental health and biodiversity conservation are vehemently advocated?

Protected areas in Ghana and Africa as a whole will survive only if they provide benefits that are substantial enough for the local communities. There is, therefore, an urgent need to address the question of equitable distribution of the benefits from protected areas. Alternatives for the local communities and development options that will increase protected area benefits must be found. These might include development of appropriate agricultural technologies and facilities to increase productivity through increasing yield per unit area rather than increasing acreage of arable land; promotion of agricultural practices that encourage forest conservation; and farming of favorite or useful wild animals or plant species, such as grasscutters (*Thryonomys swindetianus*) and chewing sticks.

Source: Yaa Ntiamoa-Baidu. (2001). Indigenous Versus Introduced Biodiversity Conservations Strategies: The Case of Protected Area Systems in Ghana. In William Weber, Lee J. T. White, Amy Vedder, and Lisa Naughton-Treves (Eds.), *African Rain Forest Ecology and Conservation: An Interdisciplinary Perspective*, p. 392. New Haven, CT: Yale University Press.

Indigenous Traditions—Asia

Asia is the largest, most populous continent, and its peoples are as diverse as its landscapes. Nevertheless, traditions of the indigenous people do share some characteristics: connection to the land and a belief in spirits, particularly ones dwelling in animals and nature. Because of these factors, conservation and protection of resources is reinforced and strengthened by the native religions.

Few generalizations can be made about Asia's vast number of indigenous minority groups. Those few, however, are important, especially for the ways in which these groups connect to the natural world and thus encourage the practice of ecological conservation and preservation. All groups are closely tied to their local landscapes, and have been (except for recently migrated groups) for a very long time. All see the landscape as full of spirits. Edward Tylor (1832–1917), recognized as one of the founders in the field of social anthropology, introduced the word *animist* to describe these societies (Harvey 2006); the term refers to the belief that all of reality is pervaded by spirits or souls, and that all reality is in some sense animate. Spirits dwell in mountains, trees, animals, and other entities. They need worship, care, and concern. Such spirits may be human-like in consciousness—other-than-human persons—or quite alien. They act on humans in ways that go beyond the everyday and direct. They are like wind or breath: invisible and intangible, yet active and felt.

Nearly universal in Asia are beliefs in powerful tree spirits. Trees and groves are worshiped from the Europe–Asia border to Tibet and Thailand. Field research conducted by the sociologists Barbara Anderson and E. N. Anderson, as well as the work of other scholars, reveals that these "tree beliefs" have influenced majority religions, especially Buddhism, in which reverence for tree spirits is often used to promote conservation of trees (Darlington 1998).

The more powerful predatory animals are also considered to be bearers of particularly powerful spirits. Wolves, bears, tigers, eagles, and similar animals are widely respected and revered. Most societies believe in "shape changing": animals can take different forms including human form, and humans with special powers can take the form of animals.

Spirits of departed humans are usually important in Asian minority groups. Many groups also worship gods—remote, powerful beings that do not reside in local tangible objects—in addition to spirits. Spirits and gods are "supramundane" rather than "supernatural." Most of these societies distinguish human and nonhuman realms, but conceptualize this differently from the "human versus nature" dichotomy of European thought.

All groups have local informal religious practitioners who contact gods and spirits, including the dead, and communicate with them. Communication often involves an altered state of consciousness—a trance (in a very broad sense) or something similar—and it requires special rituals, different from and more elaborate than communication with living humans. In many societies, the religious person is a shaman, one who sends his or her soul to the realms of the supramundane beings. In others, the spirits enter the religious practitioner—a spirit medium—in a "possession trance." Many societies have both shamans and spirit mediums; occasionally the same individual will serve as both. Some indigenous societies have priests: formal, organized officiants who intercede, hold ceremonies, and worship without the need to enter an altered mental state.

In these societies, conservation or protection of resources is motivated or strengthened by religion. This ranges in importance. Small, low-density groups in Malaysia and Indonesia may be minimally motivated to conserve. Some do not practice obvious conservation. Many small-scale traditional societies around the world do not protect biotic resources, at least not effectively (Hames 2007). In Asia, however, almost all groups at least make the effort. Many groups effectively protect whole sacred mountains and forests. No Asian minority religions maintain that destroying plant and animal environments is a positive good, as do many developers and political regimes in Asia and elsewhere.

Beyond these generalizations, Asia's indigenous minorities are as varied a set of peoples as the world affords. They speak hundreds of very different languages. They live in environments ranging from arctic coasts to tropical mountains. Some live in scattered hunting-gathering bands, others are densely populated societies practicing intensive agriculture. Some are completely nonliterate, while others retain ancient literary traditions. Some have religions based largely on remote gods, others are purely concerned with local spirits.

All are culturally closer to neighboring or nearby majority cultures than to distant minorities. There was never a barrier to contact between neighboring groups, and religious ideas and practices have always flowed from local minority to majority groups and vice versa. Old ideas of cultural isolation or cultural dependence have long been abandoned. So has the belief that the minorities retained ancient forms of majority beliefs. Research has shown that both majority and minority groups in a given region often developed their religion from similar origins, and both have thus influenced each other.

Asia's minorities can be broadly classified into three great geographical assemblages: North Asia (north of central China and of the Islamic world of central Asia); Southeast Asia; and the Indian subcontinent. Outliers include remote groups in Indonesia and the Philippines.

North Asia and Shamanism

North Asia is the home of shamanism: for years the classic source on the subject has been Mircea Eliade's 1964 book *Shamanism: Archaic Techniques of Ecstasy*, but more recent sources are to be preferred for Asian research. The word, which has its origin in Tungus, a language spoken from far north China to the Arctic, has been loosely used for any folk religious practitioner who goes into trance, and thus for all manner of disparate people worldwide, but careful scholarship reserves it for North and East Asian soulsenders and their Native North American counterparts. The remote Turkic groups of southern Siberia are also shamanistic. Mongush B. Kenin-Lopsan's *Shamanic Songs and Myths of Tuva* (1997) presents a particularly good "insider's" account with details on environmental thought.

Societies that have practiced shamanism in recent times are largely hunting-gathering, fishing, or herding peoples,

though many societies with long-established agriculture share the system. Historical evidence suggests that China, Japan, Korea, and Tibet were dominantly shamanistic in very early times. In China the ancient word *wu*, originally meaning a shaman, now means a spirit medium, implying a rather dramatic change in religion (Waley 1955). Shamanism survives today in Japan (Blacker 1986) and is the ultimate source of many of the widespread shape-changing stories about the fox and the *tanuki* ("raccoon dog," often mistranslated as "badger"). Shamanism also survives in minority religions in China (the Hmong and Mian, for example) and Tibet. It is often absorbed into majority religions, as in bön, the oldest spiritual tradition of Tibet (Snellgrove 1967). Spirit-mediumship in Korea is so obviously closely related to Tungus and Mongol shamanism that the spirit mediums (*mudang*) are almost always called shamans in Western-language literature (Kendall 1988). At these points the distinction between shaman and spirit medium becomes blurred. After extreme repression under Communism, shamanism has experienced a huge revival in Russia, where many dubiously qualified persons, if not to say outright frauds, have capitalized on its new popularity (Balzer 1990).

Shamans are usually healers. They visit the otherworld to find causes of illness. If the causes are seen to be violations of social and ritual rules, social harmony is served; the cause may also be witchcraft, in which case identifying the witch may cause social conflict. The shamanic journey is long and hard (Humphrey 1996), especially if a whole tribe suffers sickness or ill luck. Real environmental landmarks and scenes are incorporated into journey narratives, which may become celebrations of the group's territory and regular travels. Widespread is a belief in a "world tree" at the center of the cosmos—its roots in the underworld, its trunk in this (middle) world, and its crown in the sky-world or heaven. Shamans often climb up or down this tree on spirit journeys.

Shamans are often shape changers, able to take the form of bears, eagles, or other "power animals" as needed. Stories of shape changing abound: all humans and nonhumans are persons, all interact and can often change into each other. The unity of humans with the rest of the world is assured, and society includes both human and nonhuman persons.

Conservation and Sacrifice

Throughout the shamanistic world, religion serves the cause of conservation. Respect is shown by proper ceremonies and by taking no more from nature than is necessary for immediate personal and family needs. Religion often protects lands and especially waters from pollution, because purity is a major ritual requirement of respect for spirits.

On the other hand, sacrifice is often important and may involve the sacred wild species. Sacrifice of wild creatures teaches respect and reverence for them, and probably leads to some conservation in the end. The Mongols sacrifice sheep and other animals, leaving the hide suspended from a pole. The Koryak of northwest Siberia sacrifice dogs suspend them on similar poles. In early historic times, human sacrifice occurred in central Asia; a leader's retainers were sacrificed to accompany him or (rarely) her in the other world.

Mongols and Shamanism

The Mongols are not really a minority since they have their own independent country, Mongolia, but they are so typical in their shamanism that they should be discussed. They speak several closely related languages within the Altaic family, which also includes the Turkic and Tungus languages. Most were traditionally herders (largely of sheep, goats, and horses, and also of yaks) but many practiced some agriculture and all hunted when possible. Like many East Asian peoples the Mongols trace their descent from powerful animals—in the Mongol case, the union of a gray wolf and a beautiful doe (de Rachewiltz 2004). The Mongols recognize a remote and impersonal sky god, Tengri, as the highest power and most revered entity, but direct more of their religious activity at more immediate spirits of good and ill. Some groups have multiple sky gods. Evil spirits of disease and ill luck cause many problems, and the shaman sends his soul—shamans in this tradition are usually male—to the other world to find what has gone wrong. (*Shamans and Elders: Experience, Knowledge, and Power among the Daur Mongols*, by Caroline Humphrey and shaman Urgunge Onon, 1996, documents such practice.)

The Mongols have always protected local forests, mountains, and waters (see the historical notes in de Rachewiltz 2004). Their concern for ritual and practical purity of water has been instrumental in conserving Siberia's Lake Baikal (Metzo 2005). Buddhism has been widely adopted by many Mongols. It has not deeply changed shamanistic practice, but it has added a new dimension of respect for life. The Mongols have not given up hunting or butchering animals, but Buddhism has strengthened traditional prohibitions against unnecessary taking of life.

The Ainu of Japan

Less typically shamanic, and unique in language and culture, are the Ainu, the indigenous minority of northern Japan living primarily on the island of Hokkaido. Until Japanese intrusion changed their lives in the nineteenth century, they supplemented a fishing lifestyle with hunting and small-scale agriculture. Their lives were tightly bound to local animal and plant life, and their religion was devoted to animal powers. They traditionally sacrificed bears in a major festival (the *iyomante*) and also sacrificed eagles, eagle owls, foxes, wolves, and other creatures whose predatory power indicated great spiritual strength (Brett L. Walker 2001). The fishing-owl was a guardian bird. The salmon, a sacred fish, offered itself to humans for food. Such divine creatures were *kamuy*, "gods" (the Ainu word is derived from—or perhaps possibly the source of—the Japanese equivalent, *kami*). Small sticks (*inau*), shaved in patterns, were ritually set up for spirits. Long and beautiful ritual songs informed people of the histories and needs of wolf, owl, and bear gods, killer whales, sharks, and other powerful animals (Philippi 1982). Healing was the most important role of Ainu religious officiants. These shamans—often or usually female—were in Japan and Korea usually spirit-mediums in actual practice. Male elders who took on priestly function presided over other rituals.

Indigenous Traditions in Southeast Asia

Southward, shamanism grades into a vast complex of spirit-based religions found throughout mainland Southeast Asia and most of the island world east of it. Here, trance is more usually spirit-mediumistic than shamanic. (China's southern minorities retain both, and share a fondness for epic and mythic chants used in rituals for curing, fertility, and life-passage rites.) Many of these chants draw heavily on parallels between natural and cultural themes—or, more accurately, between the wider society (animals, plants, spirits, geographic phenomena) and the narrower human one.

The Akha and Cultivation Practices

A particularly well-studied group is the Akha, a Tibeto-Burman people (Sturgeon 2005). They live at middle elevations in the mountainous regions where China, Burma, Thailand, and Laos come together; they are divided between the four countries. They live by shifting cultivation and, increasingly, settled agriculture and tree cropping. (Shifting cultivation is a system in which land is cleared, burned, used to grow a mixture of agricultural crops for a few years, and then abandoned for a fallow period; tree cropping refers to growing trees that produce food.) The forests of the Ahka were preserved carefully until recently; they still hold a few elephants, tigers, and other "charismatic megafauna" (large creatures whose popular appeal makes them the convenient focus of environmental activists and conservation campaigns wishing to raise funds or draw attention to more humble endangered species), as well as hundreds of species of birds and small mammals. The forests are the abode of the spirits. Some are highly sacred, others less so. Certain trees are particularly revered. Origin and migration stories link the Akha closely to their homelands. Until recently the Akha maintained high population densities while preserving their landscape, through ritually regulated wise use; today, political pressures in these borderlands have had a devastating effect. This is one the clearest cases of an extremely sophisticated traditional ecological system eroded by outside pressures. The culturally related Sani, Lahu, and Yi have broadly comparable beliefs about nature, forests, and conservation, and they too have suffered heavy environmental losses in recent years. A wide range of the plants and animals living today in southwest China are mentioned in the Lahu creation myth (Arthur R. Walker 1995).

In south China and Southeast Asia most minority groups live by shifting cultivation. With this practice of cutting down small areas of forest, burning them, and planting crops in the ash, fertility is exhausted in a few years, and a new area is cut. Usually the rotation period is long-term, with a field re-cut every twenty to fifty years. This practice, as well as the more drastic slash-and-burn cultivation, has been blamed for deforestation, but most groups have religious rules against overcutting. In fact, deforestation has been done largely by majority cultures, especially by large-scale logging and agribusiness interests. Only a few minority groups with high populations and fewer ties to the land have overcut forests. In fact, the existence until modern times of magnificent forests, in spite of high population densities of shifting cultivators, is a tribute to the religiously coded management practices of both minority and majority peoples. Until the last two generations, Southeast Asia was unique in supporting huge, densely populated, ancient civilizations, as along with the small societies considered here, and yet maintaining 90 percent forest cover with high biodiversity.

Spiritual Practices

Throughout Southeast Asia, nature spirits are all-important, with tree spirits often taking pride of place. Sacred trees and groves get varying degrees of protection. Some are absolutely protected, others cropped for fuel, construction timber, fruit, rattan, and other goods. Sacred status keeps them from being leveled for agriculture or clear-cut logging, and thus protects local wood supplies. In most areas certain kinds of trees—often wild fig trees (*Ficus* spp.)—are sacred wherever found and also protected to varying degrees. (Sacred groves were also important in Africa and Europe, but links with Southeast Asia are tenuous.) Mountains are central presences, and in Indonesia, where volcanoes abound, these fire-peaks have major religious significance.

Animals are less revered but generally respected, and, as usual, powerful predators have varying degrees of taboo or respected status. In northern Southeast Asia, animal ancestor myths are common; many groups trace their descent to a dog or similar being. "Merit feasts" involving sacrifice of buffaloes or cattle exist among many minority peoples, and those who host such feasts get social and religious recognition. The worshipers share the sacrificial meat according to kinship; often, each category of kin gets a particular cut of the animal.

Concerns with growth and fertility, especially the all-important rice, are almost universal, and much art and ceremony is dedicated to rice and other staple crops. Along with environmental phenomena, ancestors are revered, especially in Indonesia, and marriage is widely important, not just to unite two individuals but to unite whole descent groups (see Tannenbaum and Kammerer 2003). Kinship is complex and all-important and is routinely projected on nature through cosmology and symbolism.

Many of Southeast Asia's minority religions are highly dualistic, with strong contrasts established between humans and spirits, men and women, wife-giving and wife-taking groups within the kinship network, and other social categories. Complex cosmological symbolism projects these on the universe; they may be represented by sacred geography, sacred biology, classes of gods, clothing designs, ritual usages, and points in the house, for example. Ethnic groups differ dramatically, making this region one of the most religiously and cosmologically rich and diverse in the world (Schiller 1997).

The Indian Subcontinent

The religions of the so-called tribal peoples of the Indian subcontinent are, if anything, even more diverse. India has the largest "tribal" population in the world, but the only real defining feature of a "tribe" is that it did not have fully literate state-level society when the British colonial regime defined them as such. There are hundreds of groups, from tiny hunting-gathering bands to ethnic groups numbering in the millions that, like the Santal, have complex societies and large towns with hierarchic political systems (Archer 1974).

The Indian subcontinent is a meeting ground of all Asian traditions. In the north, Tibetan-related groups often have shamanic religions (Snellgrove 1967). In the east, the "tribals" of eastern India and northern Bangladesh are culturally Southeast Asian, grading westward into more typical Indian cultures. In the southern mountains of India are groups who worship gods associated with cattle herding, hunting, and farming. In general, the "tribals" share varying degrees of belief in gods and sacred animals with the majority caste Hindus. For at least 2,500 years sages have equated tribal gods with the major Indian trinity of Brahma, Vishnu, and Shiva; tribal gods are seen as incarnations of these. Goddesses embody the feminine aspects of the trinity.

Some specialized indigenous groups in India focus their spiritual practices on particular concerns or aspects of their daily lives. The very small Toda group of far southern India, a specialized dairying group, has made milking their special breed of water buffaloes and processing the milk in dairies an integral part of their religion. The dairies serve as temples of varying degrees of sanctity (Arthur R. Walker 1986).

Afghanistan–Pakistan Borderlands

The "Kafirs" (Arabic for "pagans") of the Afghanistan–Pakistan borderland are the sole group in west Asia to have preserved a non-Abrahamic, non-Iranic religion. (They were the subject of the renowned 1896 study *The Kafirs of the Hindu-Kush*, by George Scott Robertson, a British soldier-surgeon attached to the Indian Foreign Service who made a year-long expedition to the remote area of what was then called Kafirstan; since Robertson wrote, the groups in Afghanistan have converted to Islam, but about 4,000 Kalasha maintain the old religion in northwest Pakistan.

The religion centered on a pantheon of gods and goddesses, including a high god Imra, a very important war god, Gish, and a goddess of cultivation and fertility, Disani or Dizne (Jettmar 1986). The Kalasha are deeply concerned with purity. Female life events, including menstruation, involve complex rituals. They share some veneration for trees and lakes (which are gates to the realm of gods), and the widespread use of the house as cosmological symbol. They sacrifice animals, including goats and cattle, often for merit feasts. Singing and dancing are very important in rituals and the many festivals. Divisions of labor—men herding and plowing, women cultivating—are religiously maintained. Relations with animals and the landscape are ritually regulated, but the Kalasha appear not to be as intensely involved with the wider natural world as are most East Asian groups. This has not spared them from being shamelessly romanticized by tourist agencies and similar interested parties, and (partly in consequence) subjected to "development" at its least sensitive level. Peter Parkes's (2000) excellent account of this could be applied, all other things being equal, to many Asian minority groups.

Challenges to Indigenous Traditions

Only one minority religious tradition (the Kafirs) survives in western Eurasia, where the Abrahamic religions—specifically Christianity and Islam (and one might add Communism, sometimes called "a Judeo-Christian

heresy")—promote conversion and do not tend to accept local traditions. In sharp contrast, Hinduism, Buddhism, and East Asian majority religions such as Daoism, Confucianism, and Shinto, have generally been highly tolerant, either leaving local peoples alone or allowing them to maintain their faiths as local manifestations of the majority ones. Thus in East and South Asia, thousands of local groups retain their own religions.

Unfortunately, many indigenous groups in the Indian subcontinent are extremely poorly known to scholarship, and the area is now in the grips of rapid religious change. Conversion to world religions has been rapid. In Indonesia, forced conversions under the dictatorship of Suharto, who was in power from 1967 to 1998, devastated local religions. Extreme forms of Islam, alien to the region until the 1970s, have propagated in Muslim areas of Indonesia and in Malaysia, presenting risks to "pagan" minorities.

As the freedom to practice indigenous traditions in these regions is endangered, so is the handing down of spiritual beliefs that long upheld conservation of the Earth's resources and the preservation of its species.

E. N. ANDERSON
University of California, Riverside

FURTHER READING

Agrawal, Arun. (2005). *Environmentality: Technologies of government and the making of subjects.* Durham, NC: Duke University Press.
Anderson, Danica; Salick, Jan; Moseley, Robert; & Xiaokun, Ou. (2005). Conserving the sacred medicine mountains: A vegetation analysis of Tibetan sacred sites in Northwest Yunnan. *Biodiversity and Conservation 14,* 3065–3091.
Archer, W. G. (1974). *The hill of flutes: Life, love and poetry in tribal India: A portrait of the Santals.* Pittsburgh, PA: University of Pittsburgh Press.
Balzer, Marjorie Mandelstam. (Ed.). (1990). *Shamanism: Soviet studies of traditional religion in Siberia and Central Asia.* Armonk, NY: M. E. Sharpe.
Balzer, Marjorie Mandelstam. (1997). *Shamanic worlds: Ritual and lore of Siberia and Central Asia.* Armonk, NY: M. E. Sharpe.
Batchelor, John. (1901). *The Ainu and their folk-lore.* London: The Religious Tract Society.
Beyer, Stephen. (1978). *The cult of Tara: Magic and ritual in Tibet.* Berkeley: University of California Press.
Blacker, Carmen. (1986). *The catalpa bow: A study of shamanistic practices in Japan* (2nd ed.). London: George Allen & Unwin.
Bogoras, Waldemar. (1904–1909). *The Chukchee* (2 vols.). American Museum of Natural History, Memoirs, 11. Leiden, The Netherlands: E. J. Brill.
Bogoras, Waldemar. (1917). *Koryak texts.* Leiden, The Netherlands: E. J. Brill.
Bogoras, Waldemar. (1918). *Tales of the Yukaghir, Lamut, and Russianized Natives of East Siberia.* AMNH Papers XX:1. New York: American Museum of Natural History.
Buijs, Kees. (2006). *Power of blessing from the wilderness and from heaven: Structure and transformations in the religion of the Toraja in the Mamasa area of South Sulawesi.* Leiden, The Netherlands: KITLV.

Chindarsi, Nusit. (1975). *The religion of the Hmong Njua.* Bangkok: Siam Society.

Darlington, Susan M. (1998, Winter). The ordination of a tree: The Buddhist ecology movement in Thailand. *Ethnology 37*(1), 1–15. Retrieved May 27, 2009, from http://ccbs.ntu.edu.tw/FULLTEXT/JR-ADM/susan.htm

de Rachewiltz, Igor. (2006). *The secret history of the Mongols: A Mongolian epic chronicle of the thirteenth century* (Vols. 1–2). Leiden, The Netherlands: Brill.

Eliade, Mircea. (1964). *Shamanism: Archaic techniques of ecstasy* (Rev. ed.). London: Routledge & Kegan Paul.

Elwin, Verrier. (1991). *The Muria and their ghotul.* Oxford: Oxford University Press.

Fitzhugh, William, & Chisako Dubreuil. (Eds.). (1999). *Ainu: Spirit of a northern people.* Washington, DC: Smithsonian Institution, National Museum of Natural History, Arctic Studies Center, with University of Washington Press.

Goullart, Peter. (1955). *Forgotten kingdom.* London: John Murray.

Guha, Ramachandra. (1993). *Social ecology.* Delhi: Oxford University Press in India.

Hames, Raymond. (2007). The ecologically noble savage debate. *Annual Review of Anthropology, 36,* 177–190. Retrieved in May 27, 2009. from http://www.unl.edu/rhames/ms/savage-prepub.pdf

Hamilton, Roy W. (2003). *The art of rice: Spirit and sustenance in Asia.* Los Angeles: UCLA Fowler Museum of Cultural History.

Harrell, Stevan. (2001). *Ways of being ethnic in southwest China.* Seattle: University of Washington.

Harrell, Stevan. (Ed.). (1995). *Cultural encounters on China's ethnic frontiers.* Seattle: University of Washington Press.

Harrell, Stevan. (Ed.) (2001). *Perspectives on the Yi of southwest China.* Berkeley and Los Angeles: University of California Press.

Harvey, Graham. (2006). *Animism: Respecting the living world.* New York: Columbia University Press.

Huber, Toni. (1999). *The cult of pure crystal mountain.* New York: Oxford University Press.

Humphrey, Caroline, with Onon, Urgunge. (1996). *Shamans and elders: Experience, knowledge, and power among the Daur Mongols.* Oxford, U.K.: Oxford University Press.

Jettmar, Karl. (1986). *Religions of the Hindukush: The religions of the Kafirs, Vol.1* (Adam Nayyar, Trans.). Warminster, U.K.: Aris and Phillips.

Jochelson, Waldemar. (1908). *The Koryak. American museum of natural history, Memoir 10.* Leiden, The Netherlands: E. J. Brill.

Kendall, Laurel. (1988). *The life and hard times of a Korean shaman: Of tales and the telling of tales.* Honolulu: University of Hawaii Press.

Kenin-Lopsan, Mongush B. (1997). *Shamanic songs and myths of Tuva.* Mihály Hoppál (Ed., Trans.). Budapest: Akadémiai Kiadó.

Lopatin, Ivan A. (1960). *The cult of the dead among the natives of the Amur Basin.* The Hague: Mouton.

Maggi, Wynne. (2001). *Our women are free: Gender and ethnicity in the Hindukush.* Ann Arbor: University of Michigan Press.

Maskarinec, Gregory. (1995). *The rulings of the night: An ethnography of Nepalese Shamas oral texts.* Madison: University of Wisconsin Press.

Maskarinec, Gregory. (1998). *Nepalese Shaman oral texts.* Cambridge, MA: Harvard Oriental Studies 35.

Metzo, Katherine R. (2005, June). Articulating a Baikal environmental ethic. *Anthropology and Humanism, 30*(1), 39–54.

Müller-Ebeling, Claudia; Christian Rätsch; & Surendra Bahadur Shahi. (2007). *Shamanism and Tantra in the Himalayas.* Rochester, VT: Inner Traditions.

Nowak, Margaret, & Stephen Durrant. (1977). *The tale of the Nišan Shamaness: A Manchu folk epic.* Seattle: University of Washington Press.

Ohnuki-Tierney, Emiko. (1981). *Illness and healing among the Sakhalin Ainu: A symbolic interpretation.* Cambridge: Cambridge University Press.

Ohnuki-Tierney, Emiko. (1999). Ainu sociality. In William Fitzhugh and Chisako Dubreuil (Eds.), *Ainu: Spirit of a northern people* (pp. 240–245). Washington, DC: Smithsonian Institution, National Museum of Natural History, Arctic Studies Center, with University of Washington Press.

Orans, Martin. (1965). *The Santal: A tribe in search of a great tradition.* Detroit: Wayne State University Press.

Parkes, Peter. (2000). Enclaved knowledge: Indigent and indignant representations of environmental management and development among the Kalasha of Pakistan. In Roy Ellen, Peter Parkes, &Alan Bicker (Eds.), *Indigenous environmental knowledge and its transformations: Critical anthropological perspectives* (pp. 253–292). Amsterdam: Harwood Academic.

Philippi, Donald. (1982). *Songs of gods, songs of humans: The epic tradition of the Ainu.* San Francisco: North Point Press.

Rangan, Haripraya. (2000). *Of myths and movements: Rewriting Chipko into Himalayan history.* London: Verso.

Rivers, W. H. R. (1906). *The Todas.* London: MacMillan and Co.

Robertson, George Scott. (1896). *The Kafirs of the Hindu-Kush.* London: Lawrence and Bullen.

Rouget, Gilbert. (1985). *Music and Trance.* Chicago: University of Chicago Press.

Roux, Jean. (1966). *Faune et flore sacrées dans les sociétés altaïques.* Paris: A. Maisonneuve.

Roux, Jean. (1984). *Religion des Turcs et des Mongoles.* [Turkish and Mongol Religion]. Paris: Payot.

Schiller, Anne. (1997). *Small sacrifices: Religious change and cultural identity among the Ngaju of Indonesia.* New York: Oxford University Press.

Snellgrove, David L. (Ed. & Trans.). (1967). *The nine ways of Bon: Excerpts from gZi-brjid.* London: University of London, London Oriental Series.

Shapiro, Judith. (2001). *Mao's war against nature: Politics and the environment in revolutionary China.* Cambridge, U.K.: Cambridge University Press.

Shutova, Nadezhda. (2006). Trees in Udmurt religion. *Antiquity 80,* 318–327.

Sturgeon, Janet. (2005). *Border landscapes: The politics of Akha land use in China and Thailand.* Seattle: University of Washington Press.

Tannenbaum, Nicola, & Kammerer, Cornelia Ann. (2003). *Founders' cults in Southeast Asia: Ancestors, polity, and identity.* New Haven, CT: Yale University Press.

Tylor, Edward. (1871). *Primitive culture.* London: John Murray.

Vainstein, Sevyan. (1980). *Nomads of south Siberia: The pastoral economies of Tuva.* Cambridge, Studies in Social Anthropology, 25. Caroline Humphrey (Ed.), Michael Colenso (Trans.). (Original work published in Russian in 1972)

van Wouden, F. A. E. (1968). *Types of social structure in eastern Indonesia.* Rodney Needham (Trans.). The Hague: Martinus Nijhoff.

Waley, Arthur. (1955). *The nine songs: A study of shamanism in ancient China.* London: G. Allen and Unwin.

Walker, Anthony R. (1986). *The Toda of south India: A new look.* Delhi: Hindustan.

Walker, Anthony R. (Ed.) (1995). *Mvuh Hpa Mi Hpa: Creating heaven, creating Earth: An Epic myth of the Lahu people in Yunnan* (Shi Kun, Trans.). Chiang Mai, Thailand: Silkworm Books.

Walker, Brett L. (2001). *The conquest of Ainu lands: Ecology and culture in Japanese expansion, 1590–1800.* Berkeley: University of California Press.

Indigenous Traditions—Australia

The spirit of sustainability is prominent within the religion and philosophy of the Australian Aboriginal people. It emphasizes the preeminence of the land and configures humankind as part of the larger whole through a worldview referred to in English as Dreaming. *Indigenous religion requires attentiveness to the needs of all things and proposes that those who destroy what has been created ultimately destroy themselves.*

The Australian Aboriginal words for the concepts at the center of their traditions and worldview have no single equivalent in English, but many indigenous people have been using the word *Dreaming* for about a hundred years, primarily as a noun, to express how the world, its features, and all of its beings came to take their shapes and connectivities. The meanings of Dreaming include creation, continuity, religious action, and ecological connectivity. A spirit of sustainability is beautifully articulated in the concept of Dreaming, although not in those English words of course. The Aboriginal philosopher Mary Graham distills Aboriginal religious philosophy into two main precepts: the land is the law, and you are not alone in the world. These two principles can be understood as an indigenous ethic and practice of connectivity. The second precept—you are not alone—situates humanity as a participant in a larger living system. The first requires that humans submit to the workings of the world; it offers joy and celebration within a mode of participation. Graham develops this precept with the further explanation that "all meaning comes from

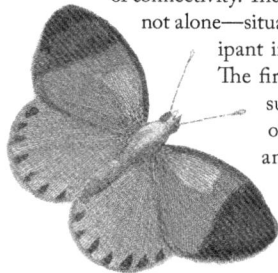

land" (Graham 2008, 181–182). Sustainability is an outcome of the practices of care that reflect these two precepts.

Dreaming

Creation stories vary across the Australian continent, yet at the same time they are connected through the travels and actions of Dreamings—the great shape-shifting creators who walked this Earth. All across the land, Dreamings made a world of form and difference; they brought into being and organized the different countries, languages, peoples, species, cultures, plant communities, and sources of fresh water.

One side of Dreaming is that which endures. Dreamings created *countries*—not as political entities in the way they are often considered today but as homes for human groups and for distinctive plants and animals and the unique landforms that sustain their lives. The landscape itself is sacred geography. The other side of this created world is ephemeral: the living things, the relationships between and among them, the waters that support their lives, the cultural forms of action and knowledge that sustain the created world. Through actions of knowledgeable living things (a category that is not exclusively human), Dreaming is actualized in present time. The enduring life of the creation is carried through contemporary time and space by ephemeral life forms.

Caring for Country

The term *caring for country* is another indigenous contribution to contemporary English. *Care* concerns relationship and responsibility. People care for their own home country, so that each country is ideally a matrix of ongoing life, moral action, and ultimate meaning. Since colonization by Europeans in the nineteenth and twentieth centuries, Aboriginal peoples' capacity to care for country has been radically diminished in many regions. As people were dispossessed and either killed or taken away from their homes, and as country was converted to private property and to industrial agriculture and pastoralism, the losses have been extreme. Ecosystems may collapse rapidly, as has happened in central Australia, where the rate of mammalian extinctions is the highest in the world (Johnson 2006, vii). They may also (or alternatively) collapse slowly, as appears to be happening in many other areas. It is difficult to sort out the variables, but in many parts of Australia the loss of Aboriginal care is causally linked to major changes in ecosystems.

Yet all over Australia, Aboriginal people continue to care for country as best they can. In areas of former reserves, where ecosystems remain relatively intact, that care continues to be expressed in daily life, ritual action, and in an underlying religious philosophy of relationship and responsibility. Caring for country is communicative. Aboriginal people say that their country calls them into action: it relays messages; they listen, smell, see, understand, and respond. The "call of country" is communicated by all the senses, and the people who are away from their home country experience sensory deprivation that feels like loss, banality, and inertness of spirit. Kathy Deveraux, an elder of the Mak Mak clan whose home is in the swamps and floodplains near the northern city of Darwin, described the experience of coming home: "You see the birds, you see the country, and your senses come back to you. You know what to do and where to go" (Rose et al. 2002, 1).

Caring for country is founded in knowledge. Many people have an encyclopedic knowledge of the plants and animals of their country, of the habitat requirements of plants, of the food and other habitat requirements of the animals, of how to interpret the tracks and other traces of life in the land. Old people, in particular, hold deep knowledge of the histories of disasters and refuges and of the communities of symbiosis that enable all the forms of life to flourish through the generations.

Care and the nurturance of ecosystems express two major ethical propositions concerning the flourishing of life in this created world. These propositions give rise to sustainable ecosystems and, in the view of many Aboriginal people, are applicable to all people in all times and places (Neidjie, Davis, and Fox 1985). The first is that a country and its people take care of each other. This proposition

emphasizes place and proximity in the organization of care and asserts that relationships of care are reciprocal. To take care of one's country is to take care of the conditions whereby country can continue to provide sustenance for living things, including the people who belong to (and take care of) the place. The second proposition is that those who destroy their country ultimately destroy themselves. This proposition follows directly from the first; attentiveness to the needs of other living things pervades this whole ethic of care.

Mutuality

Ecological knowledge is coded into iconography, song, and story; a great deal of myth and ritual articulates ecological knowledge for a given country. The more complex ritual performances include not only song, dance, and designs applied directly to the body, but sacred objects that bear designs, some of which are permanently inscribed and some of which are painted. Iconographic representation of a plant or animal species speaks to relationships between a group of people and that species. At the same time, images of plant or animal species also concern that species quite directly: the image speaks to a site that is part of the creation story for that species and to care that ensures the flourishing of that species.

Aboriginal fire ecology is one of the best examples of caring for country. Mandated by Dreaming action and stories, Aboriginal people's use of fire aims to produce a mosaic effect of patches of country at various stages of regrowth after fire. The effect is to increase habitat diversity and thus to facilitate biodiversity. The burning of vegetation is carried out country by country in accordance with local knowledge. Because fire ecology is linked to local conditions, the timing, frequency, and organization of fires varies across the continent. People's explanations for why they burn vary, but hunting is an important component. There is a mutuality to burning: it improves the lives of other creatures by increasing habitat diversity and removing desiccated vegetation to make way for nutritional green growth. At the same time, it also improves the lives of humans, not only by improving the health of animals which will be hunted, but also by making the country easier to travel through. An aesthetic of "clean" country refers to country that has been properly burnt: cleared up but not wiped out.

April Bright, a Mak Mak clan Elder whose home country has experienced continuous Aboriginal burning through the era of colonization, explains: "'Burn grass' takes place after the wet season when the grass starts drying off. This takes place every year. The country tells you when and

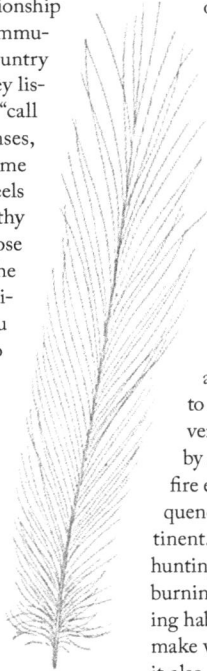

where to burn. To carry out this task you must know your country. You wouldn't, you just would not attempt to burn someone else's country. One of the reasons for burning is saving country. If we don't burn our country every year, we are not looking after our country" (Rose et al. 2002, 25).

Respect

For over 40,000 years, indigenous people in Australia have lived in and cared for the driest inhabited continent on Earth. During the time of human inhabitation there were periods that were more arid and periods that were wetter; the seas pulled back and then came in again. In a few regions in the far south, ice sheets pushed people out, but most of the continent has been continuously inhabited through many ecological changes. In the course of millennia, people developed a philosophical-religious ecology that is located in country, in ecosystems, and in ongoing creation. Dreaming is all about this living world—how it came into being and how it continues to come into being. People's religious life, as much as their economic life, celebrates the joy and plenitude of life in country.

Since colonization, Aboriginal people and Australian ecosystems have suffered enormously. And yet even in the most devastated areas, the spirit of responsibility remains. Phil Sullivan, an Aboriginal man whose home is on the Darling River in a region of drought and failing irrigation ventures, speaks of his experience of trying to sustain relationships between people and country: "We may lose our . . . language, even the rock art may fade, but we

will never lose what's inside our hearts—our spiritual connection to country. The outward things may pass but the respect, the thing inside, will last. We respect our animals and our land. That's what I call our last line of defence. The last line of defence is respect" (Rose, Watson, and James 2003, 102).

Deborah Bird ROSE
Macquarie University

FURTHER READING

Graham, Mary. (2008, November). Some thoughts on the philosophical underpinnings of Aboriginal worldviews. *Australian Humanities Review, 45*, 181–194. Retrieved January 19, 2009, from http://www.australianhumanitiesreview.org/archive/Issue-November-2008/graham.html
Johnson, Chris. (2006) *Australia's Mammal Extinctions: A 50,000-year history*. Melbourne: Cambridge University Press.
Neidjie, Bill; Davis, Stephen; & Fox, Allan. (1985). *Kakadu man: Bill Neidjie*. Queanbeyan, New South Wales, Australia: Mybrood.
Rose, Deborah. (1996). *Nourishing terrains: Australian Aboriginal views of landscape and wilderness*. Canberra, Australia: Australian Heritage Commission. Retrieved March 30, 2009, from http://www.environment.gov.au/heritage/ahc/publications/commission/books/pubs/nourishing-terrains.pdf
Rose, Deborah; D'Amico, Sharon; Daiyi, Nancy; Deveraux, Kathy; Daiyi, Margaret; Ford, Linda; et al. (2002). *Country of the heart: An indigenous Australian homeland*. Canberra, Australia: Aboriginal Studies Press.
Rose, Deborah; Watson, Christine; & James, Diana. (2003). *Indigenous kinship with the natural world*. Sydney: National Parks and Wildlife Service, New South Wales. Retrieved March 30, 2009, from http://www.environment.nsw.gov.au/resources/cultureheritage/IndigenousKinship.pdf

ABORIGINAL CONCEPTS OF COUNTRY

While studying the peoples in Western Australia and New South Wales, Deborah Bird Rose was inspired by the twentieth-century philosopher Emmanuel Levitas's term "nourished terrain." She developed her own definition of how Aboriginals experience "country" as a place that gives and receives life. "Not just imagined or represented," she writes, "it is lived in and lived with."

Country in Aboriginal English is not only a common noun but also a proper noun. People talk about country in the same way that they would talk about a person: they speak to country, sing to country, visit country, worry about country, feel sorry for country, and long for country. People say that country knows, hears, smells, takes notice, takes care, is sorry or happy. Country is not a generalised or undifferentiated type of place, such as one might indicate with terms like 'spending a day in the country' or 'going up the country.' Rather, country is a living entity with a yesterday, today and tomorrow, with a consciousness, and a will toward life. Because of this richness, country is home, and peace; nourishment for body, mind, and spirit; heart's ease.

Source: Deborah Bird Rose. (1996). Nourishing Terrains: Australian Aboriginal Views of Landscape and Wilderness, pp. 7. Canberra, Australia: Australian Heritage Commission. Retrieved October 1, 2009, from http://www.environment.gov.au/heritage/ahc/publications/commission/books/pubs/nourishing-terrains.pdf

Indigenous Traditions—
North America

A common belief among indigenous peoples of North America is that everything on Earth and in the universe has a soul and is animated by spirit—although with over 560 recognized tribes in the United States alone, there is considerable variation to the theme. Many peoples consider land and water and everything that lives on it and in it to be sacred, a belief that often—but not always—lends itself to a sustainable lifestyle.

Native Americans today practice a wide variety of religious traditions, from their original indigenous ways to Christianity and combinations of the two in unique forms of syncretism. It is important to note that most North American tribal spiritual leaders do not refer to their practices as "religion"; instead, they refer to "spiritual traditions," "sacred ways," and "spiritual ways of life." The term *religion* is often associated with European, Middle Eastern, and European-American institutions based on holy texts, prophets, and monotheism. This differs significantly from the sacred ways of native peoples who have site-specific, Earth-centered, spiritual ethics and practices based on intergenerational oral teachings often referred to as "traditional knowledge," "natural laws," or "original instructions."

With 4 million reported American Indians and 562 recognized American Indian and Alaskan native nations in the United States, the range and diversity of spiritual traditions is immense. In Canada, there are 1,172,790 reported aboriginal people living in more than six hundred First Nation, Métis, and Inuit bands and off-reserve communities. In Mexico, there are approximately sixty distinct indigenous groups that speak over sixty unique languages. The indigenous cultural diversity within and between these three North American nation-states is vast and complex—vast because of inherent cultural diversity (ethnic, linguistic, philosophical, and artistic) and complex because of the severe changes in traditional practices due to numerous waves of colonialism which tribes responded to, accommodated, and resisted in numerous resilient ways.

There is an almost unfathomable variety of indigenous religious and spiritual expressions in North America—from Inuit traditional shamans in northern Canada to Mormon Paiutes in the U.S. Great Basin; from Yaqui syncretic Catholics in the southwestern United States and Mexico to Lakota Sun Dancers in the plains of the United States; from Native American Church worshippers to urban mixed-blood (Métis, Mestizo, Creole) pan-spiritualists in major North American cities. From this vast diversity, the major Native American spiritual practices can be grouped into four main categories: (1) traditional, (2) Christian or other major religion, (3) syncretic—a unique combination of Christian and traditional spiritual practices, and (4) pan-tribal—an intertribal blend of varied spiritual beliefs, practices, and ceremonies. This article will focus on the first category, the traditional spiritual teachings of North America—the precolonial spiritual philosophies, ethics, and ceremonies.

Key Concepts

Given all of the geographic, ethnic, cultural, and linguistic diversity of Native American spiritual traditions, some consistent key concepts can be generalized and summarized.

These teachings originate in the oral tradition and can now be found in published forms. In terms of philosophy and belief, most native spiritual traditions are considered holistic and animistic. They originate in ideas that the spiritual and material worlds are intimately entwined and that nature is an embodiment of sacred and spiritual energies. Therefore, everything on Earth and in the universe—plants, animals, clouds, humans, rocks, and so forth—has a soul and is animated by spirit. This belief is also often called pantheistic, meaning that the source of the universe, the universe itself, and nature (including humans) are all merged as part of one sacred, spiritual creation. These teachings support the idea that the divine or sacred is both immanent and transcendent, with the emphasis on immanent, prioritizing a more personal and intimate relationship with the sacred in daily life.

Native Americans often refer to their teachings as the "original instructions" because, according to their cosmologies and cosmogonies, they were the first spiritual teachings given to them, in their own languages, by their Creator or Creators in the Creation Time. Each native language serves as the foundation and medium for distinct philosophical, psychological, and intellectual perspectives that are often impossible to interpret within a Western worldview and the English language. These original, oral instructions are like the holy texts of other religions except they are more spoken, personal, and dynamic. Within these oral instructions are specific ethics, values, lessons, and worldviews that explain how to live a spiritually healthy, balanced, and good life in harmony with other humans and the Earth. These spiritual values are infused with practical science and observation to support the survival and regeneration of the people and all that the people need to survive—food, water, shelter, clothing, and medicine. To support this regeneration, many Native nations, like the Yurok Tribe of northern California, practice world renewal ceremonies to literally "keep the Earth in balance." These values and practices could also be called an embodied sustainability in the sense that they help a particular group of people sustain themselves within a specific ecosystem and traditional homeland.

A common spiritual instruction that Native Americans share is the perception and understanding that a Great Power and Great Mystery exists in the universe that is ultimately unknowable to the human mind. This power reminds humans to be humble and grateful for the gifts of life. In dreams, visions, death, darkness, and the unknown, there is a Great Mystery that must be revered and placated. This value in, and respect for, Mystery helps humans realize that they are part of a larger universal cycle of life and death, creation and destruction, and that reverence, humility, and humor are aids for peaceful living.

Two other interrelated concepts central to Native American spiritual traditions are kinship and reciprocity. Native peoples understand that they are intimately and personally connected, as if in a family, to the extended family of the natural world. Through food, water, breath, and other needs, humans depend on the plants, animals, soils, climate, and sun for their nourishment and continuance. Therefore, they are holistically interrelated to all that lives, especially to the "kin" in their local environment. The Raramuri ethnoecologist Enrique Salmon has called this "kincentric ecology": "Indigenous people view both themselves and nature as part of an extended ecological family that shares ancestry and origin. It is an awareness that life in any environment is viable only when humans view that life surrounding them as kin" (Salmon 2000, 1327). Since humans depend on nature for survival, they must treat it with care, respect, and honor, and make offerings and sacrifices to these other life forms and their spirits. For example, when a Cree hunter prepares to hunt, he makes special prayers and offerings to the Moose Spirit so that it will give up its life to sustain the hunter and his family. After he kills the moose, he sings a song to it to help its spirit be at peace and offers a sacred herb such as tobacco, sweetgrass, or sage to symbolically and literally thank the moose and reciprocate for the gift of its life. This emphasis and practice of reciprocity is extremely important and exhibited in numerous ways when gathering, collecting, or hunting food or medicine. It is also expressed when exchanging gifts or trading with friends, family, or folks at traditional gatherings, ceremonies, or powwows. This spirit of kinship and reciprocity is also encouraged with all peoples, including strangers and people from different backgrounds. In this sense, Native American spiritual traditions teach about the importance of cultural pluralism, intercultural respect, and the gift economy.

Traditional Rituals and Ceremonies

According to Carl Waldman's *Atlas of the North American Indian*, the North American religious traditions "can be seen as a diffusion and cross-fertilization of two distinct cultural traditions: the Northern Hunting tradition and the Southern Agrarian tradition" (Waldman, 67). Animal worship, shamanism, ritual healing, and interspecies communication characterize the Northern Hunting tradition. The Southern Agrarian tradition is part of elaborate seasonal and agricultural cycles of planting, growing, and harvesting foods at certain times. In these tribal systems, priesthoods and religious institutions are more formalized and hierarchical with secretive and esoteric forms of worship.

Many of the ceremonies and rituals practiced by Native Americans from both of these generalized traditions involve sacrifice, the quest of a vision, and use of music, dance, art, and plant and animal medicines to shift one's consciousness from the ordinary to the supernatural. Sacrifice is emphasized in the Lakota sweat lodge and Sun Dance ceremonies where fasting is required and one is purified through intense heat, sweating, dancing, and prayer. Fasting is very common in many tribal traditions where a young person enters a rite of passage and seeks a vision through fasting alone in nature for a specific period of time, often for four days and nights. This practice is often called a vision quest. Other ceremonies involve group activities where the four elements (air, fire, water, earth) are used with particular songs and dances to make offerings to ancestors, plants, and animals, or Earth spirits. The Pueblo Corn Dances of the American and Mexican Southwest are examples of these group rituals of giving thanks to the Corn Mother through elaborate group songs, dances, and offerings. The Huichol of Mexico use their sacramental plant peyote as a medicine to induce altered states of consciousness and communication with unseen spirits and energies.

All of these rituals and ceremonies require an intimate understanding of the local ecology and web of relationships. Therefore, land and water and the life that lives on and within them are considered sacred and personal. The landscape must be cared for and tended in a familial and regenerative way. The Hopi of Arizona use certain clays and dyes in their ceremonies and sacred arts; thus, they must have a practical and scientific understanding of geology, soils, and geography for sustainably harvesting these clays over thousands of years. Likewise, Midé priests, Ojibwe traditional healers, use the oil from bear and sturgeon, two totem animals, in special healing ceremonies. They must have a detailed knowledge of the life cycles, physiological stages, anatomy, and behavior of those animals to harvest, extract, and utilize those oils in healing ways. In this sense, native religion, science, and art merge as a holistic way of living.

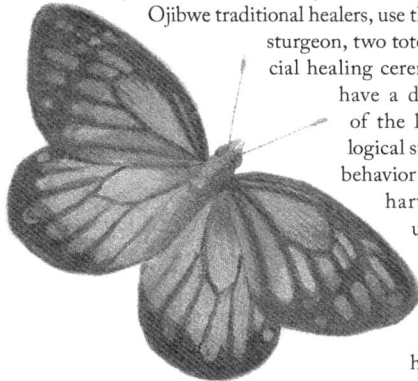

All of these rituals occur in sacred places in specific native lands and waters. Therefore, the concept of holy lands and sacred places is central to all Native American traditions.

Kinship Ecology and the Ecological Indian

For food, medicine, clothing, shelter, sacred practices, and daily nourishment, Native Americans historically practiced extensive and intensive land management that was guided by ethics of restraint, sacrifice, moderation, reciprocity, gratitude, and celebration. Due to their elaborate belief systems revolving around kinship and reciprocity and practical expressions and behaviors involving offerings to the natural world, Native Americans have often been called the "first ecologists" or "original environmentalists." The label of the "ecological Indian" is met with both approval and disdain by native peoples of North America. On one hand, indigenous peoples throughout the world are the only groups of humans who have demonstrated living sustainably within their local ecosystems for thousands of years before colonialism radically disrupted their ways of life. On the other hand, some native groups have also overexploited natural resources and either moved or disappeared due to that overexploitation. Regardless of which position one takes, it is still considered a stereotype to label Native Americans as ecologists rather than getting to know who they are as individual modern people with diverse views, opinions, and practices. Even though many native peoples have expressed highly complex and sophisticated ecological philosophies and practices, to say "all Native Americans are ecological" is overly romantic, essentialistic, and problematic.

Religious Freedom Struggles and Controversies

Native Americans today face ongoing threats to their sacred ways as many tribes struggle to maintain relationships with their sacred places and have access to their traditional medicines and ancestral lands. Religious freedom is still difficult and controversial for Native Americans as many non-natives misunderstand, stereotype, and discriminate against native peoples and their spiritual beliefs and practices. For example, the people of the Winnemem Wintu nation of northern California struggle to protect their sacred sites from being again flooded by the expansion of a river dam. Another threat to Native American spiritual traditions is the New Age Movement where "white shamans" and "plastic medicine men" fake Native American traditions and charge non-natives large amounts of money to participate in so-called ceremonies. Extractive industries such as mining, logging, damming, and military uses continue to threaten and destroy Native American shrines, burials, emergence places, and origin sites at an alarming rate. Industrial land uses, New Age commercialism, cultural stereotypes and ignorance, and governmental restrictions are some of the main factors that threaten the religious freedom of today's Native Americans.

Despite these and other major challenges to Native American religious freedom and spiritual expression, today's Native Americans continue to practice traditional sacred ways. As the Ojibwe activist Winona LaDuke has stated, these time-tested spiritual traditions illustrate a worldview not based on conquest. They demonstrate a much needed philosophy, ethics, and embodied practice of ecological kinship and intergenerational responsibility.

Melissa K. NELSON
San Francisco State University

FURTHER READING

Beck, Peggy V., & Walters, Anna L. (1988). *The sacred: Ways of knowledge, sources of life*. Tsaile, AZ: Navajo Community College Press.

Caldicott, J. Baird, & Nelson, Michael R. (2004). *American Indian environmental ethics: An Ojibwa case study*. Upper Saddle River, NJ: Pearson Education.

Deloria, Vine, Jr. (1994). *God is red: A native view of religion*. Golden, CO: Fulcrum Publishing.

Deloria, Vine, Jr. (2006). *The world we used to live in: Remembering the powers of the medicine men*. Golden, CO: Fulcrum Publishing.

Graham, Harvey. (2006). *Animism: Respecting the living world*. New York: Columbia University Press.

Grim, John. (1998). *Indigenous traditions and ecology: The interbeing of cosmology and community*. Cambridge, MA: Harvard University Press.

Kelley, Dennis F., & Crawford, Suzanne J. (2005). *American Indian religious traditions: An encyclopedia*. Oxford, U.K.: ABC-CLIO.

Kidwell, Clara Sue. (2001). *A Native American theology*. Maryknoll, NY: Orbis Books.

Martin, Joel. (2001). *The land looks after us: A history of Native American religion*. New York: Oxford University Press.

Nabokov, Pete. (2007). *Where the lightning strikes: The lives of American Indian sacred places*. New York: Penguin.

Nelson, Melissa K. (2008). *Original instructions: Indigenous teachings for a sustainable future*. Rochester, VT: Bear & Company/Inner Traditions.

Niezen, Ronald. (2000). *Spirit wars: Native North American religions in the age of nation building*. Berkeley: University of California Press.

Salmon, Enrique. (2000). Kincentric ecology: Indigenous perceptions of the human–nature relationship. *Ecological Applications, 10*(5), 1327–1332.

Smith, Huston. (2007). *A seat at the table: Conversations with American Indian leaders on religious freedom*. Berkeley: University of California Press.

Sullivan, Lawrence. (1989). *Native American religions: North America*. New York: Macmillan Publishing Company.

Treat, James. (1996). *Native and Christian: Indigenous voices on religious identity in the United States and Canada*. New York and London: Routledge.

Vecsey, Christopher. (1991). *Handbook of American Indian religious freedom*. New York: Crossroad Publishing Company.

Waldman, Carl. (2000). *Atlas of the North American Indian*. New York: Checkmark Books.

Wessendorf, Kathrin. (2008). *The indigenous world 2008*. Copenhagen: International Work Group for Indigenous Affairs.

Indigenous Traditions—Oceania

In Oceania indigenous beliefs and practices reflect an awareness of the interdependence of all life. Ritual (such as the Hawaiian hula) and dynamic concepts (such as the Dreaming of Australia) celebrate habitats and engage the individual and community in life-giving power. Western resource exploitation and rising seawaters that threaten to submerge some island homelands are among the dangers to ecological and cultural sustainability in the area.

The indigenous peoples of Oceania follow both the ways of their ancestors and the Christianities brought to them by missionaries. In some places indigenous lifeways and introduced faith are well integrated while in others they constitute separate and competing ways of living in the world. Overall, styles of religion in the Pacific emphasize social and ecological relationships. Traditional environmental knowledge among indigenous peoples in Oceania and elsewhere emphasizes a reciprocity between people and other life-forms; this give-and-take structures traditional myth and ritual and influences Pacific appropriations of Christianity. The region of Oceania, extending from the large island of New Guinea in the west to Hawaii and Rapa Nui (Easter Island) in the east, includes the islands of the Pacific Ocean and the landmass of Australia. Indigenous ways of life in the region are conditioned by its diverse environments, from the deserts of central Australia to the rainforests of New Guinea to the coral atolls of the central Pacific. In ritual practices people seek their own well-being and that of their land, crops, and animals, and in mythic narratives they tell of how the land was shaped, how people came to dwell in their particular territory, and how social institutions arose. Sustaining fertility and well-being in the present and maintaining the cosmic order handed down from the ancestors is of ultimate concern both individually and socially. The physical diversity of the region is echoed in the social diversity, which includes societies led by chieftains and more egalitarian communities with a variety of kinship patterns. These intersect with modern political systems introduced in the colonial era. Throughout Oceania spirit beings of various kinds—ancestral ghosts, creator gods, and spirits dwelling in trees and pools and features of the landscape—are understood as active players in the social world. With the introduction of Christianity the triune Christian God and Christian saints have been incorporated into that world.

Religion from an Ecological Point of View

Classic Western definitions of religion emphasize relationship to God or gods and speak of beliefs, practices, values, and symbols. These approaches to religion can be used in exploring the ways of life of the peoples of Oceania. But an ecological orientation toward religion—an orientation that construes religion as the linking and empowerment of the many domains of experience—is preferable. Rather than negating other perspectives it suggests that religion is awareness of the interdependence of all of life. Actions to sustain life and to tap into life-giving power flow from such awareness. While the term "religion" has no exact equivalent in traditional Oceania there are indigenous notions that share in its significance. Among them are the "Dreaming" in indigenous Australia and *mana* and *tapu* in Polynesia and parts of Melanesia. All three terms have ecological import and, as a consequence of colonial and missionary incursion into the Pacific, all three have had an influence on how contemporary scholars of religion think about their subject.

The "Dreaming" is an English term adopted by Australian indigenous peoples to represent ideas about origins and the ongoing empowerment of the world. It refers at one level to an epoch in which beings with extraordinary powers, such as the Rainbow Snake, appeared from below the ground or from the sky or from over the horizon. These powerful beings shaped the earth, distributed plants and animals and water, and established human cultures. They are themselves called Dreamings. Each person and group has associations with particular Dreamings. The work of the Dreamings is narrated in myths and enacted in rituals that transmit their power to the landscape and to the community. Australian indigenous religion is more concerned with place than with time. Within their own "country" (territory, land) people are aware of Dreaming tracks, paths along which the Dreaming figures traveled, and Dreaming places where the powerful beings rested or engaged in creative actions. In the Dreaming perspective people belong to their country and share life with all the other species that inhabit it. It is the responsibility of the people to tell the stories and to perform the rituals so that the community of land, animals, plants, and people will flourish. People understand themselves as belonging to the land and bearing a responsibility to sustain it through carrying out the rituals given to them in the Dreaming.

Through the work of Émile Durkheim (1858–1917) and others the terms *mana* and *tapu* have entered the lexicon of religious studies and taken on a wider significance. (Durkheim 2008 [1912], 140–152, 221–242). In the Pacific *mana* is a quality of being in which a person or an object is, temporarily or permanently, under the influence of gods, spirits, or other powers. The Anglican missionary R. H. Codrington (1830–1922) characterized Melanesian religion as a process of acquiring *mana* (Codrington 1891, 118–121, 191–193). Whereas *mana* suggests a manifestation of power and is often glossed as "supernatural power," *tapu* implies a restriction or curbing of power. *Tapu* is usually rendered in English as "taboo" and glossed as "forbidden." Objects, persons, and behaviors that are seen as dangerous to ordinary people are said to be *tapu* (taboo). Thus, places where spirits dwell are potentially dangerous and are usually *tapu*. When it is necessary to venture there, for instance to harvest fruit or nuts or to hunt, people carry out protective rituals. The historian and linguist Anne Salmond observes that Polynesian words like *mana* and *tapu* and *atua* (god) are "highly theory-dependent, and correspondingly difficult to interpret and translate." She points out that they arise "from an explanatory project which in this case takes the physical experience of mating, reproduction, and growth, and from that base develops a genealogical description language to account for the relations among entities of all kind (e.g., people; their ancestors and ancestor-gods; plants and animal species; and phenomena such as the stars, sky, earth, the sea, land, the mountains and the wind) and the emergence of the cosmos itself" (Salmond 1989, 57).

Symbolic Words and Works

In Oceania most indigenous people either live in rural areas or retain links with rural communities. Many sustain themselves, as their ancestors did, by gardening, hunting, and fishing. In daily life people communicate in "ordinary" language and perform "ordinary" labor to provide food. But in rituals to sustain the land (and sea) they use multivalent words and actions to forge fruitful connections across the many domains of experience and particularly with the spirit beings. Everyone uses symbolic words and symbolic works, and some societies entrust their most significant myths and rituals to specialists such as healers and priests. For example, as Michael Young discusses in *Magicians of Manumanua*, in the Massim society of Kalauna in Papua New Guinea the "guardians" of the community are hereditary ritual specialists who know the myths concerning food and who conduct rituals to banish famine and to promote the supply of food. In symbolic words, such as spells for gardens and prayers for the growth of children, and in symbolic works for healing and renewal, ritual specialists and their clients work to achieve balance and prosperity.

In adopting Christianity, peoples of the Pacific accommodated traditional rituals, such as the Hawaiian hula, to changing circumstances. Prior to the arrival of missionaries in 1820, the hula, a combination of dance and chant, which according to one legend was instituted by the goddess Laka, was performed to honor the gods, to pay tribute to chiefs, and to celebrate nature and the community. Hula chants and dance movements evoke the natural environment with its valleys and forests and rivers, its ferns and flowers and fruits. Missionaries were offended by the sexual imagery of the hula, which depicted both human love and the fruitfulness of nature, and denounced it as heathen. Traditional forms of hula declined, but there was a resurgence during the reign of King David Kalākaua (1874–1891) in which a form of hula, the *hula ku'i,* combined traditional and new elements. To appeal to tourists in the twentieth century hula was presented as an entertainment with a focus on the exotic charms of the dancers. Since the 1960s with the Hawaiian Cultural Renaissance there has been renewed interest in the study and practice of ancient hula that have accompanied a struggle for land, a reclamation of traditional forestry and farming practices, and a return to Polynesian voyaging.

Environmental Ethics

Religions provide guidance on how to live in the natural world that may be couched in a Pacific ethic of reciprocity, or in a Christian ethic of stewardship of the Earth, or in other terms. Pacific and Christian ways are not without common ground, and both are tested by contemporary realities. Traditional communities used both manual labor and symbolic processes to maintain balance in their environment but sometimes, as on Rapa Nui, they failed in their efforts. Polynesians, who settled on Rapa Nui perhaps as late as 1200 CE, felled trees to create fields for agriculture and to use in the transport of huge stone statues called *moai*, which represented their sacred chiefs and gods and the unity of their community. Over time destruction of forests led to erosion of topsoil and a decline in agricultural productivity. By the 1830s, competition for resources and loss of confidence in the chiefs had led to internecine wars and the collapse of the society. In most parts of Oceania, however, people were able to adjust to the constraints of their environment. From the chiefly societies of Polynesia to the more egalitarian societies of highland New Guinea an ethic of reciprocity prevailed, but not everyone was equal in the social network. In the chiefly societies lower status people lacked the privileges of the higher status people, and in most societies women were considered inferior to men. The networks of relationships making up the worlds of meaning of Pacific peoples were not static. They constantly needed adjustments and corrections that rituals of healing and reconciliation provided.

In the more than two centuries of Western presence in the Pacific the traditional ethic and Christian assertions about social justice and ecological responsibility have been severely challenged by labor recruiters, whalers, miners, loggers, and bio-prospectors. The Western incursion into the Pacific has seen profound transformations and severe dislocations of traditional community life. For example, in Fiji there are difficulties in the relationship between indigenous Fijians and Indo-Fijians, the descendants of the Indians brought in the nineteenth century to work in the sugarcane plantations established by the British. Indo-Fijians are either Muslim or Hindu while indigenous Fijians follow both Christianity and traditional ways. Meanwhile, in New Guinea many people who once made gardens and kept pigs now earn wages by working for mines and logging companies. In most Pacific states there is a tendency to rely on economic opportunities afforded by resource exploitation. Some leaders resist the multinational companies, railing at their desecration of sacred places and exploitation of native labor. Others urge accommodation and cooperation in order to negotiate deals that are beneficial to both sides. International resource-extracting companies have been concerned primarily with returns to their shareholders and not with benefits to local communities or protection of the environment.

Nuclear testing in Oceania was part and parcel of colonialism, a matter of outsiders using and abusing the region in their Cold War strategies. The sponsors of nuclear testing in the region (Great Britain, the United States, and France) had little regard for the health of indigenous peoples living in remote areas or for the likelihood of environmental damage. The United States exploded bombs over Bikini and Enewek atolls in the Marshall Islands from 1946 to 1958 and over Johnston Atoll and Kirimati (Christmas Island) in 1962. Great Britain carried out testing between 1952 and 1958 at Maralinga and Emu Field in south Australia and in the Monte Bello Islands and Kirimati off the west Australian coast. France, having been forced out of the Sahara by Algeria, carried out testing in French Polynesia from 1966 to 1996. At the beginning of nuclear testing the two major powers in the region, Australia and New Zealand, were allied with Great Britain in the enterprise. But from the 1970s an antinuclear sentiment developed in the Pacific island nations, and in Australia and New Zealand, leading to the signing in 1985 by member states of the South Pacific Forum of the Rarotonga Treaty for a South Pacific Nuclear Free Zone. The treaty bans the use, testing, and possession of nuclear weapons within the zone. It was signed, and subsequently ratified, by Australia, the Cook Islands, Fiji, Kiribati, Nauru, New Zealand, Niue, Papua New Guinea, the Solomon Islands, Tonga, Tuvalu, Vanuatu, and Western Samoa. The Pacific Council of Churches was a strong advocate for the nuclear-free zone. Although nuclear testing in the Pacific ended in 1996 there are still people and places suffering its aftereffects. Nuclear threats, such as shipment of nuclear wastes through the Pacific, proposals to dump nuclear waste on Pacific atolls, and uranium mining in Australia continue. Commenting on the campaigns seeking redress for nuclear testing, the journalist and researcher Nic Maclellan observes that they "have common demands, calling on the nuclear weapons states: to acknowledge their responsibility for the health and environmental impacts of past nuclear tests; to introduce or extend programs for monitoring, cleanup, and rehabilitation of former nuclear test sites; to open up their archives to allow independent researchers access to documentation and studies on the health and environmental impacts of testing; to compensate former test-site workers, and civilian and military personnel at the sites, and neighboring local communities; to continue long-term funding for the necessary programs of monitoring, cleanup, rehabilitation, compensation, and reparations" (Maclellan 2005, 368–369). Opposition to nuclear testing has been an important element in the forging of common identity among the indigenous peoples of Oceania and settler peoples who today call the region home (Mara 1997).

Oceania and the Global Community

Oceania now consists of independent nations as well as of states and territories that are part of external countries such as the United States and France. Within Oceania there is a marked contrast in economic opportunity between those who live in the Pacific islands and those who live in the more prosperous nations of Australia and Aotearoa / New Zealand or in the state of Hawaii. Yet even in those places the indigenous citizens have less opportunity than the settler citizens. The indigenous peoples are caught, as it is often put, "between the local and the global." Both their cultural survival and the survival of their habitats are at stake. Rising sea levels resulting from global warming will almost certainly submerge the low-lying homelands of some island dwellers. In August of 2008, religious leaders from various faith groups within Australia united with their counterparts from the Pacific islands to challenge the Australian government to take immediate action on climate change to assist the Pacific's small island nations. In an open letter to the Australian government they stated that Australia has a moral obligation since it has an historical responsibility for this serious situation.

Like the peoples of Oceania, indigenous people in many parts of the world have seen their resources seized and their ways of life changed by colonial intrusion. The Declaration of the Rights of Indigenous Peoples, adopted by the United Nations in September of 2007, addresses some of the issues that arise from the colonial experience. The declaration sets out the individual and collective rights of indigenous peoples including their rights to culture, identity, language, employment, health, and education. It asserts the right of indigenous peoples to maintain and strengthen their own cultures and religions and prohibits discrimination against them. The declaration is nonbinding but, nevertheless, it represents an important step in the formulation of relationships between indigenous peoples and the global community. Religion, an integral part of traditional culture in the Pacific, and, in the form of Christianity, an integral part of Pacific life today, offers perspective on the local/global relationship. The indigenous ethic of reciprocity and contemporary Christian understandings of social justice and ecojustice provide frames within which to discuss the environmental violations of the mining and logging companies and the matter of biopiracy. It is the hope of many of the religious bodies within Oceania that their cooperation within the region and their engagement with the global community can contribute to sustaining the lands and cultures of the Pacific.

Mary N. MacDONALD
Le Moyne College

FURTHER READING

ABC Radio Australia. (2008, August 18). Faith groups in Pacific climate change appeal. *Pacific Beat*. Retrieved June 5, 2009, from http://www.radioaustralia.net.au/programguide/stories/200808/s2334303.htm

Barker, John. (Ed.). (1990). *Christianity in Oceania: Ethnographic perspectives*. Lanham, MD: University Press of America.

Boutilier, James A.; Hughes, Daniel T.; & Tiffany, Sharon W. (1978). *Mission, church, and sect in Oceania*. ASAO Monograph No. 6. Ann Arbor: University of Michigan Press.

Connell, John, & Waddell, Eric. (Eds.). (2007). *Environment, development and change in rural Asia-Pacific: Between local and global*. London and New York: Routledge.

Codrington, Robert Henry. (1891). *The Melanesians: Studies in their anthropology and folk-lore*. Oxford, U.K.: Oxford University Press.

Durkheim, Émile. (2008 [1912]). *The elementary forms of religious life*. Carol Cosman (Trans.), Mark S. Cladis (Ed.). Oxford, U.K.: Oxford University Press.

Emerson, Nathaniel Bright. (1965). *Unwritten literature of Hawaii: The sacred songs of the hula*. Collected and translated, with notes and an account of the hula (rev. ed.). Rutland, VT: Tuttle.

Feld, Steven. (1990). *Sound and sentiment: Birds, weeping, poetics, and song in Kaluli expression* (2nd ed.). Philadelphia: University of Pennsylvania Press.

Grim, John A. (Ed.). (2001). *Indigenous traditions and ecology: The interbeing of cosmology and community*. The Center for the Study of World Religions' Religions of the World Series. Cambridge, MA: Harvard University Press.

Herda, Phyllis; Reilly, Michael; & Hilliard, David. (Eds.). (2005). *Vision and reality in Pacific religion*. Canberra, Australia: Pandanus Books.

Maclellan, Nic. (2005) The nuclear age in the Pacific Islands. *The Contemporary Pacific, 17*(2), 363–372.

Mageo, Jeannette Marie, & Howard, Alan. (Eds.). (1996). *Spirits in culture, history, and mind*. New York: Routledge.

Mara, Ratu Sir Kamisese. (1997). *The pacific way: A memoir*. Honolulu: University of Hawaii Center for Pacific Islands Studies, East-West Center Pacific Islands Development Program.

Meigs, Anna S. (1984). *Food, sex, and pollution: A New Guinea religion*. New Brunswick, NJ: Rutgers University Press.

Overton, John, & Scheyvens, Regina. (1999). *Strategies for sustainable development: Experiences from the Pacific*. Sydney: University of New South Wales Press.

Rappaport, Roy A. (1984). *Pigs for the ancestors: Ritual in the ecology of a New Guinea people* (2nd ed). New Haven, CT: Yale University Press.

Salmond, Anne. (1989). Tribal words, tribal worlds: The translatability of *tapu* and *mana*. In Mac Marshall & John L. Caughey (Eds.), *Culture, kin, and cognition in Oceania: Essays in honor of Ward H. Goodenough* (pp. 55–78). Washington, DC: American Anthropological Association.

Strathern, Andrew; Stewart, Pamela J.; Carucci, Lawrence M; Poyer, Lin; Feinberg, Richard; & Macpherson, Cluny. (2002). *Oceania: An introduction to the cultures and identities of Pacific Islanders*. Durham, NC: Carolina Academic Press.

Swain, Tony, & Trompf, Garry. (1995). *The religions of Oceania*. London and New York: Routledge.

Young, Michael W. (1983). *Magicians of Manumanua: Living myth in Kalauna*. Berkeley: University of California Press.

Young Leslie, Heather E. (2007). A fishy romance: Chiefly power and the geopolitics of desire. *The Contemporary Pacific, 19*(2), 365–408.

United Nations. (2007). Declaration on the rights of indigenous peoples. Retrieved April 29, 2009, from http://www.un.org/esa/socdev/unpfii/en/drip.html

Indigenous Traditions— South America

South America is among the richest continents in terms of biodiversity. Its spirit of sustainability lies in the sustainability of spirit generated by indigenous peoples who resisted colonial and neocolonial powers that threatened not only their environment but their cultures. These people, with a worldview based on the cyclical process of cultivation nurtured and encouraged by pachamama (Mother Earth), have thus become some of the most important actors in promoting sustainability.

In South America, particularly the Andean region, spirituality and sustainability have been inextricably interwoven within the land-culture of its indigenous peoples. The term *land-culture* refers to the way in which indigenous peoples' histories and lives are tied to specific landscapes. Because indigenous peoples have defined themselves as descendants of those who inhabited the land before colonial societies conquered and appropriated it, the destruction of their landscapes, or their resettlement on reservations away from their native landscape, is to them quite literally an obliteration of their culture. Thus for many indigenous peoples of South America, environmental preservation is considered cultural preservation.

The Andean region as discussed here is not the one mapped by the north-south longitudes of the Western-colonial intellectual tradition. The Andean region from a precolonial view and practice is transregional, comprising western coastal lowlands, the highlands, and the eastern tropical lowlands of the Amazon—regions whose ecological niches interact within the cyclical process of *pachamama* (Mother Earth). The spirituality and sustainability expressed in this region are intrinsic to a particular way of knowing, being, and being related to the world that has existed for the last 10,000 years. This indigenous worldview embodies the system of cultivation that the peoples' land-cultures have sustained spiritually for millennia; it is fundamentally different from the dominant Euro-American worldview.

Land-Culture versus Colonization

South America's indigenous population, whose lands (and thus land-cultures) have been appropriated and exploited, view the past and current Euro-American world as a mechanistic, positivistic, homogenizing, unsustainable way of knowing and being. That the concept of sustainability has been foreign to such a dominant, colonial worldview for the last five hundred years suggests why we are facing a global environmental, ecological, spiritual, moral, and ethical crisis for the first time in human history. For South America the spirit of sustainability and the sustainability of the spirit are deeply rooted in the perdurability of indigenous peoples, their worldview, and their land-cultures. The sustainability blueprint for today's Latin America is present, alive, and regenerating within the various strongholds of these land-cultures, languages, and *cosmovisions* (worldviews), a situation that may not be visible to the world's population at large.

The past and current colonization process has had a significant negative impact upon the lives, cultures, lands, territories, and natural resources of Latin America, whose total population of around 580 million individuals live mostly in urban areas, detached from nature, land-culture, and a holistic sense of place. According to conservative estimates, 40 million people (or less than 10 percent of the total population) are indigenous. The total surface area controlled by indigenous peoples throughout the Americas has shrunk significantly due to nation-state building. Indigenous peoples were removed from their lands in order to make room for the emerging national citizens and their descendants, who inherited the colonial mentality reflected at the hemispheric level. We thus must attend to the outgrowth of a space-based (as opposed to place-based) mentality, which creates monocultures of the mind-spirit-land. This spatial, detached view of land and nature challenges the spirit of sustainability and the sustainability of the spirit of indigenous peoples rooted in specific places. In contrast to space-based, nonsustainable monocultures, indigenous regions in South America continue to nurture cultural places through the spiritual values of the *ayllu*, a word of the Quechua and Aymara (the two most populous indigenous peoples of the Andean region), which literally means "extended family / community," but embodies the meaning that all living beings take shelter in, and value, their communal place. Here, at the core of Andean collective life, all visible and nonvisible living beings—such as plants, animals, deities, rocks, mountains, rivers, and humans—are nurtured and sustained by *pachamama*.

Cultural Diversity / Biodiversity

South America is among the richest continents in terms of biodiversity. Its spirit of sustainability lies in the sustainability of spirit generated by indigenous peoples who resisted colonial and neocolonial powers. The indigenous people of South America have thus become some of the most important actors in promoting sustainability.

For South America, and particularly for the Andean-Amazonian region, indigenous places are the crux of biological and cultural diversity. This region is populated by more than four hundred ethic groups of indigenous peoples, each with its own distinct language, social organization, and *cosmovision*. For these peoples, who live in 80 percent of the ecologically protected areas in Latin America, cultural diversity is highly correlated with both biological and agricultural diversity. From a Westernized perspective, most of these Latin American groups are considered "peasants" or subsistence farmers, a Western term suppressing the fact that such "peasants," the ones who foster the region's biological and agricultural diversity, are the sources of information the agriculture industry relies on for monetary profit. For hundreds of years, Western economies have expropriated and exploited the food security generated by the indigenous peoples, a process known as "biopiracy."

Preserving the Spirit of Sustainability

Indigenous movements of political autonomy and cultural affirmation are part of the political and intellectual labor necessary for protecting this spirit of sustainability. Movements and organizations aligned with the interests of indigenous communities in a process of *acompañamiento* (simplistically and roughly translated, a method of apprenticeship), such as the Andean Project of Peasant

Technologies (PRATEC), walk side by side with and facilitate the collection and systematization of indigenous knowledge grounded on an understanding of sustaining the resources of *pacha* (the Earth). PRATEC, a nongovernmental organization established in 1987, supports the resurgence of indigenous Andean "ritual agriculture" practices that have been challenged by anthropocentric-based methods of Western industrialism, and thus helps preserve this spirit, which is itself sustained by *pachamama*.

While Western epistemologies consider economy, society, and politics to be discrete concepts, the traditional forms of communal and collective existence that persist today for indigenous peoples, such as the *ayllu*, integrate these concepts into what could aptly be called *the sustainability of spirit* or *the spirit of sustainability*. For the vast majority of indigenous peoples this integrative worldview emerges from a ritual cycle of cultivating the land. It has now been extended into urban sectors through an indigenous ethnic diaspora. The designation *campesino* (or "peasant" farmers) has for several decades been used to characterize these displaced indigenous peoples as powerless. More problematically, the term "peasant" has further limited and confined the Andean cultivator of Andean land to a paradigm of feudal organization that is European and colonial, and which denigrates the activity of the human person who cultivates (*runa*) by reducing it to techno-bureaucratic, class-based, political analyses. The Andean *runa* lives in equity with all other living members (and persons) of the other collectivities, procuring harmony with them through continual, daily, and sometimes ritualized conversation. But indigenous peoples have been active participants in their own history (outside of the Western class and gender structures imposed on them), and there is no evidence that a derogatory or demeaning characterization will damper their spirits as they engage in the active process of recovery and affirmation. All Andean indigenous life centers on the regeneration of life as a whole; in Andean cultures nature is very distinctly lived rather than analyzed.

Quechua Natural Order

The Andean/Amazonian region's *ayllu*-cultural practices could be said to center on a Quechua "natural order" from which the Quechua people gather their language, traditional knowledge, or spiritual practices within specific landscapes. This Quechua Andean/Amazonian natural order, still accessible today, is shared with Aymara and many other native peoples. Its path—its life-way—traverses the coastal region, the Andean highland region, and the Amazonian region. Those who cultivate the land in these places are not "farmers" according to the contemporary definition, practice, and understanding of the way in which Western farmers often farm: Quechua and other indigenous peoples do not lease or own land or property and therefore do not remain tethered to the same plot of land or the same crop. The Quechua/Aymara cultivators conceive of their labor as cyclical and in a state of permanent motion—as transterritorial and transregional. The Quechua and Aymara person (*runa* and *haqi*, respectively) walks with *kawsay mama*—the living mother, the living seed—in its multiple paths, through which diversity as a spiritual practice of sustainability is cultivated.

The paradigm for this world order is a cycle of conviviality—of all beings sustained by spirit in an elliptical transverse motion, tilted in accord to the movements of all living beings (on *pacha* and in place and time) dwelling with and protected and harbored by *pachamama,* or the spirit of sustainability. This natural order renders the world both in whole and in distinction, in unity and diversity. It does not do this by dividing beings from Being (or Essence), as in many Western understandings of unity and diversity, but rather as an integrated whole whose plenitude is manifest as the conviviality of all beings, at the same time both distinct and in communion. Nor is the Essence or Being of any being considered dualistically. In terms of the division of the animate in contrast to the inanimate, for instance, all beings are animate and within spirit—*ayllu, kawsay mama, pachamama,* and *pacha.*

The Spanish word *mestizo* comes from a Latin root word (*miscere*) meaning *mixed.* Its common usage refers to a person as being of mixed, or "part" Spanish and "part" indigenous, descent and implies a sense of dismembering that does not reflect the essence of identity in the Quechua natural world order. For the Quechua/Aymara, identity involves the "re-membering" that takes place in a cycle of movement sustained by and in spirit. The identity of all beings in spirit is determined rather by the confluence of distinct beings of undifferentiated value, in equity, in a sustainable movement of harmony and balance. *Allin kawsay,* well-being, is the way that the *ayllu* welfare of all beings may be practiced through cultivation and nurturance, in an endless cycle meant to achieve balance. This integrative spirit can be seen as far back as the Inca, whose personage is the cultivator, as is any person (*runa/haqi*), in place and time on *pacha.* Neither the republican *criollo,* as a liberated colonial subject, nor the *mestizo,* as a split identity, are at play in the Andean world; Andean languages respond to the need to regenerate the whole. The *mallku* (an Andean human of authority charged with overseeing the *ayllu*) *is* the *ayllu* in the sense that he protects the *ayllu* and the *ayllu* protects *him*; the *mallku* performs *mullu,* the act of walking from household to household in the *ayllu* to converse with mothers and fathers and children about their welfare— and is said to be following the path of the seed, which is also called *mullu*—in order to achieve *ayllu* welfare, *allin kawsay.* The *mallku* follows the path of *kawsay mama* (living mother, living seed). This Quechu/Aymara way is the spirit of sustainability of *pachamama* as much as it is the sustainability of spirit of *kawsay mama.*

Tirso GONZALES
University of British Columbia Okanagan

Maria E. GONZALEZ
University of Michigan

FURTHER READING

Andean Project of Peasant Technologies (PRATEC). (2001). *Comunidad y biodiversidad. El ayllu y su organicidad en la crianza de la diversidad en la chacra.* Lima, Peru: PRATEC.

Choque, M. E., & Mamani, C. (2001). Reconstitucion del Ayllu y derechos de los pueblos indigenas: El movimiento indio en los andes de Bolivia. *Journal of Latin American Anthropology, 6*(1), 202–224.

Deruyttere, Anne. (1997, October). *Indigenous Peoples and sustainable development: The role of the Inter-American Development Bank* (No. IND97-101). Washington, DC: Inter-American Development Bank.

Escobar, Arturo. (1995). *Encountering development: The making and unmaking of the third world.* Princeton, NJ: Princeton University Press.

Escobar, Arturo. (2001). Culture sits in places: Reflections on globalism and subaltern strategies of localization. *Political Geography, 20*(2), 139–174.

Gonzales, Tirso A. (1999). The cultures of the seed in the Peruvian Andes. In S. B. Brush (Ed.), *Genes in the field: On-farm conservation of crop diversity* (pp. 193–216). International Plant Genetic Resources Institute. International Development Research Centre, Ottawa, Canada: Lewis Publishers. (Also retrieved May 26, 2009, from http://www.idrc.ca/en/ev-98735-201-1-DO_TOPIC.html)

Gonzales, Tirso A. (2008). Renativization in North and South America. In Melissa Nelson (Ed.), *Original instructions:Indigenous teachings for a sustainable future* (pp. 298–303). Rochester, VT: Bear & Company.

Grillo, Eduardo. (1998). Cultural Affirmation: Digestion of imperialism in the Andes. In Frédérique Apffel-Marglin with PRATEC (Eds.), *The spirit of regeneration: Andean culture confronting western notions of development.* London: Zed Books.

Grim, John A. (Ed.). (2000). *Indigenous traditions and ecology: The interbeing of cosmology and community.* Cambridge, MA: Harvard University Press.

Gutiérrez Leguía, Benjamín. (2007). La formalización de la propiedad rural en el Perú. Período 1996–2006, lecciones aprendidas. Retrieved June 20, 2008, from http://www.catastro.meh.es/esp/publicaciones/ct/ct60/60_5.pdf

IAASTD LAC Sub-global SDM. (2008). Retrieved May 26, 2009, from http://www.agassessment.org/

Ishizawa, Jorge and Grillo Fernández, Eduardo. (2002). Loving the world as it is: Western abstraction and Andean nurturance. *Revision, 24*(4), 21–26. Washington, DC: Heldref Publications.

IUCN. (1997). Chapter 2: What is Sustainability? In *Inter-Commission Task Force on Indigenous Peoples. Indigenous peoples and sustainability: Cases and actions.* Indigenous Peoples and Conservation Initiative. Utrecht, The Netherlands: International Books.

Kloppenburg, Jack Ralph. (1988). *First the seed: The political economy of plant biotechnology, 1492–2000.* New York: Cambridge University Press.

Lizarralde, M. (2001). Biodiversity and loss of indigenous languages and knowledge in South America. In Luisa Maffi (Ed.), *On biocultural diversity: Linking language, knowledge, and the environment.* Washington, DC: Smithsonian Institution Press.

MacCormack, Sabine. (1991). *Religion in the Andes.* Princeton, NJ: Princeton University Press.

Valladolid, J. (2001). Andean cosmovision and the nurturing of biodiversity in the peasant chacra. In John A. Grim (Ed.), *Indigenous traditions and ecology. The interbeing of cosmology and community.* Cambridge, MA: Harvard University Press.

Indigenous Traditions—
The Arctic

Indigenous peoples of the Arctic recognize the spirit of beings other than humans and practice ritual respect for all beings. From their beliefs and values emerge two key ideas of interest to environmental scientists and related to sustainability: humans as an integral part of ecosystems, and the importance of continuing to use resources to maintain respectful relationships and stewardship traditions.

There is no single accepted definition of the Arctic. The *Arctic Human Development Report* (AHDR) defines the Arctic as: all of Alaska; Canada north of the sixtieth parallel, plus northern Quebec and Labrador; Greenland; Iceland; the northernmost counties of Norway, Sweden, and Finland; and the northern parts of Russian Siberia. The AHDR Arctic covers an area of 40 million square kilometers or about 8 percent of the surface of Earth, with a population of about 4 million people, almost half of them in the Russian Arctic.

People of the Arctic

Humans have occupied large parts of the Arctic at least since the Ice Age, and from as early as 40,000 years ago in the European Arctic. Contemporary residents of the Arctic include indigenous populations and recent arrivals. Some countries such as Iceland have no indigenous populations; others such as Greenland have a majority; the Canadian Arctic has an equal split; and all others (United States/Alaska, Russia, Norway, Sweden, and Finland) have a minority of indigenous peoples. Indigenous peoples are those who show one or more of the following characteristics: they identify themselves as indigenous; they speak a language different from that of the dominant society; their cultures are different from that of the dominant society;

and they often diverge from the mainstream society by being hunters, nomads, or pastoralists.

Prior to World War II, many Arctic societies led a relatively self-sufficient way of life based on extended families or kinship groups, and in some cases, small communities. Livelihoods were based mostly on hunting, trapping, fishing, gathering, and herding, and the trading of products from these pursuits. These activities provided a strong connection to the environment, and this connection was important for two reasons. First, it was a matter of survival; animals were important for food and for the local economy. Second, traditional pursuits were important for maintaining social relationships and cultural identity. For example, seal hunting not only provided food for sharing; it was a way of life and a symbolic part of Inuit culture.

After World War II, most indigenous societies were impacted in a variety of ways. The introduction of mandatory education and establishment of permanent villages made it difficult to pursue the seasonal round of activities on the land. Transportation and communications changed at an increased pace after World War II. Motor boats, snowmobiles, and four-wheel all terrain vehicles (ATVs) became common. Television became available in most Arctic households and provided exposure to new lifestyles and role models.

Culture and Religion

Arctic indigenous societies have been in a rapid social and economic transition since World War II, but religious transition started even earlier. The vast majority of Arctic indigenous people are affiliated with some form of Christianity. The major periods of religious conversion were the eighteenth and nineteenth centuries. In many cases, the adoption of Christianity did not mean the complete

replacement of one religion with another. Rather, in most indigenous societies, elements of old and new beliefs were mixed together, and the resulting system still retained some traditional values and beliefs. But generalizations are difficult to make because there are large differences from region to region, and in some cases, even between adjacent communities.

The Arctic indigenous world is diverse. The mixing of indigenous groups with one another and with the more recent European immigrants has produced a melting pot of cultures. Despite this mixing, indigenous Arctic values and beliefs vary by area. Most indigenous pre-Christian beliefs were characterized by animism, the idea that humans, animals and plants, in addition to other natural phenomena that Westerners consider inanimate, such as mountains, springs, rivers, and glaciers, all share a spirit that energizes them; belief in spiritual beings; and more broadly with pantheism, the doctrine that identifies the universe with the Creator.

With animism at the core of their belief systems, most indigenous peoples believed that humans were not the only beings capable of independent action. For example, the Tlingit in the area of St. Elias Mountains, a glacier field that straddles Alaska, Yukon, and British Columbia, tell stories in which glaciers are sentient and responsive. Many Arctic and other Northern peoples consider animals to be capable of deciding to make (or not to make) themselves available for the hunt. Since survival depended on the ability to hunt wildlife and marine mammals, it was rather important for hunters to maintain the cooperation of their prey. The belief among some indigenous groups such as the Dene and the Cree of Canada was to maintain a reciprocal relationship between humans and animals. Animals gave themselves willingly to hunters, but for their part, humans needed to maintain a relationship of respect and to observe certain rituals to take care of the spirits of the animals.

In many parts of the Arctic, people observe rituals signifying respect—rituals in which the remains of animals are returned to the environment to ensure the continuation of the spiritual cycle of life. For example, in Barrow, Alaska, a proper practice is to return the lower jawbone of a hunted bowhead whale to the sea. The Dene and the Cree hang beaver bones on trees or return them to the lakes and rivers they came from. Other practices of ritual respect include talking to the animals to ask for their permission for the hunt, and making offerings at the time of the hunt or during consumption of the animal. Some animal parts are taboo for certain people, but this practice varies widely.

In addition to animals, certain areas of the land also receive respect because traditional beliefs and practices are often tied to the land. Some mountains, springs, or parts of the land where certain ceremonies take place may be considered sacred. Sacred sites are found in many regions and cultural groups, almost universally across the Arctic. For example, 263 sacred sites were identified in one district alone in the Yamal-Nenets area in Russia. Such sacred sites have been receiving attention from the International Conservation Union as potential additions to national and international conservation networks.

Sustainability Principles

The recognition of the spirit of beings other than humans and practices of ritual respect for beings may be considered two principles of Arctic indigenous traditions. They give rise to two further key ideas or insights regarding sustainability. The first is the notion that humans are integral part of ecosystems, sharing the land with other beings as their kin. Many indigenous groups, and not only the ones in the Arctic, hold a community-of-beings worldview in which animals and other beings are related to humans. They are nonhuman persons but persons nonetheless and kin. Many indigenous cultures see humans and nature, not in an adversarial relationship involving domination and control, but in a symbiotic relationship with mutual obligations involving respect. This is a very different worldview from the Western concept of an external environment separate from human society, which leads to the dualism of nature/culture, mind/matter, and eventually to the idea of human domination and control of nature.

The wisdom of indigenous cultures is consistent with scientific ecology on the interrelatedness of all life forms and their biophysical environment. Many of the words in Northern indigenous languages that usually get translated as "land" (*ashkii* in Cree, *aski* in Ojibwa/Anishinaabe, *ndeh* in Dene) carry a meaning that goes well beyond land as physical landscape to encompass the living environment including humans. The literature on ecosystem-based management and social-ecological systems embraces a view of ecology similar to indigenous worldviews that considers humans as part of an integrated, interdependent entity in which the natural world and the human world sustain one another over time.

The second idea or insight suggested by Arctic indigenous environmental ethics is the importance of continuity of resource use to maintain respectful relationships and stewardship traditions. Using the environment and resources is important not only for obtaining food and maintaining culture, but also as a way of building ecological knowledge and relationships. Such practical engagement with the environment may be the basis for putting humans back into the ecosystem. It involves the knowledge, skills, and sensitivities that developed through long experience in a particular environment.

Many indigenous people have remarked that they have to use a resource to respect it. This is the basis of an indigenous conservation ethic for sustainable use. Loss of indigenous traditions or the imposition of a preservationist ethic can break the link between use and respect. From an indigenous viewpoint, non-use preservation only serves to alienate people from the land and, thus, from their stewardship responsibilities. The lesson from Arctic indigenous people is that the relationships of respect and reciprocity are essential for the stewardship of the environment and for sustainability.

Outlook for the Twenty-First Century

Arctic societies are increasingly tied to national policies and to the global economy. Rapid economic, political, and demographic changes; resource development; trade barriers; and animal rights campaigns have all produced shocks and stresses. For example, ocean pollution in the Arctic, mainly from long-range atmospheric transport of pollutants, threatens food sources through the accumulation of toxic substances in the food web. Hunting, fishing, and herding are threatened by climate change that is affecting animal distributions and interfering with the ability of people to predict the weather and seasonal animal distributions.

Globalization and the volatility of world markets for raw materials such as oil and gas result in boom-and-bust cycles that have come to characterize Arctic economies. The narrow economic base of most Arctic communities has made them vulnerable to political and economic decisions made elsewhere. The rapid shrinking of the pack ice of the Arctic Ocean has stimulated shipping activity, which, in turn, may further stimulate oil and gas development. Such amplifying relationships between global environmental change (such as climate change) and globalization (the "shrinking" of the world) have produced a "double exposure" to vulnerabilities affecting human security.

Against this backdrop, indigenous peoples throughout the Arctic have been adapting to change in a number of ways. They are pursuing land claims, resource rights, and regional government powers. Arctic indigenous people have become world leaders in the struggle for indigenous rights, co-management of resources, and the recognition of the importance of indigenous knowledge. They are revitalizing their languages and traditional practices to help maintain their connection to the environment.

These efforts often involve the pursuit of political autonomy as a first step. Greenland has home rule. Native land claims in Alaska and the Canadian Arctic have been settled. The Norwegian Saami have regional government powers. Assimilation pressures in the post-Soviet Chukotka (and elsewhere) have declined. With these changes, many Arctic indigenous cultures are undergoing revitalization. Cultural reaffirmation is not simply a reactivation of old customs but a rediscovery of cultural roots to anchor people in a rapidly changing world. Adapting to the contemporary Arctic lifestyle means a blurring of the opposition between tradition and change, indigenous culture and Western culture, and town living and harvesting the land.

Fikret BERKES
University of Manitoba

FURTHER READING

Arctic climate impact assessment. (2005). Cambridge, U.K.: Cambridge University Press. (Also retrieved September 24, 2008, from http://www.acia.uaf.edu)

Arctic human development report. (2004). Akureyri, Iceland: Stefansson Arctic Institute.

Berkes, Fikret. (2001). Religious traditions and biodiversity. In *Encyclopedia of biodiversity*, Vol. 5, pp. 109–120. San Diego, CA: Academic Press.

Berkes, Fikret. (2008). *Sacred ecology.* (2nd ed.). New York: Routledge.

Berkes, Fikret; Huebert, Rob; Fast, Helen; Manseau, Micheline; & Diduck, Alan. (Eds.). (2005). *Breaking ice: Renewable resource and ocean management in the Canadian North.* Calgary, Canada: University of Calgary Press.

Brightman, Robert A. (1993). *Grateful prey: Rock Cree human-animal relationships.* Berkeley: University of California Press.

Cruikshank, Julie. (2005). *Do glaciers listen? Local knowledge, colonial encounters and social imagination.* Seattle: University of Washington Press and Vancouver: University of British Columbia Press.

Csonka, Yvon, & Schweitzer, Peter. (2004). Societies and cultures: Change and persistence. In *Arctic human development report* (Chapter 3). Akureyri, Iceland: Stefansson Arctic Institute.

Fienup-Riordan, Ann. (1990). *Eskimo essays: Yup'ik lives and how we see them.* New Brunswick, NJ: Rutgers University Press.

Freeman, Milton M. R. (Ed.). (2000). *Endangered peoples of the Arctic: Struggles to survive and thrive.* Westport, CT: Greenwood Press.

Krupnik, Igor, & Jolly, Dyanna. (Eds.). (2002). *The earth is faster now: Indigenous observations of Arctic environmental change.* Fairbanks, AK: Arctic Research Consortium of the United States.

Nuttall, Mark, & Callaghan, Terry V. (Eds.). (2000). *The Arctic: Environment, people, policy.* Newark NJ: Harwood Academic Publishers.

Oozeva, Conrad; Noongwook, Chester; Noongwook, George; Alowa, Christina; & Krupnik, Igor. (2004). *Watching ice and weather our way.* Washington, DC: Arctic Studies Center, Smithsonian Institution.

Turner, Nancy J. (2005). *The earth's blanket: Traditional teachings for sustainable living.* Seattle: University of Washington Press.

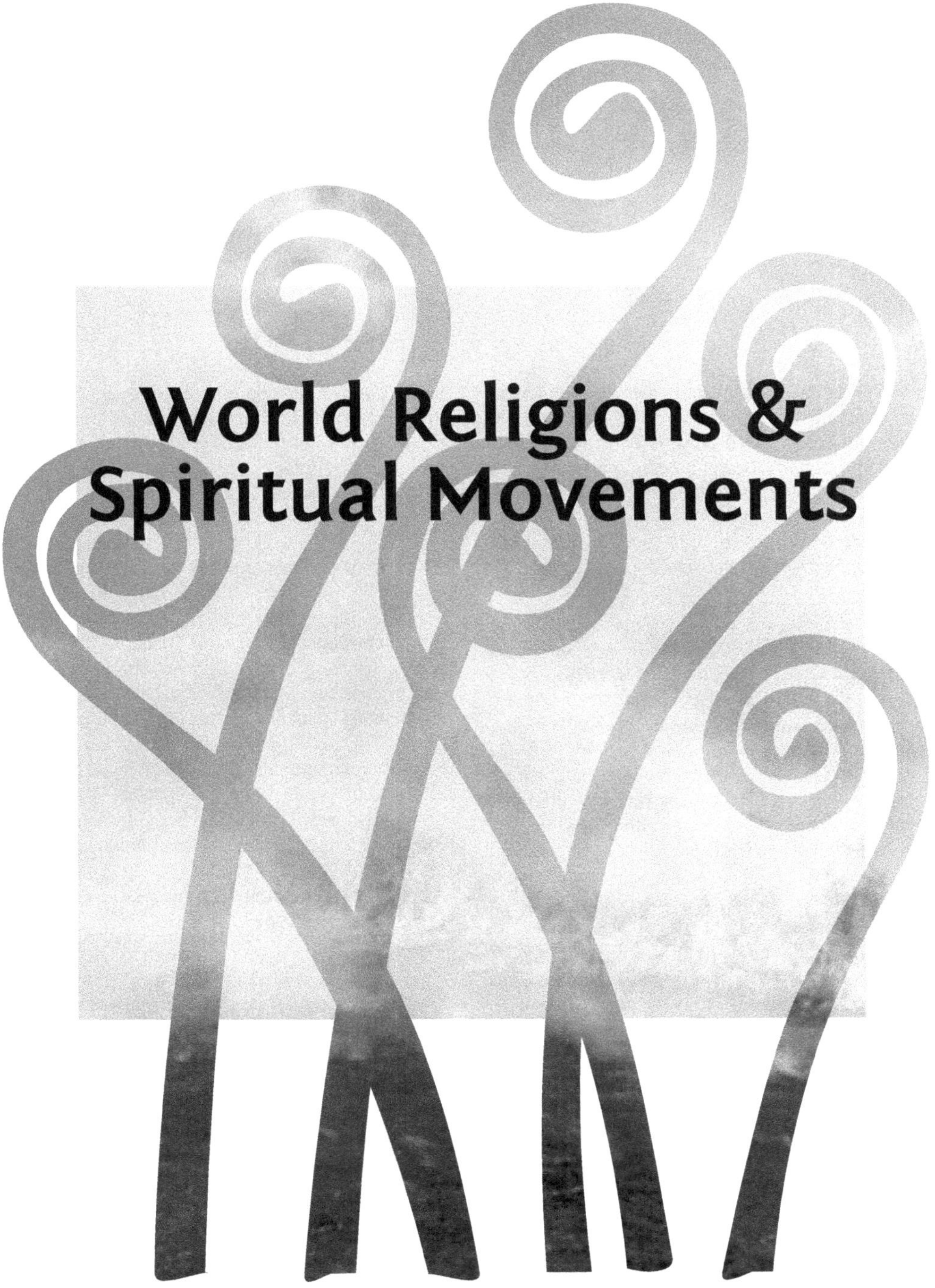

World Religions & Spiritual Movements

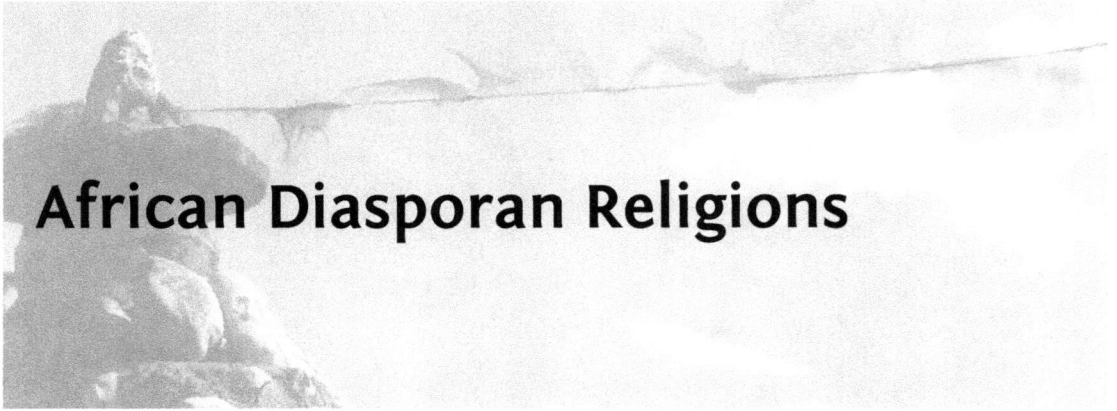

African Diasporan Religions

After West Africans were transported as enslaved persons across the Atlantic, African diasporan religions evolved in the Americas. Focusing on a Supreme Being recognized as the creator of all on Earth, and a community comprising all that is creation, the beliefs of these religions encourage practices of sustainable living. African American churches have been especially central to fostering a stewardship model to support God's provisions.

Traditional African worldviews are inherently religious, focusing on a Creator God, spirits, ruling powers, and human beings; some African indigenous religions have a pantheon of Gods. African religious thought is not monolithic, but varied, connecting the metaphysical and nonphysical sphere to the physical. Many Africans trafficked to the Americas practiced indigenous religion, Christianity, or Islam. When the African diaspora took place over nearly four centuries, transporting millions of West Africans in slave trade across the Atlantic to the Americas and the Caribbean islands, these scattered African populations managed to retain their customs, cultural identities, and belief systems as they struggled to adapt to new surroundings that were often hostile to (or derisive of) African philosophies and spirituality. African diasporan religions in these regions—while still drawing primarily on their indigenous traditions, a belief in a Supreme Being, and the importance of community—continued to be over the centuries influenced by Islam, Catholicism, Protestantism, and Pentecostalism, as well as traditions that emphasized divination and healing. In the twentieth century, Rastafarianism developed with a sociopolitical agenda. African Americans in the United States experienced a diaspora of their own after slavery was abolished and blacks were able to migrate to areas other than the South; a diaspora occurred to another extent after desegregation. How the philosophy and practices of African American faith communities and black churches—historically at the core of empowerment and political action—pertain to sustainable ways of living in the twenty-first century is the primary focus of this article.

Views of sustainability within African diasporan religions in general involve holistic, spirituality-based ecological strategies, processes, and attitudes concerning the viability, health, wellness, healing, and covenantal stewardship of God-given resources—humanity, natural resources, and all creation—in a world in which its adherents have been taunted by systemic racism, sexism, and class oppression. Stewardship, a model for a liberating, committed way of living, holds one accountable for the just, equitable, fiscally responsible, and loving use of God's provisions. Within this ethos, a heightened awareness of responsible use of resources prompts us to configure our human activity in a way that will ensure that life with complex diversity continues across all of our lived environments.

African Americans and the Environment

African American life and moral views—shaped by politics, social action, and spirituality—determine unique environmental concerns that often differ from European American views. Black churches, historically at the center of empowerment and political action, remain the major independent black institutions of influence for most African Americans. African philosophy (which lacks boundaries between sacred and secular), a legacy of racial injustice, and the historical, institutional black church contribute to the twenty-first-century black church "reality" as it functions today. Some faith communities or sects have been more separatist and not engaged in politics; some have a more otherworldly, apolitical, conservative stance. But by embracing a traditional African worldview of communalism and a social morality instilled by the minister and the church tenets themselves, faith communities embody a sense of divine protection, empowerment, and hope.

Alienation from North American Land

Mark Stoll—the editor with Dianne G. Glave of *To Love the Wind and Rain* (Glave and Stoll, 2006), a work that displaces the old colonialist studies of African Americans and examines how these blacks have historically conceived, utilized, and managed to survive in their environmental space, both rural and urban—posits that enslavement helped alienate Africans from the land of North America. Even with the symbolic metaphorical Exodus motif and Promised Land, African Americans have not had mythic connections to land, as many European Americans have had with Plymouth Rock, Stone Mountain, or Yosemite Valley. Symbolic import has not fueled a commitment to veneration or preservation, making human beings, not nature, monumental in black sacred history, and signaling the wilderness Moses, not Adam and Eve in paradise. Moses and the children of Israel wandered through the wilderness and experienced enslavement, followed by divine liberation. Having been plucked from Africa, African diasporan peoples could not possibly experience a sense of paradise in the Americas, even though most African diasporan Christians see Adam and Eve as the first humans. With African American migration from the rural South to the North, Midwest, and West—from the post–Civil War period, during World War II, and then postdesegregation—came declining activism in some arenas, although blacks' beliefs in a system of social morality continued to exist.

Components essential to African Americans' perceptions and experiences of sustainability closely relate to class, ethnicity, gender, and race—the factors that have shaped where and how African Americans have been forced to live, work, and play: Blacks have had, for example, limited access to certain geographic areas; they have been subject to peonage (the use of laborers bound in servitude) and relegated to segregated public spaces. Thus environmental justice concerns the liberation of black people—a focus involving a relationship with the environment and depending on the sociopolitics surrounding it—where community is broadly cast, pursuit of collective rights important, and environment connected to production and work. Ironically, while often denied access to recreation in parks, forests, and the wilderness, many African Americans have appreciated the health and spiritual benefits of healing and wholesomeness from working and being out of doors.

Although the effect of desegregation has been far less detrimental to the environment than the larger movement of industrialization in the United States and globalization itself, the increasing migration of African American populations to so-called more liberal havens or neighborhoods has often resulted in ecological injustice, actions, beliefs, and other processes antithetical to sustainability. Heightened greed and use of the land without "giving anything back" have predominated in many instances of integration, especially in urban areas. With migration and superhighways moving populations of all classes and races in all directions, people have become disconnected from the land and prone to general disregard for the planet; the effect is exacerbated for most African Americans who were stolen from African and forced into enslavement, to have to be uprooted yet again when they already felt at odds with their new landscape. While many immigrant populations also relate to such estrangement, systemic, oppressive racism has historically stacked the deck (and continues to do so) against healthy, sustainable African diasporan communities. Detrimental to African diasporan environmental justice are the urban realities of middle-class flight, spiritual blight, industrial pollution, and alienation in neighborhoods where disconnectedness leads to self-absorption. Edicts like "No Child Left Behind," which force teachers to teach students to pass standardize exams, further dampen African diasporan children's capacity to learn and be competitive; such programs, along with cultural insensitivity, the belief that black children cannot perform well, and unfair sentencing that places more and more poor black youth in jail, ultimately create a pipe line from cradle to prison.

The Poverty Factor

A significant threat to sustainability within any group, particularly African peoples, is poverty. Some biblical proverbial traits and behaviors seen as the root causes of the poverty that threatens family and community include immoral sexual behavior, laziness, stinginess, wasting time and land, failure to change, injustice, idle talk, oppression, procrastination, inattentiveness, hastiness, lack of compassion, luxurious living, unwise borrowing, exploiting people, addictions and uncontrolled appetites, poor-on-poor oppression, corrupt government, greediness, pride, and disdain; often these characteristics are unfairly projected onto a poor population, especially one of color. Therefore, too often, a community's racial makeup can be the single variable that best predicts placing commercial hazardous waste facilities in their midst. Classism and racism ensure that too many poor and people of color experience greater environmental and health risks than the general population; they

have less access for clean drinking water, clean air, parks, playgrounds, or safe working environments. The death to holistic life, especially in places like Cancer Alley on the Gulf Coast, where industry involving the use of toxins is rife, has resulted in deep losses of self, family, employment, space, place, communities, and land—a predicament often forged by spiritual dis-ease as well as physical sickness caused by pollution.

Sustainability, Harmony, Stewardship—and the Black Church

A tenet of African diasporan religion, as it has evolved into the institution of the black church, holds that as people focus on the right relationship with God, significantly they are to be in right relationship with the Earth. To affect sustainability requires engendering hope, making stewardship programs part of the black church, and partnering with civic agencies that can help work for ecologically friendly public policies. (The term "black church" is used here to embody the numerous sects and communities in which African Americans express their faith.) In the church's worldview, imbalance and injustice are fueled by heterosexism, classism, racism, sexism, and other phobias that encourage people to make someone who is different from them "other." Church members are encouraged to love themselves and love the planet that provides them living space, and to resist greed and systemic oppressions. "The Earth is the Lord's and the fullness thereof" becomes a rubric where one is continuously in God's presence, God's sanctuary. Thus nature and created order must not be abused or harmed. Sustainability involves living a harmonious, balanced life where people are one with God, themselves, and their neighbors, appreciating the planet for the abundant life it affords. According to Karen Baker-Fletcher, a professor of theology, a profound reason for this deep appreciation of the Earth is that we humans are dust (earth) and spirit, where our birth and our death connect us to everything that happens in, on, from, and around the Earth. As divine creative freedom shapes and exudes beauty through all creation, being stewards or holding the Earth in trust requires immense responsibility.

Robert E. Franklin, author of *Another Day's Journey: Black Churches Confronting the American Crisis*, (1997), envisions this responsibility amidst a unique African diasporan spiritual ecology that cultivates hope and endorses public activism—comprised of multisensory worship; intimate communal prayer; cathartic expressivism engaged, for instance, in therapeutic singing; sociopolitically framed religious education; and prophetic, imaginative preaching. Such practices galvanize congregants toward God's reign and commonwealth. Related to these are complex, diverse spiritualities—from Evangelical, Holiness, and Charismatic movements to social justice, Afrocentric, contemplative, and new age philosophies—that shape the black church social witness: pragmatic accommodationism, prophetic radicalism, redemptive nationalism, grassroots revivalism, and positive-thought materialism. With twenty-first century changes, including decline in denominationalism, growth of Word churches, growth of Afrocentrism, and contemporary life and communal challenges, the traditional African American church institution might well need to assess how its ministries can effectively help to sustain the spiritual survival of its people as well the planet. Fundamental to sustainability is embracing a worldview that appreciates and connects God with all creation, environment, rituals, stewardship, community, and environmental justice, with a keen awareness of who we are and who God is.

African diasporan religions see the lack of awareness about who we are as a result of disconnecting from the land and ultimately from ourselves, each other, from spirit, and from God. Possessions and status become more important than relationships and the Earth. If our relationship with God dictates our lives, and if God is the generator of all creation, creation is to be revered. Just as farmers rotate crops so that the land can renew itself, people too need to renew their appreciation, connections, and commitment to the total healing of humanity and all creation. The noted author Alice Walker invites us to plant a tree when someone does great harm to one we love.

Sustainability and Activism

Dianne D. Glave, co-editor of *To Love the Wind and Rain*, notes that many activists have used a Christian framework to shape their endeavors, especially following Martin Luther King's nonviolent protest. Thus black environmental liberation theology, mentioned earlier in the context of freeing black people from environmental racism, can work to protect African diasporan peoples from exposure to toxic sewage plants, landfills, garbage dumps, and auto mechanics' shops. Glave notes that levels of environmental racism on people of color inequitably have caused birth defects, stillbirths, miscarriages, cancer, and autoimmune and stress-related illnesses (Stoll and Glave 2006). Skewed biblical interpretations of dominion implying stewardship *over* rather than *for* the Earth have allowed abuse, the abandonment of fiduciary (trusting) responsibilities involved in making a covenant with God, and thus the lack of care and displacement of many sentient beings. Preservation and conversation of resources and wildlife must include all human beings and creation. This work envisions engaging a sociocultural, moral geography, where destruction of

creation is wrong. Working with the National Council of Churches (NCC), many African American church leaders have focused on quality of life and health issues in the African American community. Often ministers provide substantial help when communities want to protest, educate about, and negotiate with companies engaged in environmental racism in the effort to alter such detrimental practices.

With heightened technology, increased population, deforestation, extinction of thousands of species each year, lowering water tables, and depletion of other natural resources, sustainability is a global issue. The prison industrial complex, drug trafficking, and bankrupt educational practices that teach for tests and stifle creativity threaten and deplete many human resources, not just those of African Americans or people of color. If these trends continue, human beings are in danger of becoming extinct, for the Earth will no longer be able to maintain life as we know it. Human activity has caused huge ecological imbalances: record heat waves, related hurricanes, tsunamis, reduced grain harvests, droughts, and increased greenhouse gases.

While African American churches have inherited a tradition of engaging in public policy, the levels of participation have varied. Most activism has focused on racial injustice and black economic development, while welfare reform, social services, health care and reproductive rights, education reform, and criminal justice receive far less attention. Commitment of time, energy, and resources to produce effective lobbying that would address these issues remains unfulfilled and yet significant for sustainability.

In nineteenth-century Brazilian Candomblé, a spirit-possession religion of the African diaspora in Brazil, leaders worked to address the imbalances within physical, spiritual, sociopolitical, and ecological systems due to oppressions, based upon their understandings of how to address causes and cures for illness. Candomblé posits a quest for right relationships among human beings—and among human beings, the natural world, and spirits. Via the Shona peoples' Mutopo principle, the worldview framing the mobilization of spirit mediums for environmental protection, the deity cares about ecological and human well-being. Candomblé, imbued with a sense of rejuvenation, provided an alternative awareness of identity and a way of thinking about reality for the enslaved, which parallels the African American enslaved experience of a God who allows one to know and take care of oneself. Both religious practices allow for joy amidst resistance, as believers cultivate individual and collective identity in opposition to the imposed subordinate status from dominant society.

African diasporan ecojustice, and thus sustainability, can be fostered when the community recognizes that its survival depends upon honoring rights of the most vulnerable, particularly the elderly, women, and children. This cosmology sees connections between God, humanity and all creation, the dead, and the yet-to-be born. Such Shona principles, together with Christianity practiced by African independent churches, create an engaging, activist response to contemporary environmental and social challenges brought on by colonialism. The church functions as a guardian for creation. For change to be affected any positions privileging power must shift to alternative value systems that do not dominate people or nature but encourage cooperative spirit of all existence. Change can be effected when the church and other faith communities challenge societal oppressions and abuses of class, race, gender, white supremacy, imperialism, and capitalism; when the desire for ecojustice presses us to work for balanced, healthy, sustainable environments and relationships; and when economic parity and development are central to ministry—all endeavoring to transform those poor in spirit and poor in material goods, honoring the world we hold in trust.

Cheryl A. KIRK-DUGGAN
Shaw University Divinity School

FURTHER READING

Amen, Ra. (2006). The role of feminism, traditional religion, and Christianity in addressing social and ecological problems in Zimbabwe. Unpublished paper. Berkeley, CA: Graduate Theological Union.

Baker-Fletcher, Karen. (1998). Sisters of dust, sisters of spirit: Womanist wordings on God and creation Minneapolis, MN: Augsburg Fortress.

Chapman, Audrey; Petersen, Rodney; & Smith-Moran, Barbara. (Eds.). (2000). Consumption, population, and sustainability: Perspectives from science and religion. Washington, DC: Island Press.

Fick, Gary W. (2008). Food, farming, and faith. Albany: State University of New York Press.

Franklin, Robert E. (1997). Another day's journey: Black churches confronting the American crisis. Minneapolis, MN: Augsburg Fortress.

Glave, Dianne, & Stoll, Mark. (Eds.) (2006). To love the wind and the rain: African Americans and environmental history. Pittsburgh: University of Pittsburgh Press.

Anderson-Stembridge, Matthew, & Radford, Phil. (2007). Bottom line ministries that matter: Congregational stewardship with energy efficiency and clean energy technologies. Washington, DC: Eco-Justice Program of the National Council of Churches.

Smith, R. Drew. (Ed.). (2004). Long march ahead: African American churches and public policy in post-civil rights America. Durham, NC: Duke University Press.

Bahá'í

Founded in the nineteenth century, the Bahá'í Faith now has over 5 million members located throughout the world, representing a microcosm of humanity. Bahá'ís recognize nature as an expression of God's will, view science and religion as complementary approaches to truth, and strive to pursue processes of individual and community development that promote unity, interdependence, social justice, and ecological sustainability.

The Bahá'í Faith is an emerging world religion concerned with the spiritual, social, and ecological challenges facing humanity in an age of increasing global integration. The Persian founder of the Bahá'í Faith, Bahá'u'lláh (1817–1892), called for humanity to recognize a coming age of global interdependence and to implement principles and practices that could serve as the basis for a more just and sustainable world order. The nascent Bahá'í community has, until recently, been focused largely on processes of internal growth, which continue to occupy much of its attention. The worldwide expansion and consolidation of the community, however, has provided it with the human resources and administrative capacity to engage contemporary social and ecological problems in a direct and systematic manner, which it has begun to do.

For instance, in 1987, the Bahá'í Faith joined the World Wide Fund for Nature's Network on Conservation and Religion. Two years later a compilation of extracts from Bahá'í scriptures and other primary texts was published, entitled *Conservation of the Earth's Resources*. Study of this document within the Bahá'í community inspired a multitude of ecological stewardship and sustainable development initiatives around the planet, including environmental education programs, conservation projects, tree-planting activities, sustainable-technology innovations, awareness-raising campaigns employing the arts, and advocacy work in various policy arenas. This document has also inspired a growing body of scholarship exploring the social and ecological dimensions of sustainability from a Bahá'í perspective, and it has prompted the formation of Bahá'í-inspired professional organizations such as the International Environment Forum, which has members in over fifty countries.

Within the U.N. system, the Bahá'í Office of the Environment actively participated in planning processes leading up to the 1992 Earth Summit in Rio de Janeiro. Bahá'í offices at the United Nations also played an active role in most of the other global U.N. summits on social and environmental issues throughout the 1990s, and a Bahá'í representative cochaired the U.N. Millennium Forum of nongovernmental organizations at the end of the decade. Meanwhile, in 1995 Bahá'ís participated in the founding of the Alliance of Religions and Conservation, and in 1998 they became founding members of the World Faiths and Development Dialogue. Membership in these organizations brought Bahá'ís into direct dialogue with other faith communities regarding the spiritual dimension of environment stewardship and sustainable development. This involvement has stimulated a range of grassroots actions within the Bahá'í community. One example is the emergence of Bahá'í-inspired "community

learning groups" among the indigenous Bribri and Cabecar peoples in Costa Rica, who are studying the relationship between moral leadership and environmental stewardship; initiating sustainable development projects such as school and family gardens, fish farms, and poultry raising; and collaborating with other local organizations to promote the conservation of natural resources.

Vision of Nature and Society

Underlying these examples of engagement is a sense of spiritual purpose derived from the Bahá'í teachings on nature and society. The Bahá'í Faith is founded on a belief in one unknowable Divine Essence—God. Bahá'u'lláh taught that although humans cannot comprehend God, the natural world is a reflection of God's attributes and an expression of God's will. Bahá'ís are thus urged to revere, contemplate, and unravel the mysteries of nature by drawing on the complementary methods and insights of both science and religion.

In this context, the Bahá'í teachings explain that while the universe is characterized by a great diversity of forms, it is nonetheless an organically integrated whole that is governed by relations of interconnection, mutuality, and balance. Likewise, humanity is understood as an organic whole that should be governed by these same characteristics. Religion, according to Bahá'u'lláh, is the one force capable of unifying humanity in this manner.

The Bahá'í teachings also liken human society to the human body, whose cells and organs, while diverse in form and function, are characterized by reciprocity and interdependence. Within the human body, the health and well-being of each part is inseparable from the health and well-being of the whole. Similarly, in the body of humanity, the interests of all individuals and groups are interdependent, and the well-being of the part is inseparable from the well-being of the whole.

This organic worldview informs the Bahá'í vision of nature and society. According to this worldview, unity and reciprocity are requisites of a just and sustainable social order. Bahá'ís thus believe that as long as human societies remain in states of conflict and competition, divided and indifferent to their organic interdependence, it will be impossible to address increasingly complex social and ecological problems in an effective and sustainable manner.

Evolutionary Perspective

According to the Bahá'í teachings, humanity has arrived at a critical historical juncture. Humanity's social evolution has led to unprecedented levels of interdependence and has dramatically increased our impact upon the ecological systems that sustain us. Yet inherited patterns of belief and behavior prevent humanity from addressing the challenges that we are now facing. As these inherited cultural codes prove maladaptive under contemporary conditions, Bahá'ís believe that the social and ecological crises facing us will continue to deepen and proliferate.

Bahá'ís hold that at this critical juncture in human history, the question facing humanity is whether we will embrace our organic unity and interdependence as a species and self-consciously adapt to the new conditions of our existence, or whether we will cling to inherited patterns of belief and behavior and learn the lessons of interdependence the hard way, through the deepening social and ecological consequences of a failure to adapt. The goal of the Bahá'í community is, therefore, to effect those changes in human culture and consciousness that will hasten the construction of a more just and sustainable social order.

Likening human society again to an individual body, the Bahá'í writings teach that we have passed through the stages of our collective infancy and childhood and have now reached the turbulent transitional period of our collective adolescence, in which we are approaching our full physical capacity but our actions are not yet tempered by the wisdom and judgment that comes with maturity. Although this transitional stage will be difficult, Bahá'ís have confidence that the long-awaited age of maturity, alluded to in various ways by all of the major religious traditions of the past, will eventually be realized.

This process, according to the Bahá'í teachings, implies an organic change in the structure of society that will reflect the underlying principle, or truth, of the oneness of humanity. This principle entails the emergence of a consciousness of world citizenship, along with the eventual federation of all nations into an integrated system of governance that can coordinate and harmonize human affairs across the planet. The principle of oneness also entails: the establishment of the full equality of men and women in all arenas of human affairs; the elimination of all forms of prejudice and discrimination based on race, religion, or nationality; the establishment of a universal currency and other integrating mechanisms that promote global economic justice and shared prosperity; the adoption of an international auxiliary language that facilitates communication and mutual understanding; the demilitarization of

the world and the redirection of massive military expenditures toward constructive social ends; and the emergence of an ethic of sustainable development that promotes the conservation and stewardship of the Earth's resources, along with the just and equitable distribution of the benefits that derive from them.

Dimensions of Change

In order to effect these changes, the Bahá'í Faith addresses itself to both individual and institutional dimensions of change. At the level of the individual, Bahá'ís engage in a number of spiritual disciplines, such as daily prayer and meditation, along with an annual period of fasting, as they strive to transcend the pull of their baser instincts and struggle to develop qualities of the spirit such as selflessness, moderation, purity of motive, and devotion to the common good—all of which they see not only as individual spiritual imperatives but as prerequisites for a just and sustainable collective future. To these ends, the Bahá'í community is also developing systematic approaches to the moral education of children, the spiritual and intellectual empowerment of adolescents, and the training of older youth and adults with skills and capacities for community service—as demonstrated by the Ruhi Institute, which has developed training materials and educational processes that are being used by tens of thousands of Bahá'ís and others around the world. In addition, Bahá'ís emphasize the education of individuals in the arts and sciences, which are recognized as powerful forces for social transformation and advancement. Examples of such an emphasis can be seen in Bahá'í-inspired projects such as the Mongolian Development Center in Ulaanbaatar, the Barli Development Institute for Rural Women in India, the Uganda Program of Literacy for Transformation, or the Foundation for the Application and Teaching of the Sciences in Colombia.

Difficult as these processes of individual education and development may be, Bahá'ís see them as necessary but insufficient conditions for the establishment of a more just and sustainable social order. Responsible and effective institutional forms are also needed. Toward this end, the Bahá'í community is constructing (at local, national, and international levels) institutional structures and practices it believes are suited to the age of maturity that humanity is entering.

For instance, the Bahá'í community, which has no clergy, employs a participatory system of governance with a unique electoral process that, while democratic in spirit, is entirely nonpartisan and noncompetitive. All adult community members are eligible for election, and every member has the reciprocal duty to serve if elected. Nominations, campaigning, and all forms of solicitation are prohibited. Voters are to be guided only by their own consciences as they exercise real freedom of choice in voting for those they believe best embody qualities such as trustworthiness, integrity, recognized ability, mature experience, and selfless service to others. Through a plurality count, the nine individuals who receive the most votes are called to serve as members of the governing assembly—even though they did not seek to be elected.

These assemblies, in turn, are guided by consultative principles that are intended to encourage decision making as a unifying rather than divisive process. These electoral and decision-making methods are used to govern the affairs of the Bahá'í community at the local, national, and international levels. With a current membership of over 5 million people drawn from over two thousand ethnic backgrounds and residing in every nation, these methods of governance are currently being learned and practiced in over ten thousand distinct communities around the globe. Based on decades of accumulated experience with these methods, Bahá'ís offer their administrative system as a model that others can learn from in their search for more just and sustainable institutional forms.

Science and Religion

As Bahá'ís focus on processes of individual and institutional transformation, they also emphasize the importance of applying scientific knowledge and methods in efforts to solve the mounting social and ecological problems facing humanity. But Bahá'ís believe only religion can inspire the vision, motivation, commitment, self-sacrifice, and unified action required to construct a just and sustainable social order that encompasses the planet.

Science and religion are thus understood by Bahá'ís as complementary systems of knowledge that can guide human development and channel humanity's intellectual and moral powers within processes of social evolution. According to this view, the methods of science have allowed humanity to construct a coherent understanding of the laws and processes governing physical reality. The insights of religion have, in turn, illuminated the deepest questions of human purpose and existence, clarified those shared values and essential principles that promote human well-being, and given constructive direction to individual and collective endeavors—including the enlightened application of scientific knowledge.

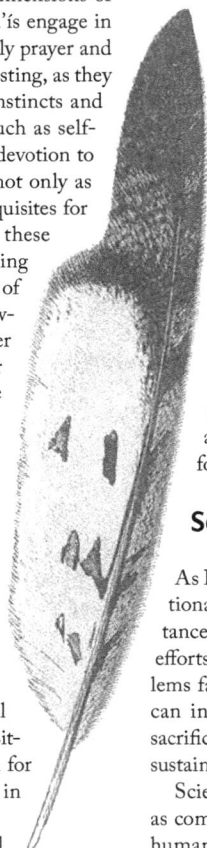

In this context, Bahá'ís interpret the purely materialistic interpretations of reality that are often advanced in the name of science as obstacles to dealing with the pressing challenges facing humanity. At the same time, they interpret the fanatical and divisive claims that are often advanced in the name of religion as equally problematic obstacles. According to the Bahá'í teachings, religion in its pure form is a single, universal, and transhistorical phenomenon that reflects humanity's ongoing response to expressions of a Divine will and purpose. Religious truth, Bahá'u'lláh taught, is revealed progressively over time according to the changing needs and capacities of ever-evolving human societies. At this stage in history, Bahá'ís believe, the purpose of religion is to renew and affirm the eternal spiritual truths that have been articulated within all past religious dispensations, while focusing humanity on the essential task of learning how to live together in a just and sustainable way, as an interdependent global community.

Future Prospects

The overarching purpose of the Bahá'í Faith is to effect the spiritual unification of the human family and establish a just and sustainable world order. To skeptics, this transformative project appears to be an expression of naïve idealism. To Bahá'ís, it appears to be the only realistic way forward at this critical juncture in history.

At this early stage in the development of the Bahá'í community, however, most Bahá'ís admit that they are still struggling to successfully apply many of their own teachings. In this regard, individual Bahá'ís vary significantly in their grasp of these teachings and in their commitments of time and energy to the work of the community. They also struggle to transcend cultural habits and inherited patterns of thought that often pull against or undermine their ideals. Bahá'í efforts to adopt more sustainable lifestyles— like the efforts of other people—are often compromised by limited understandings of the issues, or by the powerful pull of consumer culture, or by the unsustainable structures of contemporary society within which they currently live. Yet as the Bahá'í community grows, matures over time, and pursues its long-term project of spiritual and social transformation, the internal discourse of the community is increasingly focused on issues of sustainability; mechanisms are being established to deepen the community's grasp of, and commitment to, the principles and practices of sustainability.

In keeping with the spirit of openness, experimentation, and systematic learning that characterizes

THE BAHÁ'Í APPROACH TO SUSTAINABILITY

Today the Bahá'í Faith promotes the oneness of humanity, equality of the sexes, international justice, and world peace—all components in the striving toward sustainable life. The Persian founder of the faith, Bahá'u'lláh (1817–1892), urged humanity to put into practice such principles in light of a coming age of global interdependence; the following excerpt comes from one of thousands of scriptural "tablets" he wrote emphasizing nonliteral interpretations of the Bible and the Quran—this one a slim book of laws.

Verily, the Word of God is the Cause which hath preceded the contingent world—a world which is adorned with the splendours of the Ancient of Days, yet is being renewed and regenerated at all times. Immeasurably exalted is the God of Wisdom Who hath raised this sublime structure . . . Say: Nature in its essence is the embodiment of My Name, the Maker, the Creator. Its manifestations are diversified by varying causes, and in this diversity there are signs for men of discernment. Nature is God's Will and is its expression in and through the contingent world. It is a dispensation of Providence ordained by the Ordainer, the All-Wise.

Source: Tablets of Bahá'u'lláh revealed after the Kitáb-i-Aqdas, by Bahá'u'lláh (1892). Haifa, Israel: Bahá'í World Centre, 141–142.

the worldwide Bahá'í community, Bahá'ís offer their ongoing experience as a vast social experiment that is open for others to study. The long-term outcomes of this experiment, however, are still too distant to assess in an empirical manner. But the initial experience and accomplishments of the Bahá'í community raise thought-provoking questions about whether, or how, humanity might eventually adapt to conditions of heightened global interdependence.

Michael KARLBERG

Western Washington University

FURTHER READING

Arbab, Farzam. (2000). Promoting a discourse on science, religion, and development. In Sharon Harper (Ed.), *The lab, the temple and the market: Reflections on the intersection of science, religion and development* (pp. 149–210). Ottawa: International Development Research Centre.

Bahá'í International Community, United Nations Office. (n.d.). Statements and reports. Retrieved April 5, 2009, from www.bic-un.bahai.org

Bahá'í International Community. (2008). For the betterment of the world: The worldwide Bahá'í community's approach to social and economic development. New York: Office of Social and Economic Development, United Nations.

Bahá'í International Community. (1987). *Statement on nature*. New York: Bahá'í International Community Office of Public Information, United Nations.

Bahá'í International Community. (1992). *Sustainable development and the human spirit*. New York: Bahá'í International Community Office of Public Information, United Nations.

Bahá'í International Community. (1992). *The most vital challenge*. New York: Bahá'í International Community Office of Public Information, United Nations.

Bahá'í International Community. (1993). *World citizenship: Global ethic for sustainable development*. New York: Bahá'í International Community Office of Public Information, United Nations.

Bahá'í International Community. (1995). *Conservation and sustainable development in the Bahá'í Faith*. New York: Bahá'í International Community Office of Public Information, United Nations.

Bahá'í International Community. (1995). *The prosperity of humankind*. Haifa, Israel: Bahá'í International Community Office of Public Information.

Bahá'í International Community. (1996). *Sustainable communities in an integrating world*. New York: Bahá'í International Community Office of Public Information, United Nations.

Bahá'í International Community. (1998). *Valuing spirituality in development: Initial considerations regarding the creation of spiritually-based indicators for development*. New York: Bahá'í International Community Office of Public Information, United Nations.

Bahá'í International Community. (2001). *Sustainable development: The spiritual dimension*. New York: Bahá'í International Community Office of Public Information, United Nations.

Bahá'u'lláh. (1982). *Tablets of Bahá'u'lláh revealed after the Kitáb-i-Aqdas*. Haifa, Israel: Bahá'í World Centre.

Bahá'u'lláh; Abdu'l-Bahá; Shoghi Effendi; & Universal House of Justice. (1989). *Conservation of the Earth's resources: A compilation by the research department of the Universal House of Justice*. Haifa, Israel: Bahá'í World Centre.

Bushrui, Suheil. (2002). Environmental ethics: A Bahá'í perspective. In David Cadman and John Carey (Eds.), *A sacred trust: Ecology and spiritual vision* (pp. 77–102). London: The Temenos Academy and The Prince's Foundation.

Dahl, Arthur L. (1990). *Unless and until: A Bahá'í focus on the environment*. London: Bahá'í Publishing Trust.

Dahl, Arthur L. (1996). *The eco principle: Ecology and economics in symbiosis*. Oxford, U.K.: George Ronald; London: Zed Books.

Hatcher, William S., & Martin, J. Douglas. (1998). *The Bahá'í Faith: The emerging global religion*. Wilmette, IL: Bahá'í Publishing Trust.

Karlberg, Michael. (1994). Toward a new environmental stewardship. *World Order*, 25, 21–32.

Karlberg, Michael. (2004). *Beyond the culture of contest: From adversarialism to mutualism in an age of interdependence*. Oxford, U.K.: George Ronald.

Lalonde, Roxanne. (1994). Unity in diversity: A conceptual framework for a global ethic of environmental sustainability. *The Journal of Bahá'í Studies*, 6(3), 39–73.

White, Robert A. (1995). Spiritual foundations for an ecologically sustainable society. *The Journal of Bahá'í Studies*, 7(2), 47–74.

Universal House of Justice. (1985). *The promise of world peace*. Haifa, Israel: Bahá'í World Centre.

Vick, Holly Hanson. (1989). *Social and economic development: A Bahá'í approach*. Oxford, U.K.: George Ronald.

Buddhism

The basic tenets of traditional Buddhism—attaining wisdom; showing compassion; doing no harm to people, animals, and the Earth—seem to fit closely the concept and practice of sustainability. Modern Buddhism, particularly Western Buddhism, has gone even further in practice as Buddhists actively engage in movements and organizations that promote sustainability.

One of the biggest threats to sustainability is destructive human economic activity, much of which finds support from underlying feelings and ideas, whether fear, greed, notions of self and world, ideologies of economic growth, or beliefs in the ability of markets to generate technological fixes for environmental problems. Because Buddhism has for 2,500 years leveled much of its religious critique at mental states, it offers resources for understanding threats to sustainability and formulating responses to those threats.

Ethicists, economists, and policy makers have diverged in their conceptions of "sustainability" as it relates to the environment, economic systems, and communities. In general, however, sustainability has to do with "the optimal scale of the macro-economy relative to the ecosystem" and "justice extended to the future" (Daly and Cobb 1994, 145–146). In 1987 the World Commission on Environment and Development (now known as the Brundtland Commission) concluded that development is sustainable when it "meets the needs of the present without compromising the ability of future generations to meet their own needs." In large part, then, sustainability concerns the extent to which human practices—chiefly but not exclusively economic—maintain healthy ecosystems and communities over time. And what is clearly unsustainable are current levels of resource depletion and pollution, especially by more "advanced" economies that value endless expansion of production while ignoring limits to growth and the importance of community.

Depletion of nonrenewable resources and pollution at levels or in forms not absorbable by the environment are exacerbated by consumerism. Consumerism can be defined as both the belief that the ability to purchase and possess certain things will make a person happy and the actions based on that belief, including certain consumer behaviors and the assigning of high status to those who possess wealth or desired objects. The Buddhist thinker and Zen practitioner Ken Jones points out that, in contrast to that value system, many traditional societies have championed such status markers as "valued skills and knowledge, integrity and wisdom, as well as a rich and varied popular culture," and he criticizes "consumer culture in which this richness and diversity has been so diminished that the commodity market (which now packages experiences as well as things) comes to bear a disproportionate weight of the human need for meaning, significance, status, and belongingness" (Jones 1993, 22). Rita Gross, a scholar of Buddhism, writes that "the key question is what values and practices would convince people to consume and reproduce less when they have the technological ability to consume and reproduce more" (Gross 1997, 335). Buddhism provides such values and practices, as well as a view of self and world that contrasts with views that bolster destructive economic activity.

An Ethic of Restraint

Rather than specific rules or formulas, Buddhism presents a set of values that is helpful in fostering sustainability. Buddhism has traditionally emphasized restraint, generosity, simplicity, nonharming, and compassion. In an essay on Buddhist environmental ethics, Padmasiri de Silva

(b. 1933), author of many books on Buddhist psychology and ethics, writes, "Buddhism calls for a modest concept of living: simplicity, frugality, and an emphasis on what is essential—in short, a basic ethic of restraint" (de Silva 1990, 15).

Buddhism restrains, among other things, the mental states and dispositions that find expression in consumerism. Buddhism especially calls into question the "three poisons": ignorance, greed, and hatred. The historical Buddha taught that we suffer because we are ignorant of the fact of impermanence and we cling to ourselves and to things that give us a false sense of identity and security. When the objects of that clinging change or prove ultimately unsatisfactory, we feel anguish—we suffer. Buddhists have also noticed that when we are attached to certain things, we also feel anger toward whatever threatens those things. While feeling attraction to certain things, we feel aversion to other things. We succumb to greed and hatred.

Like others who have reflected on sustainability, Buddhists emphasize transforming our mindsets away from greed and acquisitiveness. They call for a focus on need, not greed, or as the Thai social activist and Buddhist Sulak Sivaraksa (b. 1933) has argued, more being rather than more having. Of course, some consumers in countries like the United States would argue that they do not get caught up in greed or believe that possessions are the key to happiness. But many middle- and upper-class Americans do in fact exhibit greed or clinging insofar as they are attached to their lifestyle and reluctant to simplify it to the extent necessary for global sustainability.

Buddhists have viewed hatred as an underlying cause of violence to other people, other species, and the environment in general. They have remedied it by cultivating loving-kindness (Pali, *mettā*), or compassion (Sanskrit, *karuṇā*), and avoiding unnecessary harming, as advocated by the first of the five Buddhist moral precepts. (The five precepts entail vows to restrain from taking life, taking what has not been given, engaging in improper sex, lying, and using intoxicants.) Hatred can be intensified in the economic arena, where the selfish pursuit of individual interests and pleasure, while in some cases making for profitable markets, can lead to conflict, if not violence, between people, or at least to a distrustful view of the other as a competitor. And in some cases, people may come together in shared selfishness and thereby constitute a collective ego, what Zen teacher David Loy (b. 1947) has called the "*we*go." When this happens, people may fail to recognize "our fear of insecurity, our nationalistic desire to 'win' at any cost, our desire to be number one, our culturally induced desire to find new frontiers to conquer" (Devall 2000, 391), all of which can lead to hatred and violence.

The economist Ernst Schumacher (1911–1977) expressed the Buddhist critique of greed and hatred in his book *Small Is Beautiful: Economics as if People Mattered* when he wrote, "The keynote of Buddhist economics . . . is simplicity and non-violence" and "the aim should be to obtain the maximum well-being with the minimum of consumption" (Schumacher 1973, 57). Richard Hayes (b. 1945), a professor of Buddhist philosophy, echoes Schumacher: "The Buddhist ideal of a life of simplicity, nonviolence towards all living beings, and non-acquisitiveness is one that human beings must learn to follow very soon if they have any interest in the continued survival of their own and countless other species" (Hayes 1990, 23). Simply put, Buddhism rejects unsustainable consumerism and materialism and offers instead a path of simplicity that, contrary to what one might expect, leads not to deprivation but to more fulfilling, nonmaterial forms of wealth and happiness.

Relational Awareness

Buddhist ethicists also argue that an underlying cause of the greed behind unsustainable economic practices is the poison of ignorance: the mistaken sense of existing as a separate individual with an unchanging essence, or soul, and only secondarily entering into relationships with other people and things. The ecophilosopher Joanna Macy (b. 1929) writes, "It is a delusion that the self is so separate and fragile that we must delineate and defend its boundaries, that it is so small and so needy that we must endlessly acquire and endlessly consume, and that it is so aloof that as individuals, corporations, nation-states, or species, we can be immune to what we do to other beings" (Macy 1990, 57). Buddhist meditation serves to uproot this ignorance and the false notion that one is a mind lording over mechanical nature.

Buddhism cultivates a relational way of knowing, a recognition that we are constituted through relationships with other things and exist thoroughly interconnected with those things. The individualistic, egotistical self is, according to Macy, "replaced by wider constructs of identity and self-interest—by what you might call the ecological self or the eco-self, co-extensive with other beings and the life of our planet. It is what I will call 'the greening of the self'" (Macy 1990, 57). Or as the professor of Environmental Studies and Zen practitioner Stephanie Kaza (b. 1947) terms it, we shift from a consumer identity to an "ecological identity." And in this way we can begin to release ourselves from ignorance, not only in the traditional Buddhist sense but also in at least five senses:

1. Lack of knowledge about human impacts on the environment.
2. Incorrect knowledge or information.
3. Ignorance or denial of sustainability issues.

4. Ideas justifying the continuation of our destructive lifestyles or justifying passivity in the face of current challenges.
5. Unawareness of and disconnection from nature.

Interrelational Arising

The transformation of our way of knowing and our identity is backed by Buddhist metaphysics, especially in terms of *pratītya–samutpāda*, interrelational arising. This doctrine holds that all "things" should be seen as temporary events constituted through causal and logical interrelationship with other events in an ongoing process of change, and hence things do not exist independently or have any essence prior to or separate from this interactive shaping. Buddhist ethicists claim that insight into *pratītya–samutpāda* has ethical ramifications, several of which are relevant to sustainability. They contend that as this insight deepens we realize that we are indeed a part of a larger reality and that, as the Thai Buddhist nun Chatsumarn Kabilsingh (b. 1945) writes, "When we abuse nature we abuse ourselves" (Kabilsingh 1990, 8). Buddhist ethicists maintain that to the extent we realize interrelational arising, we also discern the pain of others, gain a greater sense of compassion, feel indebtedness to the countless things that nurture us, engage in fewer harmful acts, and, recognizing how our actions have countless effects on the world around us, acquire an enhanced sense of responsibility. Along these lines the writer and activist Allan Hunt Badiner argues, "With its emphasis on cooperation and interdependence, Buddhist practice can inspire the building of partnership societies with *need*-based, sustainable economies rather than *greed*-based, growth economics" (Badiner 1990, xvii).

Monastic Ideals

Some writers have championed Buddhist monasticism as a model for building such societies. The following list is adapted from the work of the educators Leslie Sponsel and Poranee Natadecha-Sponsel (1997, 49), who state that an ideal *sangha* (monastic community) embodies the following "ecologically appropriate attributes":

1. Population that is small and controlled.
2. Egalitarian communal life based on cooperation and mutual respect.
3. Limited resource consumption and the use of self-restraint in satisfying basic needs, wants, and desires—actions aimed at achieving sufficiency and sustainability.
4. An economy based on cooperation, reciprocity, and redistribution rather than competition.

5. Stewardship practices that limit environmental impact.
6. Holistic (systems), organic (ecology), and monisitc (regarding the unity of human nature) worldview that rejects accumulating material things in favor of enhancing the quality of life.
7. Values that promote harmony within the society and between society and nature, such as reverence (inherent worth), compassion or loving-kindness (*mettā*), and nonviolence (*ahiṃsā*) toward all life.
8. Self-examination, self-realization, and self-fulfillment—actions to nurture the "deep self."

Cognizant of these features of their tradition, Western Buddhists have emphasized the need to create *eco-sanghas* that are ecologically responsible and committed to their bioregions.

Practices and Activism

Buddhists around the world are engaging in practices and forms of activism that contribute to sustainability. Complementing a range of writings on Buddhist economics, the Bhutanese have adopted a novel economic indicator, Gross National Happiness, which takes into account just and sustainable social and economic development. The Sarvodaya movement in Sri Lanka has hammered out an alternative form of economic development aimed at sustaining the environment, village communities, and core moral and aesthetic values. In Thailand, conservation monks have protected forests by "ordaining" trees. Other Buddhists have expanded the precepts, as evidenced by the Vietnamese Zen Tiep Hien Order's fourteen mindfulness trainings, which include such guidelines as the eleventh, "Aware that great violence and injustice have been done to our environment and society, we are committed not to live with a vocation that is harmful to humans and nature," and the thirteenth, "Aware of the suffering caused by exploitation, social injustice, stealing, and oppression, we are committed to cultivating loving-kindness and learning ways to work for the well-being of people, animals, plants, and minerals" (Thich Nhat Hanh 1998, 20–21).

Cognizant of traditional *gathas* (short verses or hymns from the sutras), the Vietnamese Zen monk and peace activist Thich Nhat Hanh (b. 1926) has crafted "earth *gathas*" one of which reads,

> In this plate of food,
> I see the entire universe
> supporting my existence. (Thich Nhat Hanh 1990, 195)

Such Buddhist institutions as San Francisco Zen Center's Green Gulch Farm, Zen Mountain Monastery in the

Catskills, Zen Mountain Center in southern California, and Spirit Rock Meditation Center in northern California have taken steps to make themselves into green communities. Buddhists have also crafted new practices, including the "earth relief ceremony" performed by the Zen Center of Rochester; backpacking retreats, known as mountains and rivers *sesshins* (meditation sessions of several days), run by the Ring of Bone Zendo; retreats led by Thich Nhat Hanh for environmentalists; Joanna Macy's Nuclear Guardianship project as a way to deal with toxic nuclear waste; and the Council of All Beings, an exercise Macy started with Australian eco-activist John Seed, in which participants speak for animals, plants, and inorganic things affected by destructive human actions. In an overview of these practices the professor of Buddhist Studies Kenneth Kraft (b. 1949) writes, "An abiding faith in the fundamental interconnectedness of all existence provides many individual activists with the energy and focus to stay the course" (Kraft 1994, 178).

Questions and Challenges

Buddhism presents a vision of an alternative way of life that is more conducive to sustainability than are the ideologies and practices powering mainline economic systems and consumerism. And Buddhists have been drawing on their tradition to speak to issues of sustainability. But it is not clear how much of a practical effect this has had. Insofar as they continue to fly and enjoy modern creature comforts, even progressive Buddhists in the West leave large eco-footprints, and the majority of Buddhists in Asia are fully plugged into dominant economic models and live in highly consumerist societies.

Another challenge is the historical lack of Buddhist critical distance from rulers, merchants, and other powerful players in societies where the religion has flourished. Buddhism does not have a tradition of criticizing people in power, and it has never engaged in any sustained discussion of social justice and what constitutes just relations in a sustainable community, a lack that has been exacerbated at times by interpreting the doctrine of karma to mean that each person is getting exactly what he or she deserves in life. One area in particular that Buddhist thinkers have rarely addressed is distributive justice (the question of who reaps benefits and who shoulders burdens), which must be factored in to approaches to sustainability to ensure that the needs of the poor are not ignored by calls to simplify, reduce consumption, or preserve certain resources. The traditional emphasis on giving to others and thereby cultivating the virtue of generosity as the antidote to the poison of greed could prove helpful as Buddhist ethicists address this topic.

But even if the majority of Buddhists were to change their lifestyles in a more sustainable direction and, in a commitment to ecojustice, work to redistribute the consumption of resources in a way that alleviates poverty, we would still be left with the question of how much of an impact that would have on the overall crisis of sustainability. Some Buddhist thinkers have started to expand their reflection beyond individual thought and action, beyond the scope of monasteries and Sri Lankan villages, and to grapple with broader structures of economic, political, and military power. And they have started to link this critical analysis to constructive delineation of what, exactly, from the Buddhist perspective, is optimal existence, whether of humans, communities, or ecosystems, and how humanity might achieve that goal, or at least live along a sustainable path that leads in that direction.

The poet Gary Snyder, a Buddhist who has written extensively on ecological issues, provides a glimpse of what a Buddhist path of sustainability might entail: "Practically speaking, a life that is vowed to simplicity, appropriate boldness, good humor, gratitude, unstinting work and play, and lots of walking brings us close to the actually existing world and its wholeness. . . . No expectations, alert and sufficient, grateful and careful, generous and direct. A calm and clarity attend us in the moment we are wiping grease off our hands and glancing up at the passing clouds" (Snyder 1990, 23–24).

Christopher IVES
Stonehill College

FURTHER READING

Badiner, Allan Hunt. (Ed.). (1990). *Dharma Gaia: A harvest of essays in Buddhism and ecology*. Berkeley, CA: Parallax Press.

Bond, George D. (2004). *Buddhism at work: Community development, social empowerment, and the Sarvodaya movement*. Bloomfield, CT: Kumarian Press.

Daly, Herman E., & Cobb, John B., Jr. (1994). *For the common good: Redirecting the economy toward community, the environment, and a sustainable future* (2nd ed.). Boston: Beacon Press.

de Silva, Padmasiri. (1990). Buddhist environmental ethics. In Allan Hunt Badiner (Ed.), *Dharma Gaia: A harvest of essays in Buddhism and ecology* (pp. 14–19). Berkeley, CA: Parallax Press.

Devall, Bill. (2000). Deep ecology and political activism. In Stephanie Kaza & Kenneth Kraft (Eds.), *Dharma rain: Sources of Buddhist environmentalism* (pp. 379–392). Boston: Shambhala.

Gross, Rita M. (1997). Toward a Buddhist environmental ethic. *Journal of the American Academy of Religion*, 65(2), 333–353.

Hayes, Richard P. (1990). Towards a Buddhist view of nature. *ARC*, XVIII, 11–24.

Ives, Christopher. (1992). *Zen awakening and society*. London and Honolulu: Macmillan and University of Hawai'i Press.

Jones, Ken H. (1993). *Beyond optimism: A Buddhist political economy*. Oxford, U.K.: Jon Carpenter Publishing.

Kabilsingh, Chatsumarn. (1990). Early Buddhist views of nature. In Allan Hunt Badiner (Ed.), *Dharma Gaia: A harvest of essays in Buddhism and ecology* (pp. 8–13). Berkeley, CA: Parallax Press.

Kaza, Stephanie, (Ed.). (2005). *Hooked: Buddhist writings on greed, desire, and the urge to consume*. Boston: Shambhala.

Kaza, Stephanie, & Kraft, Kenneth. (Eds.). (2000). *Dharma rain: Sources of Buddhist environmentalism*. Boston: Shambhala.

Kraft, Kenneth. (1994). The greening of Buddhist practice. *Cross Currents, 44*(2), 163–179.

Loy, David R. (2003). *The great awakening: A Buddhist social theory*. Boston: Wisdom Publications.

Macy, Joanna. (1985). *Dharma and development: Religion as resource in the Sarvodaya self-help movement* (Rev. ed.). West Hartford, CT: Kumarian Press.

Macy, Joanna. (1990). The greening of the self. In Allan Hunt Badiner (Ed.), *Dharma Gaia: A harvest of essays in Buddhism and ecology* (pp. 53–63). Berkeley, CA: Parallax Press.

Schumacher, Ernst F. (1973). *Small is beautiful: Economics as if people mattered*. New York: Harper & Row.

Snyder, Gary. (1990). *The practice of the wild: Essays by Gary Snyder*. San Francisco: North Point Press.

Sponsel, Leslie, & Natadecha-Sponsel, Poranee. (1997). A theoretical analysis of the potential contribution of the monastic community in promoting a green society in Thailand. In Mary Evelyn Tucker & Duncan Ryuken Williams (Eds.), *Buddhism and ecology: The interconnection of Dharma and deeds* (pp. 45–68). Cambridge, MA: Harvard University Press.

Thich Nhat Hanh. (1990). Earth Gathas. In Allan Hunt Badiner (Ed.), *Dharma Gaia: A harvest of essays in Buddhism and ecology* (pp. 195–196). Berkeley, CA: Parallax Press.

Thich Nhat Hanh. (1998). *Interbeing: Fourteen guidelines for engaged Buddhism* (3rd ed.). Berkeley, CA: Parallax Press.

Tucker, Mary Evelyn, & Williams, Duncan Ryuken. (Eds.). (1997). *Buddhism and ecology: The interconnection of Dharma and deeds*. Cambridge, MA: Harvard University Press.

World Commission on Environment and Development. (1987). *Our common future*. Oxford, U.K.: Oxford University Press.

Christianity—Anabaptist

The Amish and Mennonites, well known throughout the United States, belong to a wider branch of Christianity known as Anabaptism. Often persecuted in the past and misunderstood in the present, Anabaptists have a long history of simple living and stewardship of the land that can relate to modern ideas of sustainability.

Anabaptist Christianity in the United States is perhaps best characterized by diversity. Those descended from the Anabaptist tradition (including Mennonites, Amish, Hutterites, and multiple Brethren groups) may be urban dwellers with advanced academic degrees who are highly assimilated into American culture, or they may be rural members of distinct Old Order communities who travel by horse and buggy, eschew electricity, and end formal education in the eighth grade. Therefore it is not surprising to find a wide range of opinions regarding environmental sustainability across the Anabaptist spectrum.

The Anabaptist movement began in Europe during the Protestant Reformation. Most early Anabaptists were sympathetic to the reform movement, but they broke from the mainline reformers over the issue of baptism. The Anabaptists (meaning "re-baptizers") believed that only adults are capable of true faith, so they rejected the practice of infant baptism. They believed that Christian discipleship means following the teachings of Jesus in daily life, and they claimed that both faith and good works are necessary for salvation. Most Anabaptists were pacifists and refused to employ violent force or support their government's use of force. They suffered great persecution from both the Catholic and Protestant churches in Europe and eventually fled to safety in rural areas. Many Anabaptists became farmers, and they continued in this occupation when they migrated to the United States in the second half of the nineteenth century. Until the 1950s most members of Anabaptist groups made a living in occupations related to agriculture. A concern for the land is a part of their religious and ethnic heritage.

Most Anabaptists focus their concern for the land through the lens of stewardship. They cite God's command to till and care for the land (Genesis 2:15, NRSV) as the foremost reason for responsibility for the natural world. Most believe that creation is a gift from God to be used by humanity, but deliberate misuse will eventually bring God's judgment. About half of Old Order Amish and Mennonites are still involved in farming as their primary profession, and many of them acknowledge that they feel closer to God when they are working in the soil. Their level of cooperation with conservation projects varies by group and area of the country, but most want to avoid any financial subsidies from the government, and some may be uninformed about effective methods. Some Old Order farmers, especially in Amish communities, are beginning to turn to grazing and organic farming but primarily for economic reasons. They are searching for an economically viable model that will sustain the small family farm.

Anabaptists not directly involved in agriculture address environmental concerns through their concern for the wider world, often characterized by simple living and concern for the least advantaged among us. Anabaptists emphasize right living (or radical discipleship)

over right doctrine, and they pattern that discipleship on the life and teachings of Jesus. They take seriously Jesus' depiction of "harsh judgment [that] fall[s] on those who build larger barns so that they can hoard their abundance (Luke 12:21) and those who feast sumptuously while their neighbors go hungry (Luke 16:19–31). Jesus calls the wealthy to sell what they own and give money to the poor so that they can come and follow Him (Matthew 10:17–30). And He proclaims ultimate blessedness to those who feed the hungry, give drink to the thirsty, welcome the stranger, clothe the naked, take care of the sick, and visit the imprisoned (Matthew 25:31–46)." For these reasons many Anabaptists seek to limit their own consumption of resources to make these resources available to others.

For most Old Order Anabaptists, concern for simple living is not based on environmental concern but on direct biblical commandments. But Anabaptists more assimilated to the wider culture are more likely to be aware of a global community and how their consumption choices impact that wider population. Their simple living and their concern for the global community is informed by the biblical commands, their concern for the least advantaged in the world, and their awareness of the impending worldwide ecological crisis.

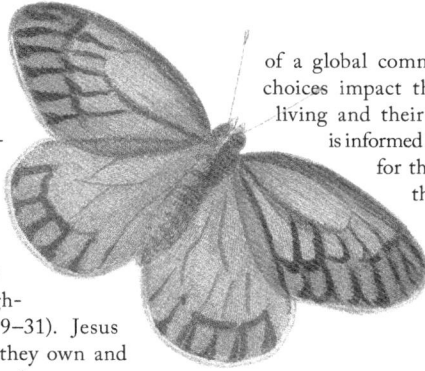

Kathryn S. EISENBISE
Manchester College

FURTHER READING

Hostettler, John. (1993). *Amish society* (4th ed.). Baltimore: Johns Hopkins University Press.

Kauffman, J. Howard, & Harder, Leland. (1975). *Anabaptists four centuries later: A profile of five Mennonite and Brethren in Christ denominations.* Scottdale, PA: Herald Press.

Kanagy, Conrad. (2007). *Road signs for the journey: A profile of the Mennonite Church USA.* Scottdale, PA: Herald Press.

Redekop, Calvin. (Ed.). (2000). *Creation and the Environment: An Anabaptist Perspective on a Sustainable World.* Baltimore: Johns Hopkins University Press.

Weaver, Dorothy Jean. (2000). The New Testament and the environment: Toward a Christology for the cosmos. In *Creation and the environment: An Anabaptist perspective on a sustainable world.* Baltimore: Johns Hopkins University Press.

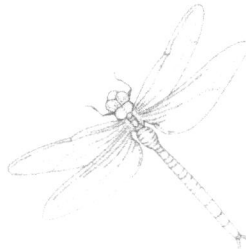

Christianity—Eastern Orthodox

Eastern Orthodox Christians believe that the predicament of the world's natural environment is not just ecological but spiritual, a problem that won't be solved unless natural resources are treated as the sacred creation and gift of God. Ascetic disciplines such as fasting—which involves learning to give rather than simply giving something up—are seen by Orthodox Christians as ways to connect to and preserve the natural world.

Orthodox Christianity retains—in its theology, liturgy, and spirituality alike— a profoundly sacred view of the natural environment, proposing a world richly imbued by God and proclaiming a God intimately involved with creation. To disconnect creation from the Creator, Orthodox Christians believe, is to desacralize both. For the way we relate to the world around us directly reflects the way we pray to "our Father in heaven." So we respond to the natural world with the same sensitivity with which we address God. All Christians understand that we must care for other human beings, as created "in the image of God." (Gen. 1:26 NRSV); it is time to appreciate the need to care for everything, as containing "the trace of God" (Tertullian, second century CE). Indeed, Orthodox Christians perceive the notion of sin as the stubborn refusal of humanity to regard the created world as a gift of communion—no less than a sacrament. In recent years, Ecumenical Patriarch Bartholomew (b. 1940), the spiritual leader of the Orthodox Church since 1991, has stigmatized environmental abuse as "sin."

In the seventh century CE, two mystics of the Eastern Christian Church eloquently described this relationship among nature, humanity, and God. Maximus the Confessor spoke of the world as a "cosmic liturgy," a magnificent altar on which human beings worship in thanksgiving and glory. The entire world comprises an integral part of this sacred song; God is praised by the sun and moon, worshipped by the trees and birds (Psalm 18:2). And Isaac the Syrian invited his spiritual disciples to "acquire a merciful heart, burning with love for all of creation: for humans, birds, and beasts." If today we are guilty of relentless waste in our world, it may be because we have lost the spirit of worship and the spirituality of compassion.

The predicament we face is not primarily ecological but in fact spiritual. It is a crisis regarding the way we imagine the world. We are treating the natural environment and its invaluable resources in an inhumane, godless manner precisely because we perceive it in this way. Unless we change the way we envisage creation, we are destined to deal with symptoms rather than with causes of the problem. One of the hymns of the Orthodox Church, chanted on the Feast of Epiphany (6 January) declares: "I have become the defilement of the air, the land, and the water."

The Orthodox Christian response to this urgent spiritual problem lies in its fundamental teaching concerning *ascesis* (or ascetic discipline). *Ascesis* is a technical term with much historical and theological baggage, whereas the word *discipline* has long been disassociated from its etymological meaning, implying the spiritual vision of a faithful disciple. Nevertheless, the intrinsic value of asceticism is discerned in the spirit of freedom and gratitude; its ultimate purpose is the rediscovery of wonder in the created world. The ascetic is one who is free, uncontrolled by attitudes that abuse the world, characterized by self-restraint and the ability to say "no" or "enough." The goal of asceticism is moderation, not repression; it looks to service and not selfishness. Without asceticism, none of us is authentically human.

An elementary example of asceticism in the Orthodox tradition is the discipline or rule of fasting. Orthodox Christians fast from dairy and meat products for half the

calendar year, in itself symbolic of reconciling one half of the year with the other—secular time with the time of the kingdom. This is because fasting entails learning to give, not simply to give up. Fasting is not to deny but to offer; it is learning to share with other human beings and to connect with the natural world. Fasting means breaking down barriers with one's neighbor and one's world: recognizing in others' faces, and in the Earth, the very face of God. Ultimately, to fast is to love; it is to see clearly, to restore the original beauty of the world. To fast is to move away from focusing on what we as individuals want and to consider first what the world needs. It is to liberate creation from control and compulsion. Fasting is to value everything for itself, and not simply for ourselves. It is to be filled with a sense of goodness, of Godliness. In the final analysis, it is a splendid summary of the Orthodox worldview and of Orthodox Christianity's approach to ecological issues because it encapsulates the effort to see all things in God and God in all things.

The ecological witness of the Orthodox tradition has been especially underscored by Ecumenical Patriarch Bartholomew, who has placed the ecological crisis at the forefront of his ministry. As spiritual leader of the Orthodox Church, which numbers over 300 million adherents, the ecumenical patriarch has been widely recognized for his pioneering work in confronting the theological and ethical imperative of environmental protection and declaring abuse of the natural environment as sinful: "To commit a crime against the natural world is a sin. For human beings to cause species to become extinct and to destroy the biological diversity of God's creation; for human beings to degrade the integrity of the Earth by causing changes in its climate, by stripping the Earth of its natural forests, or destroying its wetlands; for human beings to injure other human beings with disease and contaminate the Earth's waters, its land, its air, and its life, with poisonous substances . . . these are sins" (Chryssavgis, 2009).

Although its ecological initiatives date back to the mid-1980s, since 1989 the Ecumenical Patriarchate—located in the ancient Christian See of Constantinople (modern day Istanbul, Turkey)—has invited Orthodox Christians throughout the world to reserve 1 September, the official opening of the church calendar, as a day of prayer for environmental preservation. Numerous Christian communions have followed suit, encouraged by the World Council of Churches. In 1995, the ecumenical patriarch established the Religious and Scientific Committee, which to date has organized seven international, interfaith, and interdisciplinary symposia in the Aegean Sea (1995) and the Black Sea (1997), along the Danube River (1999) and in the Adriatic Sea (2002), in the Baltic Sea (2003) and on the Amazon River (2006), as well as in Greenland and the Arctic (2007). In 2002, Ecumenical Patriarch Bartholomew co-signed the "Venice Declaration" with Pope John Paul II, the first joint statement by the two world leaders; although the text of the declaration did not outline any binding action, it stated that protecting the environment is a moral and spiritual duty, and that Christians and other believers have a role to play in educating people about the ecological awareness—a responsibility toward self, toward others, and toward creation.

John CHRYSSAVGIS
Greek Orthodox Archdiocese of America

FURTHER READING

Bartholomew, Ecumenical Patriarch. (2008). *Encountering the Mystery.* New York: Doubleday Books.

Chryssavgis, John. (2009). *Cosmic grace, humble prayer: Ecological initiatives of the Green Patriarch Bartholomew,* 2nd rev. ed. Grand Rapids, MI: Eerdmans.

Kallistos of Diokleia. (1997). *Through the Creation to the Creator.* London: Friends of the Centre Papers.

Limouris, Gennadios. (Ed.). (1990). *Justice, peace, and the integrity of Creation: Insights from Orthodoxy.* Geneva: WCC Publications.

Sherrard, Philip. (1990). *Human image, world image.* Ipswich, U.K.: Golgonooza Press.

Zizioulas, John. (1989). Preserving God's Creation: Theology and ecology. *King's Theological Review* 12.

Christianity—Evangelical and Pentecostal

The concept of a faith-based sustainability has emerged from a number of Christian denominations, including Evangelicalism and Pentecostalism. Although still somewhat fragmented in theology and practice, an environmental movement based mainly on New Testament perspectives has begun to take shape among Evangelical and Pentecostal thinkers, leaders, and congregants.

Since the 1960s, Evangelicals and Pentecostals have become an increasingly diverse and politically significant voice in efforts to build a sustainable future. The terms *Evangelical* and *Pentecostal* are often contested and defined in a variety of ways. Evangelicals root their theology, ethics, and values in scripture, particularly the New Testament. Pentecostals do likewise but also place a heavy emphasis on the active role of the Holy Spirit. Both terms can also refer to particular denominations that identify themselves as Evangelical or Pentecostal—such as the Southern Baptist Convention or the Assemblies of God—but also can refer to congregations or individuals within Catholicism and mainline Protestantism.

There is strong debate on the relationship between Evangelicalism or Pentecostalism and sustainability, both from within and from without the churches. Most attention has been placed on Evangelicals, who, along with Pentecostals, have tended to show less environmental concern than other religious groups in the United States. With Pentecostals in particular, it is often assumed that an emphasis on the imminent return of Christ leads to a devaluation of the world and a license for unsustainable practices. But theological work is beginning to appear that connects the Pentecostal focus on the Holy Spirit and healing to environmental concerns. Within broader Evangelicalism, furthermore, a robust environmental movement has emerged, bringing with it unique perspectives on sustainability.

History

Evangelical entry into environmental issues began with publications such as the conservative Protestant theologian Francis Schaeffer's (1912–1984) *Pollution and the Death of Man* (1970), accompanied by voiced concern from major Evangelical institutions. An early organizational backbone for Evangelical environmentalism later arose with the formation of the Au Sable Institute of Environmental Studies, which provides environmental science education for students in Christian colleges.

Evangelical environmentalism gained momentum in the 1990s with the formation of several organizations, including the Evangelical Environmental Network (EEN). In 1993, the EEN drafted the Evangelical Declaration on the Care of Creation, which argues that "biblical faith is essential to the solution of our ecological problems."

As a sign of the growing success of Evangelical environmentalism, several sharp critiques have emerged. Most notably, the Acton Institute, which promotes free-market capitalism and wise-use environmental ethics, helped to organize the Interfaith Council of Environmental Stewardship (ICES) in 2000 and produced the Cornwall Declaration on Environmental Stewardship, written in response to the EEN's Evangelical declaration and arguing that the Earth is a resource to be

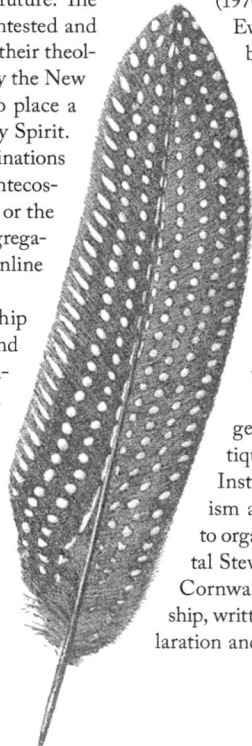

properly managed into fruitfulness. The Interfaith Stewardship Alliance emerged out of the ICES in 2005, and now is known as the Cornwall Alliance for the Stewardship of Creation.

Theological Contributions

At least three perspectives are distinctive to Evangelical understandings of sustainability. First, as Evangelical faiths are rooted in the biblical tradition, environmental sustainability is primarily understood through interpreting the Bible. This biblical emphasis also leads to a strong wariness about worshiping nature instead of God and an accompanying ambivalence toward mainstream environmentalism. Second, *stewardship* is the key Evangelical term for approaching sustainability issues. Stewardship ethics are commonly based in the first and second chapters of Genesis, whereby God gives humanity dominion over the rest of creation and, later, the responsibility of tending to the Garden of Eden. In the EEN's Evangelical declaration, stewardship is understood primarily in terms of caring for a creation in which all creatures are valued; it concludes by observing, "We are called to be faithful stewards of God's good garden, our earthly home." This caring for creation is, at its root, part of being a servant of God. The Cornwall declaration, on the other hand, understands stewardship in terms of the economic development of the Earth so that it is increasingly more productive for humanity. Third, recent Evangelical activism, especially as it has shifted toward climate change, has made sustainability into a matter of caring for the poor, an issue with a long history and much resonance among Evangelicals.

The contributions of Evangelicalism and Pentecostalism to sustainable practices are ambiguous, as there is no unified voice for these movements. Nonetheless, the work of organizations such as Au Sable and the EEN demonstrates that they carry unique strategies for grounding sustainability in a faith tradition.

Richard R. BOHANNON II
College of St. Benedict and St. John's University

FURTHER READING

DeWitt, Calvin. (1998). *Caring for creation: Responsible stewardship of God's handiwork.* Grand Rapids, MI: Baker Books.

Gabriel, Andrew. (2007). Pneumatological perspectives for a theology of nature: The Holy Spirit in relation to ecology and technology. *Journal of Pentecostal Theology, 15*(2), 195–212.

Kearns, Laurel. (1997). Noah's Ark goes to Washington: A profile of evangelical environmentalism. *Social Compass, 44*(3), 349–66.

Sharp, Kelly. (2006). Voices in the space between: Economy, ecology, and Pentecostalism on the US/Mexico Border. *Ecotheology, 11*(4), 415–430.

Christianity—Mainline Protestant

Protestantism has obtained a reputation for promoting industrial growth, through the application of the Protestant ethic, with little regard for the effects on the environment. A closer look at Protestant theology, however, reveals a notion of societal transformation that may be crucial in order to adopt more sustainable practices.

In a famous essay titled "The Historical Roots of Our Ecological Crisis" (1967), the U.S. historian Lynn White Jr. (1907–1987) concluded that Christianity, particularly Protestantism, bears "a huge burden of guilt" in this regard. Although this essay has been widely criticized, those who agree with White's claim point out that those Western countries that are largely responsible for environmental problems—such as climate change, ozone depletion, toxic waste piling, and various forms of pollution—are also countries where Protestantism has historically been influential. This begs the question whether Protestantism provided religious legitimacy to industrialized economic growth and why it failed to confront unsustainable economic practices. It also sheds new light on how to assess the impact of what the German sociologist Max Weber (1864–1920) called the Protestant ethic (based on diligence and frugality) on the accumulation of capital.

The widespread sense of environmental crisis also provides Protestantism with an opportunity for renewal and reformation. As the Protestant axiom of *ecclesia reformata semper reformanda* (a reformed church is always reforming) indicates, such reformation is common to this tradition. This is perhaps the core Protestant intuition on sustainability; namely, it becomes possible not so much through conservation, preservation, or protection but through ongoing change, adaptability, and fruitfulness. At best, it stimulates not so much a sense of awe when confronted with the sacred and the untouchable but a spirit of protest over what is: the

many faces of evil in society. But for ecosystems to be sustainable, there is a need for both stability and adaptability. The Protestant tradition is engaged in an ongoing struggle to come to terms with this recognition. Ironically, it has been at its vigilant best when protesting against what is wrong in church and society, and at its worst when its calls for stability ended up in Protestant forms of orthodoxy, conservatism, and fundamentalism. Such an emphasis on stability is easily abused to defend a particular sociopolitical status quo and to reinforce forms of domination, including the ways in which humans have appointed themselves to "subdue" the Earth and to "rule" over it.

Although the ecological footprint of Protestant institutions remains by and large unsustainable and their commitment to issues of sustainability somewhat questionable, there has emerged since the 1960s numerous calls for an ecological reformation of Protestantism. While some have tried to defend their own traditions against accusations that they are anthropocentric (human centered), and that they promote human alienation from the Earth community and endorse unsustainable practices, many others have recognized that a Christian confession of guilt, and not a reiterated confession of faith, may be the more appropriate response.

Various levels of such calls for ecological transformation may be identified. Following are some examples:

1. Liturgical renewal: the production of sermons, guidelines, and interpretive material on environmental themes.
2. The inclusion of environmental concerns in Christian education.
3. Resolutions and declarations adopted by local church councils, synods, church leaders, and ecumenical bodies, such as the World Council of Churches, the

Lutheran World Federation, and the World Alliance of Reformed Churches.

4. Numerous local faith-based earth-keeping projects in the areas of sustainable agriculture, tree planting, water harvesting, organic vegetable gardening, recycling, indigenous church gardens, outdoor youth and family activities to promote the love of nature, nature conservation, and job creation in the field of applied technology.

5. The often neglected work of the laity wherever they live and wherever they are employed in various professions.

6. The cultivation of ecological virtues and forms of spirituality at home and through various youth movements, Bible study groups, and cell groups.

7. Theological reflection through the development of teaching material, conferences hosted, and the production of a large corpus of academic publications.

Although the value of theological reflection may well be overestimated and its own ecological footprint underestimated, this is perhaps the most distinct and visible aspect of a Protestant response to environmental concerns. Individual theologians within particular confessional traditions in the wider Protestant world have made many contributions:

1. Günter Altner, Sigurd Bergmann, Ulrich Duchrow, Norman Habel, Phil Hefner, Gerard Liedke, Christian Link, Klaus Nürnberger, Larry Rasmussen, Paul Santmire, and Joseph Sittler in the Lutheran tradition.

2. T. J. Gorringe, Colin Gunton, Michael Northcott, and Peter Scott in the Anglican tradition.

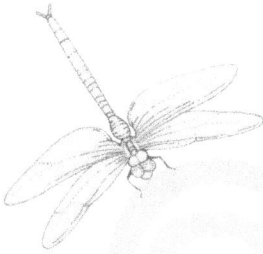

WORLD COUNCIL OF CHURCHES AND SUSTAINABLE DIALOGUES

The World Council of Churches (WCC) was an early adopter of the vocabulary of sustainability. The concept was first discussed in its 1974 Bucharist consultation of theologians and scientists. Then at its Nairobi Assembly in 1975, it initiated a program unit entitled "Toward a Just, Participatory and Sustainable Society," which was meant to address three core issues on the social agenda of the church: economic injustice, political oppression, and ecological degradation. In 1983 at its Vancouver Assembly, the WCC redeveloped the program under the themes "Justice, Peace and the Integrity of Creation." It used that motto to organize a series of conciliar dialogues for a process culminating in the World Convocation on Justice, Peace, and the Integrity of Creation, which met in Seoul in 1990. Discussions at the World Convocation debated priorities and connections among the three core social issues. Since then, the WCC continues to pursue initiatives linking issues such as climate change, human rights, access to water, poverty, and international peace.

WILLIS JENKINS

3. Steven Bouma-Prediger, Martien Brinkman, Ernst Conradie, James Gustafson, Douglas John Hall, Dieter Hessel, Jürgen Moltmann, and Michael Welker in the reformed tradition.
4. John Cobb, Jay McDaniel, Sallie McFague, and James Nash within the Methodist tradition.
5. Sam Berry, Susan Bratton, Calvin DeWitt, Ron Sider, and Loren Wilkinson in an evangelical context.
6. Christian Redekop in the Anabaptist tradition.
7. Scholars such as Marthinus Daneel on indigenous churches in Africa and George Tinker on Native American Christianity.

Some of these scholars (especially in the case of the Anglican and Methodist traditions) are noted more for the theological schools to which they belong than for their confessional identity. Such a confessional point of departure also tends to obscure the reflective wisdom and the environmental theories and practice emerging from outside the Western world.

Such scholarly work may also help to retrieve the core insights on sustainability within a Protestant context. At first sight, theological concepts—such as covenant; divine election; God's sovereignty in church and society; justification through faith, law, and gospel; or *sola scriptura* ("scripture alone")—may hold little promise for ecological reformation. Perhaps the concept used most often is that of "covenanting," for example in the context of the World Convocation on Justice, Peace and the Integrity of Creation held in Seoul (1990). (See sidebar.) Despite the solemn language used here, it remains unclear what impact the dissemination and reception of this covenant had within the context of member churches.

Nevertheless, the transformative potential of the Protestant vision for the world should not be underestimated. The Lutheran notion of two kingdoms and the Calvinist vision on God's just rule in "every square inch" may harbor serious dangers, but they have also been employed to promote economic justice, peace, and a sustainable society. Ultimately such a vision becomes possible through seeing God's presence "in, with, and under" (as Martin Luther would say) the whole created world. If God's hand were to be withdrawn, the whole of creation would collapse. In terms of the Protestant vision, God's caring hand may be regarded as the ultimate source of sustainability.

Ernst M. CONRADIE
University of the Western Cape

FURTHER READING

Bouma-Prediger, Steven. (2001). *For the beauty of the Earth: A Christian vision for creation care*. Grand Rapids, MI: Baker Academic.

Conradie, Ernst M. (2006). *Christianity and ecological theology: Resources for further research. Study Guides in Religion and Theology 11.* Stellenbosch, South Africa: SUN Press.

Fowler, Robert B. (1995). *The greening of Protestant thought*. Chapel Hill: University of North Carolina Press.

Nash, James A. (1991). *Loving nature: Ecological integrity and Christian responsibility*. Nashville, TN: Abingdon Press.

Nash, James A. (1996). Towards the ecological reformation of Christianity. *Interpretation, 50*(1), 5–15.

Santmire, Paul. (1985). *The travail of nature*. Philadelphia: Fortress Press.

Christianity—Roman Catholic

From the first church statements on environmental deterioration and human deprivation by Pope John Paul II in 1979 to subsequent writings and teachings of Catholic clergy and laity about sustainability, care for all creation and concern for all people are evident. Catholic ecological teachings from diverse sources continue to promote the close relationship of social and economic justice to environmental concerns and care.

Sustainability in Catholic thought integrates care for all creation—Earth and the biotic community—with concern for all people, which includes a "preferential option for the poor," in the words of the Latin American bishops' Puebla Conference. Catholic thought includes official church pronouncements from sources such as the Vatican, national conferences of bishops, individual bishops, and organizations established by the preceding. It also includes unofficial statements and writings from the broader church community, including Catholic laity and clergy speaking either as representatives of some part of the community of believers, or as individual theologians, ethicists, scientists, or social scientists.

Teachings from the Institutional Church

Pope John Paul II issued the earliest global church statements on environmental deterioration and human deprivation. In his first papal journeys in 1979, he discussed themes for upcoming Jubilee year celebrations in 2000. In Cuilapán, Mexico, when he participated in the Latin American bishops' Puebla Conference, the pope declared that all private property has a "social mortgage" (it is, effectively, on loan from the broader community whose needs it should meet directly or indirectly), and that governments might expropriate unused lands from the wealthy, with

appropriate compensation, and redistribute them to landless peasant farmers so that they might provide food for their families and their communities. (The phrase "preferential option for the poor," which has become significant for Catholic social teaching, was first elaborated during this conference, as part of the Latin American bishops' "Puebla Document.") In Des Moines, Iowa, John Paul affirmed the efforts of heartland region bishops to conserve family farms. He urged farmers to conserve the land so that its agricultural productivity would be sustained to benefit future generations. Throughout his papacy, John Paul II continued to speak and write about environmental concerns, and the relationship of social justice to environmental stewardship; he made a significant contribution to Catholic thought in this regard. Perhaps his most influential statement was his World Day of Peace message, *The Ecological Crisis: A Common Responsibility* (1990), in which he declared that care for creation was an "essential part" of Christian faith. The latter phrase was highly significant: it elevated creation care to a requirement for Catholics, rather than leaving it as an option. This stimulated greater church involvement in environmental issues.

The wide dissemination of *The Ecological Crisis* had global impacts, including in the United States, where the Catholic bishops issued *Renewing the Earth* (1991). The bishops described creation as a "sacramental universe," revelatory of its Creator; they extended the Catholic understanding of sacraments beyond the traditional seven *ecclesial* sacraments, to include the *natural* sacraments of creation. The bishops declared, too, that they wanted to explore the relationship between concern for people and concern for Earth, and between natural ecology and social ecology.

National conferences of bishops in several countries addressed environmental concerns due to increased awareness of the unsustainable impact of human industrial, commercial, and economic practices. Among national bishops' statements, the Dominican Republic bishops promulgated the *Pastoral Letter on the Relationship of Human Beings to Nature* (1987), and the Guatemalan bishops issued *The Cry for Land* (1988), both released prior to John Paul II's message. The Australian bishops issued later *A New Earth: The Environmental Challenge* (2002).

In the United States, a series of regional bishops' pastoral letters, focused on area concerns, began when the bishops of Appalachia issued *This Land Is Home to Me* (1975). The document's particular focus was on the regional economic and ecological harm wrought by the coal industry. Subsequent regional documents included *Strangers and Guests: Toward Community in the Heartland* (Midwestern bishops, 1980), which focused on saving the owner-operated family farm, preventing industrial harms to Earth and people, promoting land stewardship, safeguarding Native American treaty rights, and emphasizing that God's ownership of land takes precedence over private ownership.

The Columbia River Watershed bishops promulgated the first Catholic bioregional and international environmental document, *The Columbia River Watershed: Caring for Creation and the Common Good* (2001). Pressing regional issues addressed in this pastoral letter included salmon extinction; racism, particularly toward Native Americans; unemployment; and impacts of energy generation. The letter's ten "Considerations for Community Caretaking" illustrated developing Catholic sustainability proposals, including consideration of the common good; conservation of the watershed as a common good; conservation and protection of wildlife species; respect for indigenous peoples' traditions; promotion of justice for the poor, linking economic justice with ecological justice; and conservation of energy and construction of alternative energy generation facilities.

Perspectives from the Church Community

Several Catholic theologians and ethicists extended church teachings beyond their traditional expressions as they explored new exegetical (text-based) approaches to the Bible and analyzed Catholic doctrine. Pioneering works in the field offered distinct but complementary foci: John Hart, in *The Spirit of the Earth: A Theology of the Land* (1984), integrated biblical teachings, Catholic social thought, Native American spirituality, and the U.S. sociopolitical tradition, and their complementary roles in promoting care for Earth and human communities; Matthew Fox, in *Original Blessing: A Primer in Creation Spirituality* (1986), offered an innovative approach to humans' integration with their Earth context, focused on the implications of Yahweh's original blessing over the first humans, as described in Genesis; Thomas Berry, in *The Dream of the Earth* (1988), explored from Catholic and comparative religious perspectives human interaction with Earth, and offered a vision of a renewed Earth; Marcelo de Barros and José Luis Caravias, in *Teologia da Terra* (1988), described exploitation of indigenous peoples in Latin America from the colonial era to the present, linked ecological degradation to oppression of the poor, described the role of transnational capitalism and corporations in this oppression, and advocated new economic structures that would incorporate economic justice for the poor in general and for indigenous peoples in particular; Rosemary Radford Ruether, in *Gaia and God: An Ecofeminist Theology of Earth Healing* (1992), advocated an ecofeminist approach to environmental issues, noted links between male domination of women and human domination of nature, and urged conversion away from exploitation of both and toward the development of ecojustice, which would include new relationships among men and women, races, nations, and social classes; from Brazil, the liberation theologian Leonardo Boff, in *Ecology and Liberation* (1996) and *Cry of the Earth, Cry of the Poor* (1997), linked economic justice with ecological justice, and advocated new economic structures and new relationships among peoples and between people and Earth; and Ivone Gebara, in *Longing for Running Water: Ecofeminism and Liberation* (1999), offered an urban ecofeminist work which deplored, from that perspective, urban poverty, exploitation of the poor, and related ecological degradation, and offered a new ecological consciousness. Complementary works published soon thereafter included John Haught's *God After Darwin: A Theology of Evolution* (2000), which discussed the complementary relationships of theology and science to evolution, ecological responsibility, and responding to the needs of the biotic community and its Earth habitat; Rosemary Radford Ruether's *Integrating Ecofeminism, Globalization, and World Religions* (2005), which developed further social justice ideals; and Thomas Berry's *The Great Work* (2000), on ecological justice, human cosmic consciousness, and a human sense of cosmic place. John Hart's *Sacramental Commons: Christian Ecological Ethics* (2006) integrated appreciation of creation as revelation of divine immanence with advocacy of an equitable distribution of Earth commons goods; it proposed natural rights for all nature and provided principles for Christian ecological ethics. (See sidebar of Francis of Assisi's "Canticle of Creation" in the entry "Sacrament" on page 127.)

Intergenerational Implications of Catholic Teachings

Catholic ecological teachings, from diverse sources, promote ideas and ideals that relate ecological justice to economic justice. They argue for an equitable distribution and use of Earth's *commons goods* (earth, air, water, minerals) in order to meet the *common good* of humanity and of the community of all life, in the present and for the future. They integrate the

well-being of creation and the well-being of community.

The focus in most official church documents has shifted from human "dominion over" (which tended toward "domination of") to human "stewardship of" God's creation. "Stewardship," too, is somewhat problematic. While the term reminds people that, ultimately, they are caring for God's creation in trust from God, stewardship seems to imply a human managerial role over all creation. Several theologians and ethicists have replaced the constructs of dominion and stewardship with concepts of interrelationship and community: among people, between humans and other species, between biota and Earth, and between cosmos and Creator.

The impact of the human population on Earth's biosphere and available natural goods is rarely noted in institutional church documents, despite Earth's obvious limited carrying capacity—its ability to provide places for people to live and work, to produce food, to have potable water, and to acquire and use energy and minerals in sustainable ways. Institutional and community church writings do rightly note the impact of selfish human consumption and consumerism, in which natural goods are exploited to satisfy the wants of the human species (Earth's minority population), rather than to meet the needs of other biota (Earth's majority population).

People and planet can benefit, overall, from the theory and practice of Catholic socioeconomic-ecological teachings. While the tradition might lag behind in advocating responsible population numbers, it does foster reduced consumption, prioritizes needs over wants, advocates just and sustainable communities and care for creation, exhorts and exercises compassion for the poor, and, in all of this, helps to promote intergenerational responsibility and ecological sustainability.

John HART
Boston University

FURTHER READING

Berry, Thomas. (1988). *The dream of the Earth*. San Francisco: Sierra Club Books.

Berry, Thomas. (2000). *The great work: Our way into the future*. New York: Bell Tower.

Boff, Leonardo. (1996). *Ecology and liberation: A new paradigm*. Maryknoll, NY: Orbis Books.

Boff, Leonardo. (1997). *Cry of the Earth, cry of the poor*. Maryknoll, NY: Orbis Books.

Christiansen, Drew, & Grazer, Walter. (Eds.). (1996). *And God saw that it was good: Catholic theology and the environment*. Washington, DC: United States Catholic Conference.

de Barros, Marcelo, & Caravias, José Luis. (1988). *Teologia da terra*. Petrópolis, Brazil: Editora Vozes Ltda.

Ferro Medina, Alfredo. (1991). *A teologia se fez terra: Primeiro encontro Latino-Americano de teologia da terra*. [*Theology from the land: First Latin-American meeting on a theology of the land*]. São Leopoldo, Brazil: Editora Sinodal.

Fox, Matthew. (1986). *Original blessing: A primer in creation spirituality*. Santa Fe, NM: Bear & Co.

Gebara, Ivone. (1999). *Longing for running water: Ecofeminism and liberation*. Minneapolis, MN: Fortress Press.

Hart, John. (1984). *The spirit of the Earth: A theology of the land*. Mahwah, NJ: Paulist Press.

Hart, John. (2004). *What are they saying about environmental theology?* New York: Paulist Press.

Hart, John. (2006). *Sacramental commons: Christian ecological ethics*. Lanham, MD: Rowman & Littlefield.

Haught, John F. (2000). *God after Darwin: A theology of evolution*. Boulder, CO: Westview Press.

John Paul II. (1990). *The ecological crisis: A common responsibility*. Washington, DC: United States Catholic Conference.

Johnson, E. A. (1993). *Women, Earth, and creator spirit*. New York: Paulist Press.

Maguire, Daniel C., & Coward, Harold. (2000). *Visions of a new Earth: Religious perspectives on population, consumption, and ecology*. Albany: State University of New York Press.

Robb, Carol S., & Casebolt, Carl J. (1991). *Covenant for a new creation: Ethics, religion, and public policy*. Maryknoll, NY: Orbis Books.

Ruether, Rosemary Radford. (1992). *Gaia and God: An ecofeminist theology of Earth healing*. San Francisco: HarperSanFrancisco.

Ruether, Rosemary Radford. (Ed.). (1994). *Women healing Earth: Third world women on ecology, feminism, and religion*. Maryknoll, NY: Orbis Books.

Ruether, Rosemary Radford. (2005). *Integrating ecofeminism, globalization, and world religions*. Lanham, MD: Rowman & Littlefield.

Smith, P. (1997). *What are they saying about environmental ethics?* New York: Paulist Press.

U.S. Catholic Bishops. (1991). *Renewing the Earth: An invitation to reflection and action on environment in light of Catholic social teaching*. Washington, DC: United States Catholic Conference.

Christianity—Society of Friends / Quakers

The fact that two of the Society of Friends' shared beliefs (testimonies) are simplicity and integrity establishes its support of sustainability. Liberal and conservative Friends—or Quakers, as they are commonly known—have always resisted the distraction of material things to be closer to God and to sense more directly the presence of God in nature. This attitude is evident even in Quaker corporate endeavors.

Concern for sustainability and a range of environmental issues—in addition to peace, nuclear, population, and biotechnology concerns—is widespread across the Society of Friends, or Quakers as they are commonly known. Quakers trace their commitment to sustainability to the inclusion of simplicity and integrity, or right relationship, as "testimonies" (central guiding shared ethical beliefs and attitudes) that have been central to their faith from the Friends' beginnings in the Protestant reform movements of the mid-1600s in England. Other central testimonies include peace and equality/community, which have an ecological aspect in contemporary interpretation; some would add sustainability or Earth/environment to the list of testimonies that have evolved from the core testimonies (Helmuth 2007). Plainness was seen as a tool of both personal discipline and spiritual practice to cultivate an inner connection to the light of Christ in one's heart, and as a path of personal virtue to avoid the distractions of worldly things and the accumulation of wealth. George Fox (1624–1691), perhaps the most influential founder of the group, argued that the accumulation of wealth contributed to war and was a form of violence; he advocated the "right sharing" of economic resources, and integrity and honesty in economic transactions, in the interests of social justice. The testimony to simplicity meant plainness in dress, speech, buildings, and lifestyle. The commitment

to simplicity not only allows the individual to be less distracted and therefore closer to God, but also to sense the presence of God in nature. A common Quaker phrase is "There is that of God (or God's Light or Spirit) in everyone"; for many, this becomes "There is that of God in everything." For more contemporary Friends, simplicity is valued as an approach to a lifestyle that is more connected to both nature and economic justice and less focused on consumption. This "sustainability" side of the commitment to the simplicity testimony reaches across the Quaker world, connecting theologically liberal and evangelical organizations of Friends.

The testimony of simplicity is not just followed by individuals in their spirituality, lifestyles, and consumption habits, but also by the Society of Friends in their various corporate expressions. Quaker meetinghouses have always been plain, unadorned, and lacking in religious symbolism, as Friends seek a place that does not detract from the inner experience of God's presence. In this same spirit, meetinghouses built in the last four decades have sought to include a predominance of natural lighting, and many feature floor-to-ceiling windows looking out onto natural settings. The incorporation of abundant natural light serves both to enhance energy stewardship, but it also has an obvious symbolic connection to the Light of God.

In the last decade, two key buildings that house Quaker organizations in the United States have been renovated with green-building and sustainability principles in mind. The newly renovated office of the Friends Committee on National Legislation (FCNL) was the first building in Washington, D.C., to be awarded a Leadership in Energy and Environmental Design (LEED) silver certification by the U.S. Green Building Council. The FCNL, founded in 1943, is the oldest registered ecumenical lobby in Washington, D.C. It represents a range of Quaker groups, and its motto (shared on the banner of its website, www.fcnl.org) is an apt summation of its vision of sustainability: "We seek a world free of war and the threat of war . . . a society with equity and justice for all . . . a community where every person's potential may be fulfilled . . . an earth restored." The renovated Friends Center, built in 1856 in Philadelphia— a historically central location for Quakers in the United States—is the first building in Pennsylvania to have a geothermal heating and cooling system. Like the FCNL building, it uses local or reused materials when possible, has a "green roof" (a roof covered with vegetation), uses geothermal energy, and has natural lighting and energy-efficient features throughout. But it is different in that it also has solar panels and uses a storm-water-runoff collection system for use in toilets and on the grounds. According to the Friends Center website (www.friendscentercorp. org), the building, scheduled for completed in July 2009, will be a "showcase for environmental sustainability."

A key organization of Friends' work on sustainability is Quaker Earthcare Witness (QEW), an outgrowth of the Friends Committee on Unity with Nature that began in 1987 in response to the work of the Quaker environmental activist Marshall Massey. QEW points out that the current concept of sustainability is already present in the Quaker understanding of "right relationship," which can be traced back to the preacher John Woolman (1720–1772): if humans are not in right relationship with the more-than-human natural world, then the Quaker dedication to a world without war and with just social relations cannot be achieved. As with FCNL, perhaps this larger Quaker vision is best summed up in the following statement (QEW 2003): "We are called to live in right relationship with all Creation, recognizing that the entire world is interconnected and is a manifestation of God . . . the Truth that God's Creation is to be respected, protected, and held in reverence in its own right, and the Truth that human aspirations for peace and justice depend upon restoring the Earth's ecological integrity."

Laurel D. KEARNS
Drew Theological School and University

FURTHER READING

Cox, Louis; Fabianson, Ingrid; Moon Farley, Sandra; & Swennerfelt, Ruah. (Eds.). (2004). *Earthcare for Friends: A study guide for individuals and faith communities.* Burlington, VT: Quaker Earthcare Witness.

Environment: Quaker authors. (n.d.). Retrieved June 1, 2009, from http://www.pym.org/pm/lib_comments.php?id=499_0_108_0_ CQEW. (2003). Quaker Earthcare Witness's vision for the future. Retrieved June 4, 2009, from http://www.quakerearthcare.org/QEWPastandFuture/QEW_Future/QEW_ Future.htm

Friends Committee on National Legislation (FCNL). (n.d.). Retrieved on June 5, 2009, from http://www.fcnl.org

Helmuth, Keith. (2007, December). Friends testimonies and ecological understanding. *Friends Journal,* 14–17.

Merkel, Jim. (2003). *Radical simplicity: Small footprints on a finite Earth.* Gabriola Island, Canada: New Society Publishers.

Spring, Cindy, & Manousos, Anthony. (Eds). (2007). *EarthLight spiritual wisdom for an ecological age.* Philadelphia: Friends Bulletin.

Steere, Douglas. (1984). *Quaker spirituality: Selected writings.* Mahwah, NJ: Paulist Press.

Confucianism

In Confucianism, one of the three major religions of China, the ultimate context for human life is found in the "10,000 things"—nature in all its variety and abundance. Confucian texts describe nature as the basis of a stable society and warn that imbalance results from not caring for it properly. Ecological dimensions of Confucianism are being explored in China and East Asia in a search for a sustainable future amidst rapid industrialization.

Confucianism conventionally has been described as a humanistic tradition focusing on the roles and responsibilities of humans to family, society, and government. Thus, Confucianism is identified primarily as an ethical or political system of thought with an anthropocentric focus. Upon further examination, however, and as more translations become available in Western languages, this narrow perspective needs to be reexamined.

Some of the most important results of this reexamination are the insights that have emerged in seeing Confucianism as not simply an ethical, political, or ideological system. Rather, Confucianism is being appreciated as a profoundly religious tradition in ways that are different from Western traditions. (This recognition may eventually result in expanding the idea of "religion" itself to include more than criteria adopted from Western traditions, such as notions of God, salvation, and redemption.) Confucianism is also being recognized for its affirmation of relationality, not only between and among humans but also between humans and the natural world. The Confucian worldview might be described as a series of concentric circles where the human is the center, not as an isolated individual but as embedded in rings of family, society, and government. This is especially clear in the text of the *Great Learning* (*Daxue*), one of the four books of Confucianism. All of these circles are contained within the vast cosmos itself. Thus in

Confucian thought, the ultimate context for the human is the "10,000 things," namely, nature in all its remarkable variety and abundance.

Historical Development

Four major periods of Confucian thought and practice can be identified. The first stage is that of classical Confucianism, which lasts from approximately the sixth century BCE to the second century before the Common Era. This is the era of the flourishing of the early Confucian thinkers, namely Confucius and Mencius. The second period is that of Han Confucianism, when the classical tradition was shaped into a political orthodoxy under the Han dynasty (206 BCE– 220 CE) and began to spread to other parts of East Asia. The Han period saw the development of the theory that explained the correspondences of the microcosm of the human world with the macrocosm of the natural world—the relationship of the human to the seasons and the stars, for example. The third major period is the neo-Confucian era from the eleventh to the early twentieth century. This includes the comprehensive synthesis of Zhu Xi in the eleventh century and the distinctive contributions of Wang Yangming in the fifteenth and sixteenth centuries. The influence of both Confucianism and neo-Confucianism as an educational and philosophical system spread beyond China and shaped East Asian societies, especially Korea and Japan, along with Taiwan, Hong Kong, and Singapore.

In the twentieth century, a fresh epoch of Confucian humanism, called "New Confucianism," has emerged. This represents a revival of the tradition under the influence of scholars who came to Taiwan and Hong Kong after Mao Zedong's ascendancy in 1949. Mao felt that Confucianism was essentially a feudal tradition, anchored in history, and, that for his own ideas to flourish, a radical break must be made with the past. The anti-Confucian campaigns during Mao's rule were virulent, especially in the Cultural Revolution of the 1960s and 1970s. But after Mao's death there was a resurgence of interest in Confucian values, in part encouraged by the government. Indeed, the International Confucian Society held two major conferences in Beijing and in Confucius's birthplace, Qufu, to explore the future of the Confucian tradition. These conferences were held to commemorate the 2,540th anniversary of Confucius's birth; they marked a renewed interest in Confucianism to balance the unsettling effects of the rapid industrialization and modernization of China. There is a growing movement in China and across East Asia to reevaluate Confucianism for a sustainable future. This has been encouraged by a number of leaders, including, as of 2009, the Chinese vice minister for the environment Pan Yue.

Models of Confucian Sustainability

Various Confucian and neo-Confucian thinkers have suggested ways for integrating spiritual practice or cultivation with action in the world and reciprocity with nature. Confucius, Mencius, Xunxi, and Zhu Xi have distinctive approaches described below.

Confucius: Moral Rectification Extending Outward

The acknowledged founder of the Confucian tradition was known as the sage-teacher Kongzi (551–479 BCE). His name was Latinized by the Jesuit missionaries as Confucius. Born into a time of rapid social change, Confucius was concerned with the goal of reestablishing political and social order through rectification of the individual and the state. The principal teachings of Confucius are contained in his conversations recorded in the *Analects*. Here he emphasized the cultivation of moral virtues, especially humaneness (*ren*) and the practice of civility or ritual decorum (*li*), which includes filiality (*xiao*). Virtue and civility were exemplified by the noble person's (*junzi*) behavior, particularly within the five relationships between ruler and minister, parent and child, husband and wife, older and younger siblings, and friend and friend. The essence of Confucian thinking was that to establish order in the society, one had to begin with harmony, filial piety, and decorum in the family. Then, like concentric circles, the effects of virtue would reach outward to the society. Likewise, if the ruler was moral, it would have a ripple effect on the rest of the society and on nature itself, like a pebble dropped into a pond.

At the heart of this classical Confucian worldview was a profound commitment to humaneness and civility. These two virtues defined the means of human relatedness as a spiritual path. Through civility, beginning with filiality, one could repay the gifts of life both to one's parents and ancestors and to the whole natural world. Through humaneness one could extend this sensibility to other humans and to all living things. In doing so one became more fully human. The root of practicing humaneness was considered to lie in filial relations. The extension of these relations from one's family and ancestors to the human family and to the cosmic family of the natural world was the means whereby these primary biological ties provided a person with the roots, trunks, and branches of an interconnected spiritual path. Humans, nature, and the cosmos were joined in the stream of filiality. From the lineages of ancestors to future progeny, intergenerational connections and ethical bonding arose. Reverence and reciprocity were considered a natural response to this gift of life from parents and ancestors. Analogously, through reverence for heaven and Earth as the great parents of all life, one realized one's full cosmological being and one's place in the natural order. This can be considered a model for sustainability from the individual radiating outward.

Mencius: Botanical Cultivation of Self and Nature

Confucian thought was further developed in the writings of Mencius (371–289 BCE) and Xunzi (c. 310–219 BCE), who both debated whether human nature was intrinsically good or evil. Mencius's argument for the inherent goodness of human nature gained dominance among Confucian thinkers and gave an optimistic flavor to Confucian educational philosophy and political theory. This perspective influenced the spiritual aspects of the tradition as well because self-cultivation was seen as a means of uncovering this innate good nature. Mencius contributed an understanding of the process required for self-cultivation. He did this by identifying the innate seeds of virtues in the human and suggesting ways in which they could be cultivated toward their full realization as virtues. Analogies taken from the natural world extended the idea of self-cultivation of the individual for the sake of family and society to a wider frame of reference that also encompassed the natural environment. This can be described as a path of botanical cultivation. In addition to his teachings on personal cultivation, Mencius advocated humane government as a means to promote the flourishing of a larger common good. His political thought embraced appropriate agricultural practices and proper use of natural resources. In particular, he urged that the ruler attend to the basic needs of the people and follow the way of righteousness, not profit.

Xunzi: Ritual Relationship of Humans and Cosmos

Xunzi contributed a strong sense of the importance of ritual practice as a means of self-cultivation. He noted that human desires needed to be satisfied, and emotions such as joy and sorrow should be expressed in the appropriate degree. Rituals provided the form for such expression in daily human exchange as well as in rites of passage such as marriage and death. Moreover, because Xunzi saw human nature as innately flawed, he emphasized the need for education to shape human nature toward the good. Finally, he had a highly developed sense of the interdependent triad of heaven, Earth, and humanity that was emphasized also by many later Confucian thinkers. He writes: "Heaven has its seasons; earth has its riches; humans have their government" (deBary and Bloom 1999, 171). Heaven here is understood as the guiding force of the universe and Earth as the natural world within which humans lived and flourished.

Zhu Xi: Forming One Body with All Things

Confucianism blossomed during a neo-Confucian revival in the eleventh and twelfth centuries that resulted in a new synthesis of the earlier teachings. The major neo-Confucian thinker, Zhu Xi (1130–1200), designated four texts from the canon of historical writings as containing the central ideas of Confucian thought. These texts and Zhu Xi's commentaries on them became, in 1315, the basis of the Chinese civil service examination system, which endured for nearly six hundred years until 1905. Every prospective government official had to take the civil service exams based on Zhu Xi's commentaries on the Four Books. The idea was to provide educated, moral officials for the large government bureaucracy that ruled China. The influence, then, of neo-Confucian thought on government, education, agriculture, land, and social values was extensive. Views regarding nature, agriculture, and management of resources were derived from neo-Confucian understandings of the importance of humans' working to cultivate and care for nature as a means to fulfill their role in the triad of heaven and Earth.

Zhu Xi's synthesis of neo-Confucianism was recorded in his classic anthology, *Reflections on Things at Hand* (*Jinsilu*). In this work Zhu formulated a "this-worldly" spirituality based on a balance of cosmological orientation, ethical and ritual practices, scholarly reflection, and political participation. The aim was to balance inner spiritual cultivation with outward investigation of things in concert with the dynamic changes of the natural world. Zhu Xi affirmed these changes as the source of transformation in both the cosmos and the person. Thus neo-Confucian spiritual discipline involved cultivating one's moral nature so as to bring it into harmony with the larger pattern of change in the cosmos. Each moral virtue had its cosmological component. For example, the central virtue of humaneness was seen as the source of fecundity and growth in both the individual and the cosmos. By practicing humaneness, one could effect the transformation of things in oneself, in

society, and in the cosmos. In so doing, one's deeper identity with reality was recognized as forming one body with all things. As the *Doctrine of the Mean* stated: ". . . being able to assist in the transforming and nourishing powers of Heaven and Earth, one can form a triad with Heaven and Earth" (deBary and Bloom 1999, 333).

Confucian Relationality and Nature: Embodied Sustainability

From the classical texts to the later neo-Confucian writings there is a strong sense of nature as a relational whole in which human life and society flourishes. Indeed, Confucian thought recognizes that the rhythms of nature sustain life in both its biological needs and sociocultural expressions. For the Confucians, the biological dimensions of life are dependent on nature as a holistic, organic continuum. Everything in nature is interdependent and interrelated. Most importantly, for the Confucians nature is seen as dynamic and transformational. These ideas are evident in the *Book of Changes* (*I Ching* or *Yijing*) and are expressed in the Four Books, especially in *Mencius*, the *Doctrine of the Mean*, and the *Great Learning*. They come to full flowering in the neo-Confucian tradition of the Song (960–1279) and Ming (1368–1644) periods. Nature in this context has an inherent unity, namely, it has a primary ontological source (*T'ai ji*). It has patterned processes of transformation (yin–yang), and it is interrelated in the interaction of the five elements (water, metal, fire, earth, and wood) and nature's "10,000 things." Nature is dynamic and fluid with the movements of material force, or qi.

The Morality of Nature: Affirming Change

For the Confucians, humans are "anthropocosmic" beings, not anthropocentric individuals, meaning that the human is viewed as a microcosm in relation to the macrocosm of the universe. This is expressed most succinctly in the metaphor of humans as forming a triad with heaven and Earth. These relations were developed during the Han period with a complex synthesis of correlative correspondences involving the elements, directions, colors, seasons, and virtues. This need to consciously connect the patterns of nature with the rhythms of human society is very ancient in Confucian culture. It is at the basis of the anthropocosmic worldview where humans are seen as working together with heaven and Earth in correlative relationships to create harmonious societies. The mutually related resonances between self, society, and nature are constantly being described in the Confucian texts and are evident in art and architecture as well.

For Confucians, nature is not only inherently valuable, it is morally good. Nature, thus, embodies the normative standard for all things; it is not judged from an anthropocentric perspective. There is not a fact/value division in the Confucian worldview, for nature is seen as an intrinsic source of value. In particular, value lies in the ongoing transformation and productivity of nature. A term repeated frequently in neo-Confucian sources is *sheng sheng*, reflecting the ever-renewing fecundity of life itself. In this sense, the dynamic transformation of life is seen as emerging in recurring cycles of growth, fruition, harvesting, and abundance. This reflects the natural processes of growth and decay in nature, human life, and human society. Change is thus seen as a dynamic force with which humans should harmonize and interact rather than withdraw.

In this context, the Confucians do not view hierarchy as leading inevitably to domination. Rather, they see that value rests in each thing but not in each thing equally. Everything in nature and society has its appropriate role and place and thus should be treated accordingly. The use of nature for human ends must recognize the intrinsic value of each element of nature, but also its value in relation to the larger context of the environment. Each entity is considered not simply equal to every other; rather, each interrelated part of nature has a particular value according to its nature and function. Thus there is a differentiated sense of appropriate roles for humans and for all other species. For Confucians, hierarchy is seen as a necessary way for each being to fulfill its function. In this context then, no individual being has exclusive privileged status in relation to nature. Rather, the processes of nature and its ongoing logic of transformation (yin–yang) is the norm that takes priority for the common good of the whole society.

Humane Society and Government: Grounds for Sustainability

Confucians were mindful that nature was the basis of a stable society, and that without carefully tending nature an imbalance would result. There are numerous passages in *Mencius* advocating humane government based on appropriate management of natural resources and family practices. Moreover, there are various passages in Confucian texts urging humans not to wantonly cut down trees or kill animals needlessly.

The establishment of humane society, government, and culture, however, inevitably results in the use of nature for housing, for production, and for governance. In this sense Confucians might be seen as pragmatic social ecologists who recognize that stable societies depend on both educational and political institutions, rather than as deep ecologists who largely focus the primacy of the natural world and the need to reduce human exploitation of nature. Nonetheless, it is clear that for Confucians human cultural values and practices are grounded in nature and part of its structure, and thus humans are dependent on its beneficence. In addition, the agricultural base of Confucian societies has always been recognized as essential to the political and social well-being of the country. Humans prosper by living within nature's boundaries and are refreshed by its beauty, restored by its seasons, and fulfilled by its rhythms. For Confucians, human flourishing is thus dependent on fostering nature in its variety and abundance; going against nature's processes is self-destructive. Human moral growth means cultivating one's desires not to interfere with nature but to be in accord with the great Dao of Nature. Thus the human mind expands in relation to the "Mind of the Way."

In short, harmony with nature is essential for Confucians, and human self-realization is achieved in relation to and in harmony with nature. The great triad of Confucianism—namely, heaven, Earth, and humans—signifies this understanding that humans can only attain their full humanity in relationship to both heaven and Earth. This became a foundation for a cosmological ethical system of relationality applicable to spheres of family, society, politics, and nature, itself. This is the relational basis for Confucian sustainability.

Mary Evelyn TUCKER
Yale University

FURTHER READING

de Bary, William Theodore, & Bloom, Irene. (Eds.). (1999). *Sources of Chinese tradition, vol. 1: From earliest times to 1600*. New York: Columbia University Press.
Tu Wei-ming, & Tucker, Mary Evelyn. (Eds.). (2003). *Confucian spirituality*. New York: Crossroads.
Tucker, Mary Evelyn, & Berthrong, John. (Eds.). (1998). *Confucianism and ecology: The interrelation of heaven, Earth, and humans*. Cambridge, MA: Harvard Center for the Study of World Religions.

Daoism

Of China's three major philosophies, Daoism may be the most environmentally oriented; its ultimate goal is that humans live in harmony and unity with nature. Daoism also celebrates the values of mercy, humility, and frugality, which support an environmental conscious- ness, and includes many teachings that seek to restrict human behaviors such as killing animals and damaging the environment.

Western philosophy has been criticized for perpetu- ating ideas, such as dualism and reductionism that promote distance from, if not outright antagonism toward, the environment. Chinese philosophy offers an alternative approach by advocating ideas, such as holism and non- dualism, that encourage living in harmony with the envi- ronment. Chinese philosophy is commonly summarized in the expression *tianren heyi* ("nature and humanity unite as one"); *tian* is usually rendered as heaven, which rep- resents the natural world in general. Nondualism is the philosophical concept that opposites are not independent dualities, but interrelated and interpenetrating, such that the universe and people form a united whole.

Confucianism, Daoism, and Buddhism are the three major philosophies of China. Confucianism advocates humans living in harmony with nature, but its main focus is social, moral, and political philosophy. Imported from India, Buddhism also promotes harmony with nature, but its primary concern is liberating people from suffer- ing by means of meditation and enlightenment. Daoism has its own moral, social, and political philosophy and its own practices of meditation and interpretation of awaken- ing, but Daoism goes beyond the other philosophies in its emphasis on living in harmony with the natural environ- ment. In this sense, Daoism is China's foremost environ- mental philosophy in that it makes living in harmony and unity with the natural environment its ultimate goal.

Historical Background

Some Daoists claim that the ideas, masters, and texts of Daoism were originally generated by the *Dao* (meaning "Way," or the ordering and creative principle of the uni- verse) in the primordial chaos of undifferentiated, pure potentiality of existence (*hundun*) from which all things are generated. Historians believe that Daoism had its con- ception in the ecstatic vision quests of the ancient shamans of southern China from about the tenth to fifth century BCE. Some see Daoism developing out of the individualistic thought of hermits like Yang Zhu (c. sixth–fifth century BCE), who believed the world formed an organic whole such that he would not remove one hair from his shin to benefit the world (that is, he thought that each and every thing was so interconnected that one could not save the whole world by destroying any part, even a tiny hair). Most com- monly, however, the origin of Daoism is usually attributed to Laozi (or Lao-tzu, meaning literally "the old master" or "master Lao"). He is believed to have lived in the sixth to fifth century BCE and is the alleged author of the book that bears his name as its title, which is also known as the *Daodejing* (or *Tao Te Ching*; in English, Classic of the Way and its Power).

The second major figure in Daoism is Zhuang Zhou (or Zhuangzi, c. fourth–third century BCE, but also translit- erated as Chuang Tzu), who is believed to have written the first seven, or inner, chapters of the text that bears his name as its title. The impact of the *Zhuangzi* on Daoist philos- ophy and religion cannot be overstated. Whether or not Zhuangzi advances the teaching of Laozi—as opposed to being simply an independent thinker in a similar vein—is currently under debate. The expression Lao-Zhuang, refer- ring to the teachings of both thinkers, was first used in the preface to another Daoist work, the *Huainanzi* (139 BCE), and it was especially popular to discuss Lao-Zhuang

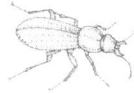

teachings during the Wei Jin period of Chinese history (220–420 CE).

In the Later Han dynasty (25–220 CE), Laozi underwent a process of apotheosis and became a celestial god. By 165 CE he was deified as Taishang Laojun, the Most High Lord Lao. This led to the development of Daoism as a religion. Zhang Daoling, a small landowner, proclaimed a new order based on revelations that he said the god Laozi made to him in 142 CE. He advocated the rule of the Three Heavens, which would deliver the world from an age of decadence and establish a perfect state for the chosen "seed people." Zhang's movement began in Sichuan Province under the name of *Wudoumi dao* (Way of the Five Baskets of Rice, a name taken from the tax levied on followers) and later became known as *Tianshi dao* (Way of the Celestial Masters). The teachings and practices of this religion and related alchemical and meditative practices underwent a complex process of change and development during the ensuing centuries. Daoism is still practiced today both in and outside of China.

Daoist Ecology

Because the early Daoist texts criticize Confucian virtues and morality, some scholars wrongly assert that Daoism lacks a morality. The early Daoist texts do in fact advocate moral ideas, proposing that the best way to live is by modeling the forces of nature and living in harmony with it. Laozi encourages people to follow the Earth as a model the way the *dao* models its own spontaneity. Emulating forces of nature is a prominent part of Daoist practices. Laozi tells us that the best people are like water, and Daoists try to emulate the virtues of water. They celebrate its softness, flexibility, and frictionless traits, its ability to erode mountains, its murky and chaotic condition when agitated, and its depth and clarity when calm. To go with the flow, literally and metaphorically, is the Daoist key to proper living.

For Daoists, people are socialized to engage in purposeful action. People are taught to work hard and to impose their willpower to achieve results. Daoists advocate acting by nonpurposive action (*wei wuwei*). The Daoist concept of nonpurposive action is closely linked to being natural, not artificial, and being spontaneous, not contrived or forced. Acting in this way allows people to be creative and to self-realize, so they will be better equipped to live in harmony with others and the natural environment.

Zhuangzi develops Daoist environmental philosophy. Some scholars postulate that Zhuangzi may have been the warden of a forest reserve; he certainly was familiar with local flora and fauna. Zhuangzi advocates a type of perspectivism: He states that each creature is limited in its understanding by the perspective from which it experiences the world. He gives numerous examples of how different creatures find different habitats and foods pleasing. He maintains that there is no single correct or privileged perspective; rather, each perspective has its unique benefits and traits. Though Zhuangzi does not consider it the highest ideal, he proposes that a person should aspire to be "a companion of nature/heaven" (Watson 1968, 56–57). The ideal for Zhuangzi is to merge with nature in what can be called an experience of nature mysticism—becoming one with nature. Ultimately for Zhuangzi this mystical experience embraces death as a natural homecoming for the human spirit. An important aspect of Daoist environmental philosophy is the recognition that opposing forces of nature, such as light/dark, hot/cold, wet/dry, and life/death are interconnected, interpenetrating, and mutually dependent. Accepting the interplay between life and death changes the context in which humans exploit the natural environment. Our lives hang in a delicate balance along with each and every other creature.

One area in which Daoism can assist modern ecology and environmental ethics is in human transformation. Many people propose that humans must change how they think about the environment and especially how they behave toward it. Daoists have developed various ideas and methods to help people embrace natural and personal transformation. Embracing change as a natural fact allows one to think and act more profoundly than does simple conservation. Instead of conservation, Daoists seek to live in harmony in the face of rapid change. For example, selective burning or removal of dead trees would be allowed if it enhanced human harmony with the forest. People are also changing; we need to transform ourselves to become even more natural and to live in harmony with nature. Daoists advocate cutting loose (*jie*) from the restrictions of social custom, psychological feelings, and divisive ideas. Cutting loose helps Daoists break free from social conventions that encourage people to exploit natural resources. Another form of personal transformation advocated by Zhuangzi is the awakening (*jue*) experience. Daoists practiced breathing exercises, meditation, sitting in forgetfulness, and losing one's self-identity. Deep ecologists (who believe that the environmental crisis is motivated by people's superficial understanding of their relationship with nature) and ecofeminists (feminists who argue that the oppression of women is intimately tied to the degradation of the environment and vice versa) would agree with Daoism's emphasis on the role of personal transformation for living in harmony with nature.

In the development of religious Daoism, a number of precepts were created to restrain people's unnatural behaviors. Some of the precepts restrict humans from disturbing, harming, or killing animals, birds, eggs, and plants. They prohibit unnecessary damage to the environment, such as wantonly destroying trees, plants and herbs, digging holes, draining wetlands or creating lakes, burning grasslands, polluting wells, springs, rivers or oceans, and making, storing, and disposing of poisonous substances. The ancient Daoist ideal of traveling without leaving a footprint has positively influenced the low-impact outdoor-sports movement (popular in the western United States, the movement wants to curtail or remove the human "foot print" from the wilderness).

Daoists celebrate mercy, humility, and frugality. From a Daoist perspective, human culture and industry are not sustainable without these three values. Human interpersonal relationships cannot be maintained without mercy and humility. Our positive interaction with the environment is enhanced and sustained through our expression of humility and frugality in exploiting resources. There is a story in the *Zhuangzi* that attempts to illustrate the Daoist ideal of frugality in working with nature. A Confucian sees a Daoist irrigating his fields with a bucket and so he tries to convince him to use a well sweep. The Daoist points out that employing machines causes people to worry about the mechanism, which in turn destroys the pure and simple life, replacing it with a mechanical one (Watson 1968, 134). Daoists are not opposed to using machines; they are opposed to the lack of humility and frugality expressed by most people who operate machinery. For Daoists, sustainable activities are those that entail mercy, humility, and frugality.

The ultimate goal for Daoists is to return to the primordial oneness of *dao,* or the way of nature. They employ a number of metaphors to express this union with nature. For example, Daoists talk about riding the wind, riding a dragon, entering water without getting wet or fire without getting burned, and living like a hermit in the mountains, only consuming dew drops. Zhuangzi expressed this union

aptly: "Heaven and earth were born at the same time I was, and the ten thousand things are one with me" (Watson 1968, 43). Daoism can awaken us to a deeper understanding of and relationship with the environment.

The impact of Daoism continues in the modern era. The ratification of the constitution of the People's Republic of China in 1982 reinstated the peoples' right to religious freedom, and people returned to worship at Daoist temples. Communist Party members downplay the value of Daoism in particular and religion in general, but there is a growing number of practicing Daoists in mainland China. Because Daoist temples and monasteries are located in forests and on mountains, Daoists claim that they have been and continue to protect at least some of China's environment.

James D. SELLMANN
University of Guam

FURTHER READING

Addiss, Stephen, & Lombardo, Stanley. (1993). *Tao te ching (Lao Tzu).* Indianapolis, IN: Hackett Publishing Co.

Ames, Roger T. (1989). Putting the *te* back into Taoism. In J. Baird Callicott & Roger T. Ames (Eds.), *Nature in Asian traditions of thought: Essays in environmental philosophy* (pp. 113–144). Albany: State University of New York Press.

Girardot, Norman J.; Miller, James; & Liu Xiaogan. (Eds.). (2001). *Daoism and ecology: Ways within a cosmic landscape.* Cambridge, MA: Harvard University Center for the Study of World Religions/ Harvard University Press.

Graham, Angus C. (Trans.). (1981). *Chuang-tzu: The inner chapters.* Channel Islands, U.K.: Guernsey Press Co.

Lau, D. C., & Ames, Roger T. (1998). *Yuan Dao: Tracing Dao to its source.* New York: Ballantine Books.

Rowe, Sharon, & Sellmann, James D. (2003). An uncommon alliance: Ecofeminism and classical Daoist philosophy. *Environmental Ethics, 25*(2), 129–148.

Watson, Burton. (1968). *The complete works of Chuang Tzu.* New York: Columbia University Press.

Hinduism

Many of the fundamental concepts and applications of Hinduism have served as a model for sustainability for the people of India. Belief in the interconnectedness of humans and the cosmos; the moral precepts of yoga; and everyday practices, many inspired by Mohandas Gandhi's view of self-sacrifice and active compassion, have guided Hindus' way of life and hold promise for India's future in the global economy.

Hinduism offers many conceptual and applied models for maintaining a sustainable lifestyle. Most Hindus live in India, a relative newcomer to the world economic stage. Most live close to the land in a self-sustaining village-based economic system. Some may regard this lifestyle to be backward and out of date, but the agricultural methods developed by small-scale farmers have proven effective and currently support more than half of India's population. Although the drive to globalization has created a growing urban class that has lost touch with its village roots, virtually all Indians are familiar with the founding values of the Indian Republic as articulated by Mohandas Gandhi (1869–1948), who believed that a life of self-sacrifice and active compassion for others would cultivate social harmony. Gandhi asserted that only true "self-rule," the result of self-control and a disciplined will, can foster economic and political self-determination.

The values required for a sustainable economic system can be seen within the traditional worldview of India. The Indic model encourages people to recognize the web of relations among humans, nature, and animals, and to develop sensitivity to the need for the protection of the Earth. The traditional Hindu emphasis on the connections between the structures of the human body and human cultures with the broader realms of creation provides a conceptual foundation for the enactment of sustainable values.

Sacrifice and Sustainability

Hinduism, like many religions, recognizes the need to perform sacrifice for the sake of the community's greater good. In the Sanskrit language, the word for sacrifice, *yajna*, derives from the root *yaj*, which means "to worship, adore, honor, consecrate, offer" (Monier-Williams 1899, 838). Hindu models for sacrifice have influenced the cultures of South Asia, and can be understood by examining three narratives: the sacrifice of the primal person (*purusa*) in the Rig-Veda; the *asva medha* (horse sacrifice) in the Brhadaranyaka Upanishad; and a twin tale of sacrificial cosmogony and anthropogeny in the Aitareya Upanishad, Each of these demonstrates a connection between human order and the larger cosmos, providing a foundational philosophy for sustainability.

In the sacrifice of the primal person in the Rig-Veda (one of Hinduism's oldest and most revered scriptures), the human person, divided up, comprises both the social order and the various constituents of the cosmos. This Vedic hymn poses a question: "When they divided Purusha, how many pieces did they prepare? What was his mouth? What are his arms, thighs, and feet called?" (Lincoln 1991, 7). The response makes direct correlations between the body parts and the now infamous Hindu caste system: "The priest was his mouth, the warrior was made from his arms; his thighs were the commoner, and the servant was born from

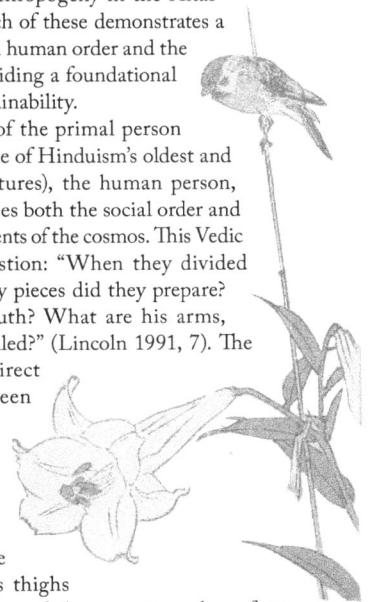

his feet." In this social order, the higher tasks performed by priests, physicians, lawyers, and teachers require a sound head. The ownership of land and the maintenance of political order require strong arms. Merchants and shopkeepers and other business folk move goods, as referred to through the extended metaphor of the legs. Servants, the "salt of the earth," perform the sort of labor required for agricultural production and construction projects. This hierarchy reflects human physiology and gives sacrificial sanction to human occupations. Civil duty (dharma) assumes religious significance.

The second part of the hymn correlates the human body with the far-flung regions of the universe:

The moon was born of his mind;
of his eye, the sun was born;
From his mouth, Indra and fire;
from his breath, wind was born;
From his navel there was the atmosphere;
From his head, heaven was rolled together;
From his feet, the earth; from his ears, the directions.

By identifying body parts with heavenly bodies, the heavens and the earth, and the elements of fire and wind, sanctity is given to both self and cosmos. Like the moon, our mind reflects and changes. Without the light of the sun, we cannot see. Our mouth proclaims our intentions and desires, and like the God of War, Indra, allows us to stake our claim in the world. Each breath we take generates and relies on the circulation of air. Our head pulls us upward; our belly gathers us toward the center and allows us to expand; our feet anchor us to the earth. Our ears orient and stabilize us within the space of the four directions. Through this sacrificial vision, each human being finds a place of importance within the cosmos. This sacrifice signals continuity between the human person, her place in society and within nature.

The horse sacrifice was performed in the twelfth year of the reign of powerful kings in India. For a full year the king would pursue a horse that had been released to the northeast of his kingdom; leaving his hair uncut, his beard unshaven, and remaining celibate for the duration of one year, he would follow wherever the horse wandered and eventually claim this territory as his own. At the end of the year, the horse would be captured and butchered in what undoubtedly was a deeply emotional ceremony. Just as in the sacrifice of the

primal person, where human body parts were matched with larger realms, so were the various portions of the sacrificial horse:

Om! Verily, the dawn is the head of the sacrificial horse;
the sun, his eye; the wind, his breath; universal fire, his open mouth.
The year is the body of the sacrificial horse; the sky, his back;
the atmosphere, his belly; the earth, the underpart of his belly;
the quarters, his flanks; the intermediate quarters, his ribs;
the seasons, his flanks; the month and half months, his joints;
days and night, his feet; the stars, his bones; the clouds, his flesh.
Sand is the food in the stomach; rivers are his entrails.
His liver and lungs are the mountains; plants and trees, his hair.
The east is his fore part; the west, his hind part.
When he yawns, then it lightens.
When he shakes himself, then it thunders.
When he urinates, then it rains.
Voice, indeed, is his voice. (Hume 1931, 73)

This description of sacrifice in the Brhadaranyaka Upanishad adds the passing of time to a description of the physical aspects of the universe, correlating the steps of the horse to day and night and the year to its whole body. In a later section of the same text, the parts of the horse are aligned with human body parts, as in the Purusa Sukta of the Rig-Veda.

Another variation on this process of worldly creation can be found in the Aitareya Upanishad. The performance of sacrificial ritual generates a form of interior, spiritual, creative heat known as *tapas*. This heat explodes the body of the primal person, creating the various parts of the universe. After the pieces of the universe have been created, they again gather, re-forming the human body.

When the man was heated, his mouth broke off, like an egg. From the mouth there was speech; from speech, fire. His nostrils broke off. From the nostrils there was breath; from breath, wind. His eyes broke off. From the eyes was vision; from vision, the sun. His ears broke off. From the ears there was hearing; from hearing, the four quarters. His skin broke off. From the skin there were hairs; from the hairs, plants and trees. His heart broke off. From the heart there was mind; from mind, the moon. His navel broke off. From the navel there was the downward breath; from the downward breath, death. His penis broke off. From the penis there was semen; from semen, the waters. (Lincoln 1991, 9)

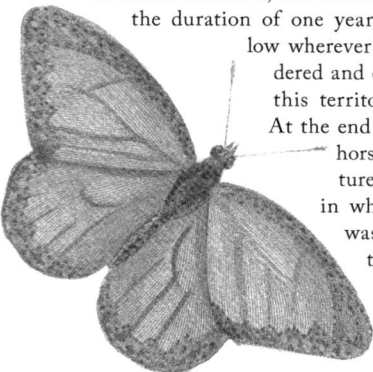

The scattering of body parts into the elements and heavenly bodies signals an intimacy between human physiology and the larger order and operation of the cosmos. As noted by Bruce Lincoln, author of *Death, War, and Sacrifice: Studies in Ideology and Practice* (1991, 10), this outward movement also has a moment of contraction in an endless pattern of expansion and contraction: "Each breath thus alternately de-creates the body while creating the world, then de-creates the world in order to re-create the body." The re-creation of the body proceeds as follows:

Fire, having become speech, entered into the mouth. Wind, having
become the breath, entered into the nostrils. The sun, having become
vision, entered into the eyes. The four quarters, having become hearing,
entered into the ears. The plants and trees, having become hairs, entered
into the skin. The moon, having become the mind, entered into the heart.
Death, having become the downward breath, entered into the navel. The
waters, having become semen, entered the penis.
(Lincoln 1991, 9)

The sacrifice of (or sacrificial, meditative attention to) the body results in the formation of or instantiation within the cosmos. The sacrifice of the cosmos results in the creation of the human body. Our body parts all eventually return and disappear into the air and earth. By recognizing these connections, one sees a common origin and a common end, body and universe.

The early sacrifices of India were dramatic and bloody, especially the horse sacrifice. Sacrifice of goats, water buffalo, and chickens still takes place in certain parts of India, particularly Bengal, Orissa, and Assam. Pressure from the Buddhists and Jainas, and more recently the British, has reduced the incidence of animal sacrifice, replacing it with ceremonies known as *pujas* that involve offerings of fruits and grains and flowers, as well as extensive cycles of prayer and chanting.

Indicating a continuity with the earlier processes documented above from the Vedas and Upanishads, a modern-day priest, Kumar Panda, described that in the process of readying himself to sacrifice a goat to the goddess Durga in a ritual conducted at Chandi Temple in Cuttack, Orissa, he transformed his body into a microcosm of the universe by correlating it to nature: *earth* is equated with parts of the body below the waist; *water* is symbolized by the stomach region; *fire* is represented by the heart; *wind* is equivalent to the throat, nose and lungs; *sky* corresponds to the brain. Kumar Panda reported a change of consciousness and the dissolution of his identity into the personage of Durga. After several hours immersed in mediation and ritual he saw lightning flashes; he then became one with the goddess, and the differences among water, fire, and sun's rays disappeared (Preston 1985, 51, 53). By becoming the goddess, his body expanded beyond the confines of ego and moved into a trance (*samadhi*) of cosmic consciousness. The feeling of deep connection in such rituals resides not only with the attendant priest but also with the tens of thousands who participate in this annual sacrifice.

Sacrifice expressed in simple ritual can be found in India in numerous ways, from the daily lighting of the kitchen fire to the creation of threshold art to the observance of a fast based on the phases of the moon. Veneration of animals can be found in the presence of cows, goats, camels, and elephants on city streets as well as in the household ritual of feeding the birds on one's windowsill before starting one's own meal. In India the excitement of large ritual moments, such as the Kumba Mela, where millions gather at the confluence of the Yamuna and Ganges rivers in Allahabad, serve to cement the religious identity of social groups. The constancy of small ritual moments, such as prayer and the maintenance of one's household shrine, serve to stabilize the family and the individual, establishing connections with the larger natural order.

The correlation of the cosmic person and the sacrificial horse to the broader forces of the universe and the ritual dismemberment of a goat in the contemporary sacrifice to the goddess Durga described above provide a different sacrificial mode. Rather than focus on loss, this approach emphasizes connectivity. These rituals do not provoke recollections of a broken past or advocate social change or tweak an individual's conscience. The exuberant rituals of India proclaim that the human person stands in solidarity with and in celebration of the great forces that drive the universe. By seeing the changing nature of the human mind in the phases of the moon, by seeing the warmth of the heart reflected in the household heart, sacrifice and ritual bring an individual to a place of identification with and empathy for the natural order.

Rituals in India evoke a primal connection between one's sensorial body and the broader powers of the universe. Much of India continues to thrive through a village-based, subsistence economy. Emotional, cultural, and physical sustainability have been achieved through a cycle of rituals and sacrifices within one's religiously sanctioned social duty (dharma). Although this system

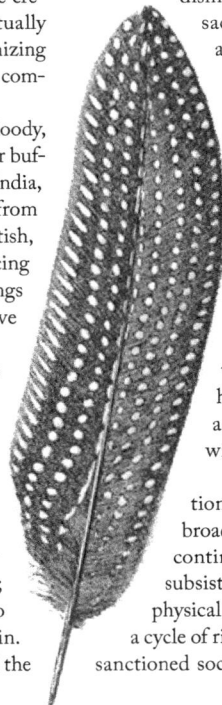

has been seen as oppressive by some, it has provided an adequate method for the sustainability of Indian culture even in the face of interkingdom conflict, waves of migration, and periods of foreign rule, including the lineage of Mughal rulers from Afghanistan who dominated northern India for centuries, and the era of the British Raj, which extended its colonial administration throughout much of the subcontinent.

As globalization extends into India and the rest of Asia, modernity threatens the rhythms of ritual and sacrificial life. India now boasts the largest middle class in the world and more than a hundred cities with populations exceeding 1 million people. Private home ownership and private automobile ownership are on the rise, but an awareness of pollution has spawned numerous environmental advocacy groups throughout India.

Mohandas Gandhi suggested that by returning to the bare necessities of life, one could disentangle oneself from the damaging effects of the British colonial system. He spun his own thread and wove his own clothing. He led "salt marches," targeted at the British Salt Tax that made it illegal for Indians to produce or sell their own salt, and thus helped to spare people from unfair taxation and reliance on imported goods. India's response to the difficulties of an enmeshed global economy might well take inspiration from Gandhi's well-known creed: "There is enough in this world for every person's need, but not enough for every person's greed."

Yoga and Sustainability

Aside from the ritual-bound traditions of India, the theories and practice of yoga offer a way to reflect on the human condition and sustainable values. Patanjali, a scholar who most likely lived circa 300 CE, codified this tradition. Yoga begins with a series of ethical values adhered to by Buddhists and Jainas as well as Hindus: nonviolence, truthfulness, not stealing, sexual restraint, and nonpossession. Gandhi advocated these as well, reinterpreting them in response to the ills of colonial occupation. In the practice of sustainability, nonviolence might be employed to help slow the pace of habitat destruction and the endangerment of species around the planet. Truthfulness might encourage the better dissemination of knowledge about the harmful effects of resource exploitation, such as deforestation, monoculture agriculture, and global warming. By recognizing how the cutting of forests, the pumping of oil, and the waste of water rob the bounty of the Earth, persons might refrain from such damaging activities. By controlling sexual impulses, the rate of population growth might be slowed. Through the minimization of possessions, people might grow accustomed to living on the bare necessities of life, a requisite step toward sustainability.

Other aspects of yoga similarly can help cultivate a sustainable lifestyle. The observances of purity, contentment, austerity, study, and devotion can help move a person from being outwardly focused and acquisitive to a place of inner stability. Refined movements of the body (*asana*) can bring one into a place of communion with nature. Control of the breath (*pranayama*) helps promote good health. Control of the senses brings an ability to concentrate, meditate, and move into a sense of deep connection with one's place in the nature. For the person established in yoga, needs are few and delights are many.

Contemporary Environmentalism in India

Environmentalists such as M. C. Mehta have acknowledged that India's traditional environmental wisdom can provide a valuable resource for moving the public to support the steps necessary to improve air quality, deal with water pollution, and slow global warming. He has commented:

> The elements of nature such as air and water are being overtaken by greed. Greed has overtaken us, leaving us under the cloak of greed. For people wearing that cloak of greed, it is very hard to come out and see real life. With correct understanding they will be in a position to respect law, and enforce it. Then we can have sustainable elements. (Personal interview with M. C. Mehta, 11 December 2006)

Hinduism's sacrificial model calls for a reconnection with the elements that have been celebrated since the Vedic period, an acknowledgment of the real connection between the human order and the cosmic order. Vandana Shiva, an ecologist and physicist, has become one of the world's most outspoken critics of globalization and has provided a critique of the "patenting" of traditional ways of knowledge for economic gain by corporations. Her activism in the realm of seed production has helped expose the excesses of the human attempt to manipulate nature. She takes a broad historical view in developing her analysis of "enclosure," or the marking off of what once held in common, to be commoditized and controlled by industrial and commercial forces.

> The "enclosure" of biodiversity and knowledge is the final step in a series of enclosures that began with the rise of colonialism. Land and forests were the first resources to be "enclosed" and converted from commons to commodities. Later, water resources were "enclosed" through dams, groundwater mining and privatization schemes. . . . The destruction of the commons was essential for the industrial revolution, to provide a supply of raw material to industry. (Shiva 2001, 44–45)

Shiva, much inspired by Gandhi, advocates what she calls living economies. One such example is Mumbai's magnificent lunch distribution system, the Mumbai Tiffin Box Suppliers Association, which delivers 175,000 lunches each day "with no documentation, no order, no bosses" and yet manages to make only one mistake every 16 million deliveries (Shiva 2005, 70). This organization has been studied by Harvard Business School as a model for human and social ingenuity. For Shiva this exemplifies the sort of people-based economy required for sustainability, joining self-determination with interdependence. Her advocacy of sustenance economy would require a shift from a corporate model to one in balance with nature, valuing partnerships, mutuality, and reciprocity.

Hinduism offers many approaches to a sustainable lifestyle. The village model still prevails throughout India, where the food is grown locally, manufactured goods are rare, and even clothing tends to be home-spun. For the growing number of urbanites who have entered into the more complex, globalized economy, some visionary pieces of legislation, particularly the use of compressed natural gas for buses and auto-rickshaws, have helped mitigate some of the deleterious effects of modernization.

To become truly sustainable, India will need to look backward to its tradition that emphasizes the interconnection between the human and the cosmic and forward to the increased generation of clean fuels, local production of food, and further innovations on the Gandhian model of self sufficiency.

Christopher Key CHAPPLE
Loyola Marymount University

FURTHER READING

Chapple, Christopher K. (1993). *Nonviolence to animals, Earth, and self in Asian traditions*. Albany: State University of New York Press.

Chapple, Christopher K. (2001). Hinduism and deep ecology. In David Barnhill & Roger Gottlieb (Eds.), *Deep ecology and the world religions* (pp. 59–76). Albany: State University of New York Press.

Chapple, Christopher K. (2008). Sacrifice and sustainability. *Worldviews: Global Religions, Culture, and Ecology, 12*(2/3), 221–236.

Chapple, Christopher K., & Tucker, Mary Evelyn. (2000). *Hinduism and ecology: The intersection of Earth, sky, and water*. Cambridge, MA: Center for the Study of World Religions and Harvard University Press.

Fuchs, Stephen. (1996). *The Vedic horse sacrifice in its culture-historical relations*. New Delhi: Inter-India Publications.

Hume, Robert E. (Trans.). (1931). *The thirteen principal Upanisads* (2nd ed.). London: Oxford University Press.

Lincoln, Bruce. (1991). *Death, war, and sacrifice: Studies in ideology and practice*. Chicago: University of Chicago Press.

Monier-Williams, Monier. (1899). *A Sanskrit–English dictionary*. Oxford, U.K.: Clarendon Press. (Available online at http://acharya.iitm.ac.in/sanskrit/dictionary/dict.php)

Preston, James. J. (1985). *Cult of the Goddess: Social and religious change in a Hindu temple*. Prospect Heights, IL: Waveland Press.

Shiva, Vandana. (2001). *Protect or plunder: Understanding intellectual property rights*. London: Zed Books.

Shiva, Vandana. (2005). *Earth democracy: Justice, sustainability and peace*. Cambridge, MA: South End Press.

Islam

The Quran teaches that humankind's stewardship of Earth is a privilege requiring profound responsibility, thus there is much in Islamic tradition to uphold an authentic environmental ethic that protects all of God's creation. Since the founding of Islam in the arid Arabian Peninsula in the seventh century CE, the Muslim world has paid close attention to water management from legal, economic, and ethical perspectives.

The Quran, Islam's primary authority in all matters of individual and communal life, as well as theology and worship, tells of an offer of global trusteeship that was presented by God to the Heavens, the Earth, and the Mountains (Sura 33:72), but they refused to shoulder the responsibility out of fear. Humankind seized the opportunity and bore the "trust" (*amāna*), but they were "unjust and very ignorant." Even so, God through mercy has guided and enabled humankind in bearing the responsibility of the *amāna*, although they have in the process also been subjected to punishment for their hypocrisy and unbelief. The Quran, however, is clear that God is the ultimate holder of dominion over the creation (e.g., Sura 2:107, 5:120), and that all things return to Him (Sura 24:42) and are thus accountable each in their own ways. In the Quran—and in the teachings and example of the Prophet Muhammad (570–632 CE), preserved in a literary form known as hadith—there is much with which to construct an authentic Islamic environmental ethic that both sustains what Muslims have achieved traditionally in this direction and leaves open a wide avenue for creative and innovative solutions in the contemporary context.

With respect to humankind's stewardship of the Earth, the privilege entails a profound responsibility. Other living species are also considered by the Quran to be "peoples or communities" (known as *ummas*; Sura 6:38). The creation itself, in all its myriad diversity and complexity, may be thought of as a vast universe of "signs" of God's power, wisdom, beneficence, and majesty. The whole creation praises God by its very being (Sura 59:24; compare with 64:1). With Him are the keys (to the treasures) of the Unseen that no one knows but He. He knows whatever there is on the Earth and in the sea. Not a leaf falls but with His knowledge: there is not a grain in the Earth's shadows, not a thing, freshly green or withered, but it is (inscribed) in a clear record (Sura 6:59).

According to the Quran, the creation of the cosmos is a greater reality than the creation of humankind (Sura 40:57), but human beings have been privileged to occupy a position even higher than the angels as "caliphs," or vicegerents (deputies) of God on the Earth. Even so, they share with all animals an origin in the common substance, water (Sura 24:45), and they will return to the Earth from which they came. The idea of human vicegerency on Earth has drawn much criticism in environmental ethics, principally since the publication in 1967 of an influential article, "The Historical Roots of Our Ecological Crisis," by the historian Lynn White Jr.; White argued that Judeo-Christian tradition encouraged exploitation of the natural world because the Bible declares human dominion over the Earth, and thus establishes anthropomorphism, and that Christianity's distinction between humankind made in God's image and the rest of a "soulless" nature make humans superior to other life forms. Muslims, as well as Jews and Christians, have had to face the intrinsic problems of such a position, historically as well as in contemporary global economic, political, and social life. But Muslims are reflecting on their fundamental and enduring religious teachings and discovering theological and moral bases for an environmental ethics that have been present, whether explicitly or implicitly, both in their sacred textual traditions and in their habits of heart, thinking, public administration, and daily life since Islam's founding. A common conviction among Muslims in this discourse is that nature is not independently worthwhile but derives its value from God. Put another way, nature is indeed incalculably worthwhile and wondrous, although according to Islam, it did not self-generate but was produced in a grand divine scheme.

Heaven and Earth

The Earth is mentioned some 453 times in the Quran, whereas sky and the heavens are mentioned only about 320 times. Islam does understand the Earth to be subservient to humankind, but it should not be administered and exploited irresponsibly. There is a strong sense in Islamic teachings of the goodness and purity of the Earth. For example, clean dust or sand may be used for ablutions before prayer if clean water is not available. The Prophet Muhammad said that the Earth had been created for him [and for all Muslims, by implication] as a mosque and as a means of purification. So there is a sacrality to the Earth; it is a fit place for humankinds' service of God, whether in formal ceremonies or in daily life. In an oft-repeated statement based a worldview very much different than that of Islam, James Watt, Ronald Reagan's first secretary of the interior, said that stewardship of the environment was not really such an urgent matter in light of the prophesied destruction of the natural order on doomsday. Those in the Muslim world would thus have recalled words the Prophet Muhammad is reported to have said, "When doomsday comes, if someone has a palm shoot in his hand he should plant it."

Muslims envision heaven as a beautiful garden, which the Quran describes in many places. Among the numerous descriptions is heaven as a garden under which streams (anhār) of pure water flow. That image is repeated some thirty-eight times and is mostly of Medinan provenance. If life on Earth is deemed the preparation for eternal life in heaven, then the loving care of the natural environment would seem to be appropriate training for the afterlife in the company of God and the angels in an environment that is perfectly balanced, peaceful, and verdant. Muslims believe that all generations will be gathered together at the Last Judgment and that in heaven the saved will enjoy the company of generations of faithful Muslims who have been rewarded with a blessed afterlife. Whether one plants a palm shoot as the end is closing in or invests in an environmentally sound way of life for the sake of posterity, it comes to the same thing: serving God through a stewardship that reflects what the Quran throughout sets forth as God's generosity, mercy, and guidance in the first place. Concerning God's reason for creating the universe, the Divine Saying so beloved by Muslim mystics, known as Sufis, declares: "I was a Hidden Treasure and I wanted to be known, so I created creatures in order to be known by them." (A "Divine Saying" is an utterance inspired by God but expressed verbally by the Prophet Muhammad.) Community between God and His creatures does not end with death; rather, it truly begins with the afterlife, according to Islamic belief. In a stirring passage describing the end of the world, the Quran details the destruction of the natural and familiar world and then declares: "When Hell shall be set blazing; and when the Garden is brought near—then shall each soul know what it has produced" (Sura 81:12–13).

"Do you not observe that God sends down rain from the sky, so that in the morning the Earth becomes green?" (Sura 22:63). The color green is the most blessed of all colors for Muslims and, together with a profound sense of the value of nature as God's perfect and most fruitful plan, provides a charter for a green movement that could become the greatest exertion yet known in Islamic history, a "green jihad appropriate for addressing the global environmental crisis." ("Jihad" means "exertion, struggle" and only by extension includes holy warfare of a military type.)

The Power of Water

Water has the highest meaning and value in the Quranic worldview, as indicated in the frequently quoted verse: "We made from water every living thing" (21:30; cf. 25:54; 24:45). References to water in its various forms and sources under the term mā' occur some sixty-three times in the Quran. Although that is not nearly as high a total of occurrences as Earth (or as the sky and the heavens), the occurrences often possess significant agency, whereas Earth

and sky—as wonderful as they are—are often the loci and channels for the passage of power rather than power itself. Water is power; indeed, it is the sine qua non of protoplasm. It is also important to note that significant references to water as the enabler of all life occur consistently throughout the chronological trajectory of Quranic revelation of some thirty-plus years—from early Meccan suras, when Muhammad was launching his prophetic career, to late Medinan times, when a stable theocratic system of faith and order had been established throughout the Arabian Peninsula.

God made all living creatures from water, and He sustains them over time and from generation to generation with that essential liquid. "And We send down pure water from the sky, thereby to bring life to a dead land and slake the thirst of that which We have created—cattle and people (*'anāsi*) in multitudes" (25:48–49). "Have you seen the water which you drink? Was it you who sent it down from the raincloud or did We send it? Were it our will, We could have made it bitter; why then do you not give thanks?" (56:68–70). God reminds us in the Quran: "Say: Have you considered, if your water were one morning to have seeped away, who then could bring you clear-flowing water?" (67:30).

The Quran principally provides a discourse on water in terms of its significance for life and as a major resource of divine providence. The treasury of prophetic statements that have been preserved in the hadith literature includes many references to water in human life in its personal, communal, civic, agricultural, legal, and commercial dimensions. An example of the first—the personal—dimension is the hadith wherein Muhammad declares: "He who serves drinks to others should be the last to drink himself" (Nawawi, reported by Tirmidhi). An example of the civic/communal dimension of water discourse in the hadith is: "All Muslims are partners in three things—in water, herbage and fire" (reported by Ibn Majah and Abu Daud). "Fire" in this hadith is usually understood to mean wood as the bearer of flame for practical uses. Another hadith adumbrates an ethic of conservation that Muslims often repeat (as translated in a contemporary Saudi Arabian source):

> It is related that the Prophet, upon him be blessings and peace, passed by his companion Sa'd, who was washing for prayer, and said, "What is this wastage, O Sa'd?" "Is there a wastage even in washing for prayer?" asked Sa'd.; and he said, "yes, even if you are by a flowing river."(*Environmental Protection in Islam* 1994, 7)

With respect to Prophet Muhammad's own ablutions—whether they are made to remove a minor impurity (by means of basic ritual washing, *wudū'*) or a major impurity (by a full ritual bath, *ghusl*)—before Salat-prayer, the Quran states: "But waste not by excess: for Allah loveth not the wasters" (6:141). Ayesha, the Prophet's young wife, reported that Muhammad used a very small quantity of water for simple ablution and a bit more for a full ritual bathing.

The Muslim world has throughout history paid close attention to water management from legal, economic, and ethical perspectives. Water in the Islamic vision is also of fundamental importance for sustaining basic human life, whether in the production of food and drink or in personal and communal piety in the purification rites that all Muslims perform on a daily basis, from cleansing one's surroundings to washing and bathing after experiencing impurity and before worship. The standard for ablution water to be used before formal worship is quite high, and the law books thoroughly treat the matter in a way that compares with extended halachic discussions of Jewish legal scholars.

The water that Muslims must use for purification, as one widely used worship guide expresses it, should be "fresh and clean like water from a tap or from a well or from the sea or from a river. Rainwater also will do." Sometimes it may take a fair amount of water to clean clothing or articles, as well as a person, from major impurity (such as contact with a pig or a dog). If one is made impure in a major way, through contact with blood and urine, for example, one must wash with water until the color, taste, and smell are removed. If a dog licks a hand or a cooking pot, as can happen, the hand or pot must be cleaned with water six times, at least, mixed with some dust. After that series of washings, the object must be washed an additional six times with fresh water without added dust. This rigorous requirement helps us to appreciate the old Persian tale of a person in the crowded bazaar who felt a moist tongue lick her bare hand as she wended her way among the other shoppers. If one cannot determine the source of the licking, one may simply declare: "Allah willing, it was a goat." Goats, like cats, are not sources of major impurity. The subject of water use in Islamic purification rituals is long and minutely detailed, but a sense of their importance has been seen from the examples given here.

Water Management in Islam

An excellent collection of essays has been published under the title *Water Management in Islam*. It is primarily based on the findings of the Workshop on Water Resources

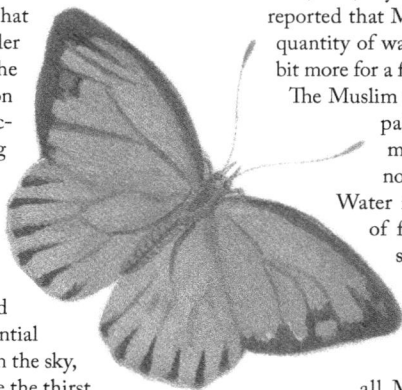

Management in the Islamic World, held in Amman, Jordan, in December 1998. (Although the Amman conference organizers sent invitations all over the world, most of the respondents were from the Middle East.) That workshop was in response to the United Nations Environment Programme (UNEP) 1992 Water Conference held in Dublin, Ireland, called Water and the Environment: Development Issues for the 21st Century; it outlined four general objectives, the "Dublin Principles" (Faruqui et al. 2001, xvi):

- Water is a social good.
- Water is an economic good.
- Water management ought to be participatory and integrated.
- Women play a central role in water management.

Some of the general, agreed-on principles of Islamic water management set forth in the book are included here appropriate categories (Faruqui et al. 2001, 1, 22, 23, 24, 25, 27, 52, 53, 87).

Water as a Social Good

Water is a gift from God and necessary for sustaining all life. Water belongs to the community as a whole—no individual literally owns water (except in containers and set apart from its natural source). The first priority for water use is access to drinking water of acceptable quantity and quality to sustain human life, and every human being has the right to this basic water requirement. The second and third priorities are for domestic animals and for irrigation.

Humankind is the steward of water on Earth. The environment (flora and fauna) has a very strong and legitimate right to water; we must minimize pollution and hold managers, individuals, organizations, and states accountable. Water resources must be managed and used in a sustainable way. Sustainable and equitable management ultimately depends upon following universal values such as fairness, equity, and concern for others.

Water Demand Management

Water conservation is central to Islam. Mosques, religious institutes, and religious schools should be used to disseminate this principle so as to complement other religious and secular efforts. Wastewater reuse is permissible in Islam, provided that treatment is appropriate for the intended purpose and not hazardous to health. This topic has generated considerable debate, and not all Muslims agree on the matter.

Recovering costs of water management is permissible for supplying, treating, storing, and distributing water, as well as for wastewater collection, treatment, and disposal. But water pricing must be equitable as well as efficient.

Islam permits privatization of water service delivery, but government must ensure equity in pricing and service. This is extremely difficult to ensure and an ongoing struggle (e.g., in Jakarta, Indonesia's capital, 20 percent of the population has access to piped, treated water, whereas the rest—approximately 80 percent—pay about 25 percent of their income for water from private vendors).

Integrate Water Resources Management

Water management requires *shura* (mutual consultation) with all stakeholders. All nation-states are obliged to share water fairly with other nation states. (There are some very difficult issues regarding water sharing today; Turkey's damming of the Tigris and Euphrates rivers, for example, threatens to cause grave shortfalls for Iraq and Syria. Iraq, especially, has been severely affected by this.)

Water management should be integrated across sectors and regions, whether among Muslim states or between Muslim and non-Muslim nations. The former should agree on basic Islamic principles, whereas the latter should seek agreements that comply with fair and just rulings by appropriate international organizations.

A major emphasis of *Water Management in Islam* is on the importance of educating the Muslim public at the most basic levels of community life in the homes, schools, and mosques and by mothers, teachers, and imams. In Jordan, the head mufti "delivered a special fatwa (expert legal opinion) that environmental education is *wājeb*, or an obligation: under such a fatwa, all Muslims are responsible for participation in environmental education. Therefore, Islam provides a dynamic forum that is capable of reaching the entire Muslim population—in the house, street, school, and mosque" (Faruqui et al. 2001, 52–53).

Water Management in Islam describes other initiatives and acknowledges that the role of women is particularly important at all levels. The editors and contributors of the book consider such initiatives to be in their infancy at present.

Facing the Future

One of the biggest problems that Muslims face, across the Afro-Eurasian world particularly, is overpopulation and mass migration from traditional rural and agricultural areas

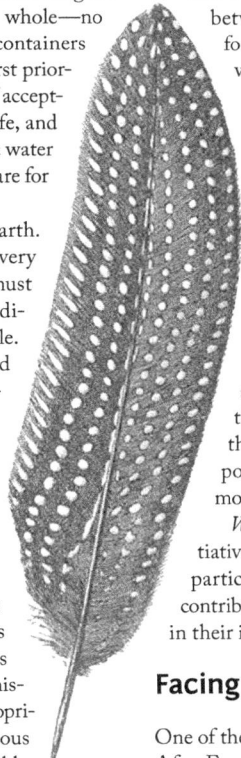

to overstressed and rundown, often squalid and neglected urban areas. And so much of the motivation and content of usually very conservative Muslim revival movements in recent decades has focused on anti-Western and anti-secular political and social matters with little if any attention paid to Islamic teachings about the natural environment. Ironically, fundamentalist types of Muslim movements readily accept modern technologies but too often without considering their effects on the natural environment.

Water stewardship in Muslim contexts has a powerful historical foundation because of the nature of the arid zone in which so many Muslims have lived since the founding of Islam in the Arabian peninsula in the seventh century CE. But thoughtful Muslims everywhere are increasingly also feeling an urgent need for developing proper stewardship of air, land, soil, plants, and animals. There is promising thinking and activism happening in some Muslim civic contexts today. Muslims realize that Allah is not interested in treating His human adult creatures like helpless children. As the Quran declares (13:11): "God does not change what is in a people until they exercise initiative in changing what is in themselves."

Frederick Mathewson DENNY
University of Colorado at Boulder, emeritus

A section of this article was adapted from "Islam and Ecology: A Bestowed Trust Inviting Balanced Stewardship"

by Frederick M. Denny, as part of the Forum on Religion and Ecology (FORE) series initiated at Harvard University's Center for the Study of World Religions; the original article can be found at http://fore.research.yale.edu/religion/islam/index.html

FURTHER READINGS

Bagader, Abubakr Ahmed; El-Chirazi El-Sabbagh, Abdullatif Tawfik; As-Sayyid Al-Glayand, Mohamad; & Izzi Deen Samarrai, Mawil Yousuf. (1994). *Environmental protection in Islam*, 2nd rev. ed. IUCN-World Conservation Union, Meteorology and Environmental Protection Administration (MEPA) of the Kingdom of Saudi Arabia, Policy and Law Paper No. 20, Rev. 1994.
Dobell, Patrick. (12 October 1977). The Judaeo-Christian stewardship attitude to nature. *Christian Century*, pp. 295–296.
Faruqui, Naser I.; Biswas, Asit K.; & Bino, Murad J. (Eds.). (2001). *Water management in Islam*. Tokyo, New York, and Paris: United Nations University Press.
Foltz, Richard C.; Denny, Frederick M.; & Baharuddin, Azizan. (Vol. Eds.). (2003). Islam and ecology: A bestowed trust. In Mary Evelyn Tucker & John Grim (Series Eds.), *Religions of the world and ecology* (pp. xliv, 584). Cambridge, MA: Harvard University Press for the Center for the Study of World Religions, Harvard Divinity School.
Izzi Deen Samarrai, Mawil Yousuf. (1990). Islamic environmental ethics, law, and society. In J. Ronald Engel & Joan Gibb Engel (Eds.), *Ethics of environment and development: Global challenge, international response* (pp. 189–198). Tucson, AZ: University of Arizona Press.
Nasr, Seyyed Hossein. (1992). Islam and the environmental crisis. In Stephen C. Rockefeller & John C. Elder (Eds.), *Spirit and nature: Why the environment is a religious issue* (pp. 85–107). Boston: Beacon Press.
White, Lynn, Jr. (1967). The historical roots of our ecological crisis. *Science 155*, 1203–1207.

If biologists believe that humans are the greatest agents of ecological change on the surface of the earth, is it not humans who, drawn from the brink, will—for their own good—abandon Mammon and listen to the prescriptions of God on the conservation of their environment and the environment of all the creatures on earth? The Islamic answer to this question is decisively in the affirmative.

MUHAMMAD HYDER IHSAN MAHASNEH

Source: Muhammed Hyder Ihsan Mahasneh. (2003). Islamic Faith Statement. Retrieved October 2, 2009, from http://www.arcworld.org/faiths.asp?pageID=75

Jainism

Some core values of Jainism, which originated in India as early as the sixth century BCE, lend themselves to sustainability, especially the focus on a living and eternal universe, the minimal use of natural resources, and ahimsa (nonviolence). The Jaina in India today, despite their small number, have the potential to advocate for change in environmental practices and policies.

The Jaina religion originated in India more than 2,500 years ago. It has survived as a minority faith and is currently practiced by approximately 4 million persons in India and several hundred thousand others scattered across the globe. Jainism espouses a philosophy that demonstrates some core teachings that accord nicely with sustainability principles. It teaches the pervasive and eternality of life forms and advocates a religious practice rooted in a nonviolent ethic. Jainism posits a living universe, uncreated and eternal. It emphasizes personal responsibility as well as an intimate, ongoing awareness of one's environment. It also advocates a parsimonious, minimalist use of resources, particularly for members of its monastic orders, who are deemed to live the ideal life.

Jaina Beliefs

Mahavira, the great Jaina leader to whom many Jaina teachings are attributed, lived during the same period as the Buddha, around the fourth century BCE. Mahavira taught close and careful observation of life: "Thoroughly knowing the earth-bodies and water-bodies, and fire-bodies and wind-bodies, the lichens, seeds, and sprouts, he comprehended that they are, if narrowly inspected, imbued with life" (Acaranga Sutra I:8.I, 11–12).

The Acaranga Sutra, the earliest known Jaina text, lists in detail different forms of life and advocates various techniques for their protection. It states, "All breathing, existing, living, sentient creatures should not be slain, nor treated with violence, nor abused, nor tormented, nor driven away. This is the pure, unchangeable, eternal law" (I:4.1). The Acaranga Sutra mentions how to avoid harm not only to animals but also to plants (by not touching them), and to the bodies that dwell in the earth, the water, the fire, and the air. For instance, Jaina monks and nuns must not stamp upon the earth or swim in water or light or extinguish fires or thrash their arms in the air.

The later philosophical tradition—as articulated in the Tattvartha Sutra written by Umasvati, a Jaina philosopher thought to have lived in the fifth century CE—states that the universe is brimming with souls weighted by karmic material (*dravya*). Many of these souls hold the potential for freeing themselves from all karmic residue and attaining spiritual liberation (*kevala*); they constantly change and take new shape due to the fettering presence of karma, described as sticky and colorful. These life forms can never be created, nor can they be destroyed. In a sense, by their very nature, they are not only sustainable but also indestructible. But they are constantly in a process of motion and change, moving from one birth to the next. To ensure their well-being, and to move toward spiritual liberation, Umasvati advocates carefully abiding by the five major vows: nonviolence, truthfulness, not stealing, sexual restraint, and nonpossession. Ultimately, if one perfects the practice of nonviolence, all karmas disperse and the perfected one (*siddha*) dwells eternally in omniscient (*sarvajna*) solitude (*kevala*).

According to Umasvati, 8,400,000 different species of life forms exist. These beings are part of a beginningless round of birth, life, death, and rebirth. Each living being houses a life force, or *jiva*, that occupies and enlivens the host environment. When the body dies, the *jiva* seeks out a new site based on the nature of karma generated and

accrued during the previous lifetime. Depending upon one's actions, one can ascend to a heavenly realm and take rebirth as a human or animal or elemental or microbial form, or descend into one of the hells as a suffering human being or a particular animal.

The Jainas were careful to observe and describe the many life forms that they hoped to spare. They cataloged them according to the number of senses they possess. Earth bodies, plants, and microorganisms (*nigodha*), at the lowest level, are said to possess only the sense of touch. Earthworms and mollusks have the senses of taste and touch. Crawling insects add the sense of smell. Moths, bees, and flies add sight. At the highest realm, Jainas place animals that can hear and those that can hear and think, including reptiles, birds, and mammals. The detailed lists of life forms provided by Jaina scholars present a comprehensive overview of life forms as seen through the prism of Jainism. As such they have presented a view of life that presages later environmental theory, resonating in its attention to detail with such writers as the U.S. environmentalist Aldo Leopold (1887–1948).

Jainism's Sustainable Worldview

The connection between Jainism and sustainability might not be obvious at first because Jainism seems most concerned with rising above karma and not with living beings—except in regard to how one's benevolence will advance one's own spiritual trajectory. Both Hindus and Buddhists have criticized Jainism as self-absorbed and even irrelevant. But the Jaina worldview powerfully evokes an emotional landscape. It states that the material world itself contains feelings and that the Earth feels and responds in kind to human presence. Animals possess cognitive faculties, including memories and emotions, and the very world that surrounds all living things feels their presence. All entities—from the water we humans drink, to the air we inhale, to the chair that supports us, to the light that illumines our studies—feel us through the sense of touch, though we might often take for granted their caress and support and sustenance. According to the Jaina tradition, humans, as living, sensate, thinking beings, have been given the special task and opportunity to cultivate increasingly rarefied states of awareness and ethical behavior to acknowledge that the universe is suffused with living, breathing, conscious beings that warrant recognition and respect. In this regard Jaina sensibilities accord well with an ethic of sustainability.

The Jainas were quite assertive in making their minority religious views known in areas of India where they gained ascendancy. To sustain their identity required great strategic thinking and action. Many of the southern kingdoms of Karnataka offered protection and patronage to the Jainas, who won several concessions regarding public laws designed to encourage vegetarianism and discourage hunting (*saletore*). Jainism exerted profound influence throughout this region from 100 CE to 1300. In the northern kingdoms of Gujarat, they experienced a golden era when Kumarapala (reigned 1143–1175) converted to Jainism. He encouraged the extensive building of temples, and under the tutelage of the Jaina teacher Hemacandra (1089–1172) became a vegetarian. He enacted legislation that reflected Jaina religious precepts regarding the sanctity of all life. In the north-central area of India, Jincandrasuri II (1541–1613), the fourth and last of the Dadagurus of the Svetamabara Khartar Gacch of Jaina monks, traveled to Lahore in 1591 where he greatly influenced the Mughal Emperor Akbar the Great (1542–1605). Akbar protected Jaina places of pilgrimage and ordered noninterference with Jaina ceremonies. Most remarkably, he forbade the slaughter of animals for one week each year. The Jainas tirelessly campaigned against animal sacrifice, which is now illegal in most states of India. Mohandas Gandhi (1869–1948), the most well-known leader of modern India, was deeply influenced by the Jaina commitment to nonviolence and adapted it in his campaign for India's political independence from Great Britain.

The Jainas have been great protectors of life within India. They have inspired legislation to protect animals over the course of centuries and have been influential in the modern government of India. Though the great struggles to ban ritual slaughter of animals and to free India from colonial rule have largely been won, Jainism appears to be well equipped to face the new challenges in regard to sustainability faced by India as it continues to pursue a course of rapid industrialization.

Jaina Environmentalism

The Jaina community has undertaken some steps toward including environmental issues within their religious discourse. L. M. Singhvi (1931–2007), a noted jurist and member of India's Parliament, published *Jain Declaration on Nature* in 1990. It quotes Mahavira's warning that observant Jainas must be respectful of the elements and vegetation: "One who neglects or disregards the existence of earth, air, fire, water, and vegetation disregards his own existence which is entwined with them" (Singhvi 1990, 7). Singhvi himself writes, "Life is viewed as a gift of togetherness, accommodation, and assistance in a universe teeming with interdependent constituents," and, stating that there are countless souls constantly changing and interchanging life forms, he goes on to note, "Even metals and stones . . . should not be dealt with recklessly" (1990, 7, 11).

Several Jaina organizations have taken up the cause of environmentalism, regarding it as a logical extension of their personal observance of nonviolence (*ahimsa*). Reforestation projects have been underway at various Jaina pilgrimage sites, such as Palitana in Gujarat, Ellora in Maharashtra, and Sametshirkhar and Pavapuri in Bihar. At Jain Vishva Bharati University in Rajasthan, a fully accredited university, the Department of Non-Violence and Peace offers a specialization in ecology. In December 1995 the department cosponsored a conference titled "Living in Harmony with Nature: Survival into the Third Millennium." Topics included the environmental crisis, ecological degradation, and unrestrained consumerism. A conference held at Harvard University in 1998 examined the topic of Jainism and ecology, and included representatives and scholars of various sects of Jainism. These activities reflect some ways in which the tradition has been refocused and newly interpreted to reflect ecological concerns: It values all forms of life in their immense diversity, not merely in the abstract but in minute detail. It requires its adherents to engage only in certain types of livelihood, presumably based on the principle of *ahimsa*.

It must be noted, however, that the observance of *ahimsa* is secondary to the goal of final liberation, *kevala*. Looking at both the ultimate intention of the Jaina faith and the actual consequences of some Jaina businesses, then, might require some critical analysis and reflection. Although the resultant lifestyle for monks and nuns resembles an environmentally friendly ideal, its pursuit focuses on personal spiritual advancement. In a sense the holistic vision of the interrelated life is no more than an ecofriendly byproduct.

In terms of the lifestyle of the Jaina layperson, certain practices—such as vegetarianism, periodic fasting, and eschewal of militarism—might also be seen as friendly to the environment and to contribute to global sustainability. But some professions adopted by the Jainas due to their religious commitment to harm only one-sensed beings might, in fact, be environmentally disastrous. The Jainas are involved with strip mining for granite and marble throughout India. Unless habitat restoration accompanies the mining, this is neither ecofriendly nor sustainable. Other industries controlled by Jainas may contribute to air pollution, forest destruction, and water pollution. In light of new evidence by the ecological sciences, the interconnection between industry, commerce, and the environment must be reevaluated. The development of a Jaina ecological business ethic would require extensive reflection and restructuring, a tradition well known within the Jaina community. The Jaina community, despite its relatively small numbers, is extremely influential in the world

of Indian business, law, and politics. If Jainas were to speak with a united voice on environmental issues, their impact could be quite profound.

Due to their perception of the "livingness" of the world, Jainas hold an affinity for the ideals of the environmental movement and are well poised to be advocates of sustainability. The Jaina observance of nonviolence has provided a model for a way of life that respects all living beings, including ecosystems. Because of their successful advocacy against meat eating and animal sacrifice, as well as their success at developing businesses that avoid overt violence, many Jainas identify themselves as environmentalists. Through a rethinking of contemporary industrial practices, and concerted advocacy of environmental awareness through religious teachings and the secular media, the Jaina tradition might help bolster a sustainable economic model.

Christopher Key CHAPPLE
Loyola Marymount University

FURTHER READING

Babb, Lawrence. (1996). *Absent lord: Ascetics and kings in a Jain ritual culture*. Berkeley: University of California Press.

Chapple, Christopher K. (1993). *Nonviolence to animals, Earth, and self in Asian traditions*. Albany: State University of New York Press.

Chapple, Christopher K. (1998). Toward an indigenous Indian environmentalism. In Lance Nelson (Ed.), *Purifying the earthly body of God: Religion and ecology in Hindu India* (pp. 13–38). Albany: State University of New York Press.

Chapple, Christopher K. (Fall 2001). The living cosmos of Jainism: A traditional science grounded in environmental ethics. *Daedalus: Journal of the American Academy of Arts and Sciences, 130*(4), 207–224.

Chapple, Christopher K. (Ed.). (2002). *Jainism and ecology: Nonviolence in the web of life*. Cambridge, MA: Center for the Study of World Religions, Harvard Divinity School, Harvard University Press.

Cort, John E. (1998). Who is a king? Jain narratives of kingship in medieval western India. In John E. Cort (Ed.), *Open boundaries: Jain communities and cultures in Indian history* (pp. 85–110). Albany: State University of New York Press.

Jacobi, Hermann. (Trans.). (1968[1884]). *Jaina Sutras: Part I. The Akaranga Sutra & the Kalpa Sutra*. New York: Dover.

Saletore, Bhasker Anand. (1938). *Medieval Jainism with special reference to the Vijayangara Empire*. Bombay, India: Karnatak Publishing House.

Singhvi, L. M. (1990). *The Jain declaration on nature*. London: The Jain Sacred Literature Trust.

Suri, Santi. (1950). *Jiva Vicara Prakaranam along with Pathaka Ratnakara's commentary* (Muni Ratna-Prabha Vijaya, Ed.; Jaynat P. Thaker, Trans.). Madras, India: Jain Mission Society.

Umasvati, Tatia. (1994). *That which is (Tattvartha Sutra): A classic Jain manual for understanding the true nature of reality* (Nathmal Tatia, Trans.). San Francisco: HarperCollins.

Judaism

Ideas embedded in the rich theological and legal litera-
ture of Judaism have informed and influenced modern
Jewish environmental ideas of sustainability: the belief
that humans are temporary inhabitants of what God
has created, and the inherent values of humility, moder-
ation, and responsibility. Many old and new traditions—Tu
b'Shvat, the Sabbath, and Sabbatical Year—celebrate care
and concern for the environment.

Judaism has, throughout its history, developed a theocentric theology while focusing much of its ethical
and legal literature on the good governance of human society, which was seen at the same time as the fulfillment of
God's will. In the earliest stages of Jewish history, found in
the Hebrew Bible, the relationship between the people, the
land, and God was conceptualized as a covenant. This was
a conditional contract in which the people had obligations
to be loyal to God alone and to follow God's commandments in return for peace and fertility on the land. Failure
to follow the contract meant exile from the land. Thus the
land-based covenant contained several important laws that
emphasized proper stewardship of the land and gratitude
to God for the bounty that the land produced under His
blessings. In later Jewish history, when many Jews lived
outside of the land of Israel, these concepts were incorporated into practices and rituals meant to remind Jews
of their ancestral connection to the land, but they could
also be applied in some part to the lands they now lived
in. It was this rich theological and legal literature that has
informed and influenced modern Jewish environmental
ideas of sustainability.

While the language of sustainability was not used
directly in Jewish environmental writing until the early
1990s, several concepts emerged in the first responses and
have continued to be the major values with which Jewish

environmentalists have found connections with the classic
elements of sustainability: God's ownership of Creation,
human stewardship of Creation, intergenerational responsibility, modesty in consumption, the common good, and
gratitude. These theological ethical concepts became part
of the organizing discourse of the Jewish environmental
movement as it began to mobilize.

Early Environmental Writings and Organizations

Jewish environmental writing began in the early 1970s as
responses to three events: the famous article in the journal
Science by Lynn White Jr., the creation of Earth Day, and
the advent of major environmental legislation. These all
occurred in North America, as Israeli environmentalism
began in the 1950s, not as a religious movement, but as
part of a secular response to development (Tal 2002). This
article will therefore focus on the Jewish religious concepts
of sustainability that were primarily developed in North
America.

The first major Jewish environmental organization was
Shomrei Adamah (Hebrew for "Guardians of the Earth,"
a reference to Genesis 2:15 in the New Jewish Publication Society's Hebrew Bible), which was founded in 1988.
Shomrei Adamah published a number of books and educational materials devoted to increasing environmental
awareness among Jews. One of its most successful activities was the popularization of the Tu B'Shvat seder. Tu
B'Shvat is the New Year for the trees, a minor event in
the Jewish calendar originally used to designate the date
when a tree's fruit became subject to tithing. In the sixteenth century, Jewish mystics created a seder or ritual
meal to mark this event, which was reinterpreted with their
elaborate cosmological system. In the twentieth century,

Tu B'Shvat was reintroduced as a kind of Jewish Arbor Day by Zionist settlers in the land of Israel. The seder was then rewritten to promote this event for Jews in the Diaspora. It was Ellen Bernstein, the founder of Shomrei Adamah, who reintroduced the mystical version of the seder within an environmental context. This ritual has spread to many Jewish communities, and Tu B'Shvat has become the de facto Jewish Earth Day. While the term *sustainability* was not originally used in the seder, the themes and practices of sustainability are now central to the seder's rituals and liturgy.

In 1992, as part of the National Religious Partnership for the Environment, the Coalition on the Environment and Jewish Life (COEJL) was founded in the United States. COEJL became a nationwide organization with many local affiliates usually connected to the organized Jewish community structures. In its founding statement, COEJL (2007) called for "mobilizing our community towards energy efficiency, the reduction and recycling of wastes, and other practices which promote environmental sustainability."

COEJL's mission statement also connected sustainability with environmental justice and the "Jewish values of environmental stewardship." The major Jewish religious denominations and rabbinical organizations in the United States have all passed numerous environmental resolutions since the early 1990s in which the language of sustainability is utilized. It is always assumed in these statements that sustainability is in consort with Jewish theology and ethics.

Ethical Obligations

It can be said that sustainability has two ethical obligations in time and space—one horizontal and one vertical. The horizontal obligation is to all humans and to all life living in the present: We must live equitably within the boundaries of what the Earth can sustain. The vertical obligation is to extend that process into the future, in other words, a commitment to generations of humans and nonhumans still unborn.

These ethical obligations can be found in the following Jewish theological assumptions upon which a Jewish concept of sustainability is based. First of all, Judaism holds that the Earth and all it contains is a creation of God. This world was not brought into being by human endeavor, nor does it exist only for human beings. For whatever reason, God created Earth and the life upon it; it all belongs to God, and human beings are temporary dwellers or tenants upon the earth (compare I Chronicles 29:11–15). This temporary tenant status also implies that humanity must leave the Earth in the same state as they entered it.

These ideas are best seen in the laws of the Sabbatical Year and the Jubilee. In Leviticus 25 (compare also Exodus

23:10), the Israelites were commanded to let the land lie fallow every seventh year. During that year—the Sabbatical Year—whatever grew on the land without human cultivation was allowed to be eaten but with the stipulation that the poor should have access to this produce as well. In a law called the Jubilee, Leviticus 25 also mandated that every fifty years, all land sold during that time was to be returned to its original owners. At the end of the stipulations of these laws it says: "But the land must not be sold beyond reclaim, for the land is Mine; you are but resident aliens with Me" (Leviticus 25:23 HB). In Deuteronomy 15:1–15, further stipulations are added to the Sabbatical Year: All debts must be cancelled and all indentured servants released. The rationale given in this source is that since the Israelites were redeemed by God from slavery in Egypt, they should imitate God and not enslave their fellow Israelites through debt. In the Torah there is also the idea of cross-generational responsibility in which the sins of one generation can end up hurting future generations (compare Exodus 20:5).

Creation is also deemed by God to be "good," which suggests a positive view of the material world. If all things created are good, then God has equal concern and delight in both human life and nonhuman life. This dual concern is found in texts such as Psalms 104 and 148. Human life, nonhuman life, and even the landscape itself form a single community in Creation. The speeches of God to Job out of the whirlwind (Job 38–41) suggest the more radical idea that humans are not the primary objects of God's concern.

Secondly, Creation has an order (in Hebrew: *seder b'reshit*.) This order is, according to classical texts such as Psalm 148, hierarchically structured with its focus toward God. But it is also horizontally structured to remind us of the interdependence of all life. Embedded in both ethical and ritual laws in the Torah is the warning against the disruption of this order (compare Genesis 4, Leviticus 18:27–30).

Thirdly, human beings have a special place and role in the order of Creation. Of all Creation, only human beings have the power to disrupt Creation. This power, which gives them a kind of control over Creation, comes from special characteristics that no other creature possesses (compare Psalm 8). This idea is expressed in the concept that humans were created in the image of God (in Hebrew: *tzelem Elohim*). In its original sense, *tzelem Elohim* means that humans were put on the Earth to act as God's agents and to actualize God's presence in Creation. But the concept also has ethical implications, which means that human beings have certain intrinsic dignities such as infinite value, equality and uniqueness, and that human beings possess God-like capacities such as power, consciousness, relationship, will, freedom, and life. Human beings are supposed

to exercise their power, consciousness, and free will to be wise stewards of Creation. They should be maintaining the order of Creation even while they are allowed to use it for their own benefit within certain limits established by God (Genesis 2:14). This ethical imperative of responsibility applies to human society as well to the natural world.

These theological concepts give rise to two ethical values in Judaism: humility and moderation. Humility calls upon human beings to recognize their place in the order of Creation. "Why were human beings created last in the order of Creation? . . . So they should not grow proud, for one can say to them, 'the gnat came before you in the Creation!'" (Babylonian Talmud, Sanhedrin 38a). While human beings do have the power to manipulate Creation, that power must be exercised carefully since humanity is dependant upon and interconnected to the rest of Creation. The second century CE Rabbi Simeon bar Yohai said: "Three things are equal in importance: earth, humans and rain." The early fourth century CE Rabbi Levi ben Hiyyata said: "And these three each consist of three letters [in Hebrew] to teach that without Earth, there is no rain and without rain earth cannot endure; while without either, humans cannot exist" (Midrash Genesis Rabbah 13:3). Humility calls humanity to understand that all actions have long-term consequences upon the Earth, that it is necessary to "tread lightly upon the Earth," and not to act out of the arrogance of power.

Moderation is a self-imposed limitation to unnecessary consumption. Moderation is a positive value that can enhance the appreciation of life. "Who is rich? One who is happy with his portion" (Mishnah Avot 4:1). One of the great Jewish texts on moderation is the *Eight Chapters* of Moses Maimonides (1135–1204), an introduction to his commentary to Mishnah Avot. Chapter Four describes the path of moderation between two extremes as the definition of virtue. And while Maimonides was especially concerned with showing how extreme asceticism is not a virtue in itself but only as a means to an end, his basic principle of understanding how destructive extreme behavior can be to the human psyche is quite relevant today in discussions about sustainability and countering the modern culture of consumerism. The Jewish tradition has never exalted poverty and has always seen material welfare as a blessing and a reward from God, but it also saw the unlimited acquisition of wealth as a danger to true spiritual and ethical values. For example, the medieval French rabbinical authority Rashi (1040–1105), in his commentary to Numbers 32:16, speaks disapprovingly of how the tribes of Gad and Reuben had more concern for their cattle and wealth than for their children. During the Middle Ages, many Jewish communities had sumptuary laws that included limitations upon extravagance in dress and as well as limitations on the amount of spending at life-cycle celebrations. One is also

not supposed to be excessive in eating and drinking or in the kind of clothes that one wears (Maimonides Mishneh Torah, Laws of Discernment, chapter 5).

It is thus easy to understand how modern Jewish environmentalism embraced the concept of sustainability within traditional theology. But Judaism has always sought to concretize its theology and ethical values within a discrete system of legal actions (in Hebrew: *halakhah*). One particular law has been part of Jewish environmentalism since its start: the mitzvah (meaning "commandment") of *Bal Tashchit* ("Do not destroy"). This law, one of the 613 commandments that Rabbinic Judaism has traditionally found in the Torah, is based on Deuteronomy 20:19–20:

> When in your war against a city you have to besiege it a long time in order to capture it, you must not destroy its trees, wielding the ax against them. You may eat of them, but you must not cut them down. Are trees of the field human to withdraw before you into the besieged city? Only trees that you know do no yield food may be destroyed; you may cut them down for constructing siege works against the city that is waging war on you, until it has been reduced.

This law was expanded in later Jewish legal sources to include the prohibition of the wanton destruction of household goods, clothes, buildings, springs, food, or the wasteful consumption of anything (see Maimonides, Mishneh Torah, Laws of Kings, and Wars 6:8, 10; Hirsch 2002, 279–280). In modern Jewish environmentalism, *Bal Tashchit* is considered the primary call to sustainable living. Thus Jews are obligated to consider carefully their real needs whenever purchasing anything. There is an obligation when having a celebration to consider whether it is necessary to elaborate meals and wasteful decorations. There is also an obligation to consider energy use and the sources from which it comes.

In classic rabbinic sources there is also a strong commitment to the common good. For example:

> Rabbi Shimon Ben Yochai taught: It can be compared to people who were in a boat and one of them took a drill and began to drill under his seat. His fellow passengers said to him: "Why are you doing this?!" He said to them: "What do you care? Am I not drilling under me?!" They replied: "Because you are sinking the boat with us in it!" (Midrash Leviticus Rabbah 4:6)

There is also the Talmudic legal principle of *geirey diley* (Aramaic for "his arrows"). In this principle, it is forbidden for a person to stand in his own property and to shoot arrows randomly while claiming that there was no intent to cause damage (Talmud Bava Batra 22b). Thus people are forbidden to establish polluting workshops in a courtyard where other people are living. This principle can also be applied to sustainability in that we cannot claim that our unsustainable consumption is morally neutral. We know that it is causing harm to other human beings in the resources extracted to create the things we consume and in the waste it produces when we throw it away. "His arrows" creates a principle of responsibility even when there is no intention of harm and even at great distances from the original act of consumption.

Lastly, Jewish environmentalism has tried to create better awareness of sustainability in Jewish liturgy and ritual practice. For example, Jewish liturgy has a large number of blessings for many different occasions: eating, celebrating, and experiencing the wonder of Creation, to name a few. Blessings and other prayers also help to create an understanding of God's ownership of Creation. When a blessing is said, a moment of holiness is created, a sacred pause. Prayer also creates an awareness of the sacred by taking people out of themselves and their artificial environments to truly encounter natural phenomena. Prayer creates a loss of control, allowing people to "see the world in the mirror of the holy," according to the twentieth-century theologian and philosopher Abraham Joshua Heschel (Tirosh-Samuelson 2002, 409). It is then possible to see the world as an object of divine concern, placing people beyond self and more deeply within Creation. Prayer also engenders a sense of gratitude for what we have and allows people to better value the things of this world.

Another important ritual aspect of Judaism that has been utilized by modern Jewish environmentalism is the Sabbath. By its restrictions of everyday work and activity and by its positive elements of prayer, rest, and celebration, the Sabbath can engender a sense of love and humility before Creation and help to foster a way to live a sustainable life. For one day out of seven, people must limit their use of resources. Traditionally people walk to attend synagogue and drive only when walking is not possible. One does not cook or shop; the day is used for relaxation and spiritual contemplation. As Rabbi Ismar Schorsch (b. 1935) once wrote, "To rest is to acknowledge our limitations. Willful inactivity is a statement of subservience to a power greater than our own" (COEJL 1994, 20).

Thus Judaism holds many traditional theological concepts, values, and actions that the modern Jewish environmental movement has connected with the value of sustainability. More and more Jewish communities and congregations are integrating these ideas into every day life and into the ritual rhythm cycle of the Jewish year and the imperatives of Jewish ethics.

Lawrence TROSTER
GreenFaith

FURTHER READING

Bernstein, Ellen. (Ed.). (1998). *Ecology & the Jewish spirit: Where nature and the sacred meet.* Woodstock, VT: Jewish Lights Publishing.

Bernstein, Ellen. (2005). Shomrei Adamah. Retrieved June 30, 2009, from http://ellenbernstein.org/about_ellen.htm#shomrei_adamah

Benstein, Jeremy. (2006). *The way into Judaism and the environment.* Woodstock, VT: Jewish Lights Publishing.

Coalition on the Environment and Jewish Life (COEJL). (1994). *To till and to tend: A guide to Jewish environmental study and action.* New York: Author.

Coalition on the Environment and Jewish Life (COEJL). (2007). Retrieved June 30, 2009, from http://www.coejl.org/~coejlor/about/history.php

Hirsch, Samson Raphael. (2002). *Horeb: A philosophy of Jewish laws and observances* (Isidore Grunfeld, Trans.) (7th ed.). London: Soncino Press.

Tal, Alon. (2002). *Pollution in a promised land: An environmental history of Israel.* Berkeley: University of California Press.

Tirosh-Samuelson, Hava. (Ed.). (2002). *Judaism and ecology: Created world and revealed word.* Cambridge, MA: Center for the Study of World Religions, Harvard Divinity School, Harvard University Press.

Yaffe, Martin D. (Ed.). (2001). *Judaism and environmental ethics: A reader.* Lanham, MD: Lexington Books.

Mormonism

Although the Church of Jesus Christ of Latter-day Saints (the Mormon Church) has not issued any official statement regarding sustainability, its sacred texts and recent institutional developments indicate a belief in divine principles that are consistent with the highest standards of sustainable living.

The Church of Jesus Christ of Latter-day Saints (also known as the Mormon or LDS Church) is a modern-revealed religion that admits the paradox of inherent, eternal value in the temporal, the corporeal, and all forms of more-than-human life. In the book of Moses, believed to be a prophetically restored account of the creation that supplements the Genesis story, the world is created spiritually before it is created physically. All things, as the LDS Church founder Joseph Smith taught, contain both spiritual and physical matter; plants and animals are "living souls" (Moses 3:9). (All scriptures cited in the article come from a three-volume set that includes *The Book of Mormon, Doctrine and Covenants,* and *Pearl of Great Price* [LDS 1983].) A belief that Earth will become heaven and that the bodies of all living things will become immortal suggests the immanence of the spiritual, not transcendence of the physical; it is a tenet that sees as holy the earthly task of sustaining all forms of life. The fall is thus fortuitous: "Adam fell that men might be; and men are, that they might have joy" (2 Nephi 2:25). Seeing the postlapsarian conditions—bringing children into the world and providing sustenance through physical suffering and labor—as blessings, not curses, has inspired Mormon economic drive

and has led in the past to an assumed obligation to have large families. Adam and Eve are told, however, that their stewardship is to work to ensure that all humankind and all of creation alike enjoy the privilege of posterity. Today, members are encouraged to plan families prayerfully, according to individual needs and inspiration.

Believers are also expected to take aesthetic pleasure in God's creations. Before Adam learns that fruits of the tree could be used for food, God intends the tree to be "pleasant to the sight of man; and man could behold it" (Moses 3:9). In a revelation to Joseph Smith, all things of the earth are given "both to please the eye and gladden the heart" (Doctrine and Covenants [D&C] 59:18). God provides for human sustenance, but human greed is kept in check by the capacity to take pleasure in natural beauty as a witness of Christ's love.

The Lord promises that there is "enough and to spare" (D&C 104:17) to feed the human family, but He is clear that it "must be done in mine own way" (D&C 104:16). This "law of consecration" involves a radical redistribution of resources so that "the poor will be exalted" and the "rich will be made low" (D&C 104:17). Key to this social aim is awareness that ownership is a merely human and secular convention. Property is made sacred by using only what is necessary for oneself and one's family and donating excess to the church welfare system (which operates without overhead costs) for redistribution to the poor in local communities and throughout the world. The sustainability of this practice, of course, would depend upon truly global and strict obedience to more modest consumption so as to lessen the ecological footprint and free up more resources for others. In the revelations of Joseph Smith, as long as natural resources are disproportionately used "the world lieth in sin. And wo[e] be unto man that sheddeth blood or that wasteth flesh and hath no need" (D&C 49:20–21).

One particularly untapped potential in Mormon practice is Joseph Smith's 1833 revelation known as the Word of Wisdom (D&C 89). Although best known for its prohibition of drugs and alcohol and strictly obeyed as such by the faithful, this dietary law instructs believers to eat a moderate and balanced diet of fruits, grains, and vegetables in season and to eat meat sparingly and to remember that God's provisions are not for man alone. With current understanding of the damaging effects of eating mass-produced meat, on both the environment and on animal life itself, and the costs of transporting food across greater distances, the need for deeper compliance to this law is becoming obvious to many believers.

Although it has made no official statement about the importance of sustainable living, the LDS Church was lauded in 2008 by the Sierra Club for its faith-based effort to create a mixed-use area, City Creek Center, as a LEED for Neighborhood Development project. (LEED is an internationally recognized green building certification system developed by the U.S. Green Building Council.) The new Church History Library meets silver LEED qualifications, and future church meetinghouses will be LEED certified. A Global Energy Management Committee also monitors and evaluates church facilities and activities worldwide. Because these efforts are not broadcast in official statements urging members to live more sustainably, they are not well known among the general membership, and the potential of LDS beliefs to promote greater sustainability is often diminished by the historically anti-environmentalist sentiment in the Intermountain West (the area in North America lying between the Rocky Mountains to the east and the Sierra Nevadas and Cascades to the west). LDS doctrines, however, are inspiring an increasing number of church members concerned about the global environmental crisis. Ad hoc developments, including the website LDS Earth Stewardship, and several recent publications, most notably *New Genesis: A Mormon Reader on Land and Community* and *Stewardship and the Creation: LDS Perspectives on Nature*, bear witness to a spirit of deeper creation care.

George B. HANDLEY
Brigham Young University

Editors' note: By listing Mormonism separately from the Christianity articles, the editors do not mean to engage in the debate about whether or not Mormonism should be considered a Christian religion. Rather, we are keeping with the organizational scheme most commonly used in academia.

FURTHER READING

Ball, Terry B.; Peck, Steven L.; & Handley, George B. (2006). *Stewardship and the creation: LDS perspectives on nature*. Provo, UT: Religious Studies Center.
Church of Jesus Christ of Latter-day Saints. (LDS). (1983). *The Book of Mormon / The Doctrine and Covenants / The Pearl of Great Price.* (3 vols.). Provo, UT: Author.
LDS Earth Stewardship. (2008, July 12). Retrieved March 21, 2009, from http://lds.earth.stewardship.googlepages.com/home
Williams, Terry Tempest; Smart, William B.; & Smith, Gibbs M. (Eds.). (1998). *New Genesis. A Mormon reader on land and community*. Layton, UT: Gibbs Smith.

19 For, behold, the beasts of the field and the fowls of the air, and that which cometh of the earth, is ordained for the use of man for food and for raiment, and that he might have in abundance.

20 But it is not given that one man should possess that which is above another, wherefore the world lieth in sin.

21 And wo[e] be unto man that sheddeth blood or that wasteth flesh and hath no need.

THE DOCTRINE AND COVENANTS 49

Source: Church of Jesus Christ of Latter-day Saints. (LDS). (1983). *The Book of Mormon / The Doctrine and Covenants / The Pearl of Great Price*. (3 vols.). Provo, UT: Author.

Shinto

Shinto, a Japanese religious tradition that emerged in prehistoric times, sees human beings, spiritual beings (kami), and nature as being harmoniously interrelated. Shinto followers, who revere this innate connection, follow rituals to communicate with the kami *manifest in living beings and natural forms or phenomena. The Shinto worldview embraces attitudes that place the world's natural environment in esteem and thus reinforce sustainable ways of living to preserve and value its resources.*

Shinto, Japan's native religion, embodies a combination of Japanese ethnic beliefs and rituals. Although Shinto has been intermittently influenced by religious traditions such as Daoism (especially the yin–yang theory), Confucianism, and Buddhism, it has developed its own worldview in which human beings, *kami* (spiritual beings), and nature are so close that "mortals, gods, and nature form a triangle of harmonious interrelationships" (Earhart 2004, 8). A discussion of the Shinto worldview, with its underlying reverence for nature and harmony, can provide perspective on the moral and ethical, philosophical, and even practical discussions of sustainability at a time when the world faces the challenge of preserving, protecting, and reestablishing the value of its natural resources.

While aspects of Shinto—such as animism, polytheism, shamanism, and syncretism—have often been emphasized as being "uniquely Japanese," they are not unique to Japan or to Shinto; rather they are characteristics of East Asian folk religion and, to a certain degree, other religions of the world. Therefore it is important to be cautious in characterizing Shinto as indigenous and unique, especially in terms of its relationship to nature.

Shinto can be divided into three types: Shrine Shinto (*jinja-shinto*), Sect Shinto (*kyoha-shinto*), and Folk Shinto (*minzoku-shinto*). Shrine Shinto has its roots in the primitive era, and today more than 80,000 shrines still exist as active places of worship. Sect Shinto has thirteen sects that were formed during the nineteenth century, and each sect conducts religious activities based on its own doctrine. Folk Shinto includes various and fragmented practices such as spirit possession, shamanistic healing, and divination based on folk beliefs in deities and spirits.

Etymology

The word *Shinto* 神道 combines two Chinese characters meaning *gods* or *spirits* and *way* or *path*, respectively, so that Shinto is often translated as "the way of the gods." When the word first appeared in Japanese history, it was used to express the system of indigenous rituals offered to the heavenly and earthly deities. The notion of such deities, or *kami*, is central to Shinto worship and pervades all aspects of Japanese culture.

The eighteenth-century thinker Motoori Norinaga created the following widely accepted definition of *kami*: "In general, *kami* refers first to the manifold *kami* of heaven and earth we see in the ancient classics, and to the spirits (*mitama*) in shrines consecrated to the same. And it further refers to all other awe-inspiring things—people of course, but also birds, beasts, grass and trees, even the ocean and mountains—which possess superlative power

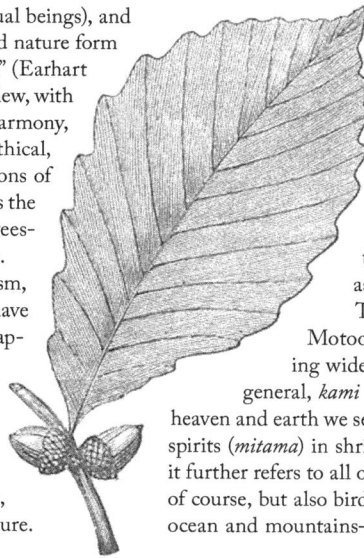

not normally found in this world. 'Superlative' here means not only superlative in nobility, goodness, or virility, since things which are evil and weird as well, if they inspire unusual awe, are also called *kami*" (Motoori 1968, 125).

Since the preliterate period the notion of *kami* has been connected with at least two meanings: the spirits of the dead and the awe-inspiring aspects of nature. While the former meaning emphasizes the closeness of human beings and *kami*, the latter meaning indicates the interrelatedness of nature and *kami*, on the one hand, and nature and human beings, on the other.

Kami in Nature

In *An Encyclopedia of Shinto* (Havens and Inoue, 2001–2006), *kami* is classified by two main categories: culture *kami* and nature *kami*. The culture *kami* can be further divided into three subcategories: (1) community *kami* worshiped by particular social groups, (2) functional *kami* related to special aspects in human life, and (3) human *kami* for historical human beings worshiped as *kami*.

The category of nature *kami* is a recognition of the "abnormal" powers or features of nature, and it can be further divided into two subcategories: celestial *kami* and terrestrial *kami*. As deified heavenly bodies and meteorological phenomena, celestial *kami* include the sun, moon, and planets, as well as wind and thunder. Terrestrial *kami* are composed of geological forms, physical processes, and plants and animals, including earth, mountains, forests, rocks, sea, rivers, islands, pine, cedar, cypress, snakes, deer, wild boar, wolves, bears, monkeys, foxes, rabbits, crows, and doves. Animal *kami* are often associated with the *kami* of natural physical phenomena and identified as the manifestations of such *kami*, while plant *kami* are often so impressive that they are easily connected with "abnormal" power.

Dwelling within natural objects or through natural phenomena and impressing human beings with a sense of awe, *kami* make humans feel the existence of extraordinary power. In other words, *kami* remain unrevealed without manifesting themselves by dwelling in natural objects. Thus, *kami* present themselves in concrete forms but not in abstract or conceptual forms. Sonoda Minoru indicates that what evokes awe "as it is" (*onozukara*) comes to be revered as *kami* (Sonoda, 2000). For instance, the spirit of the rice grain (*kokurei*) is one of the most important *kami* because it is the source of life for both the divine and human realms. Likewise, as the prayers recorded in the *Engi shiki* (*Procedures of the Engi Era*, 927 CE) show, the ancient Yamato court executed special festivals for the *kami* protecting paddy fields, the *kami* of forests and water, and the *kami* of water sources. The *Hitachi-kuni fudoki* (*Official Report from the Government Office of Hitachi Province*, eighth century CE)

tells stories in which the people of antiquity regarded wild animals such as snakes as *kami* and worshiped them when they reclaimed rice fields.

As modern linguistics suggests, the word *kami* is related to *kuma* (corner, nook) and *kumu* (to hide) and originally referred to the spiritual quality of the mountains and valleys that were the sources of water. The people of mountainous Japan have thus revered the spirituality hiding in the forests and mountains as *kami*, and they have transformed the landscape into a living cosmos in which human beings, *kami*, and nature are interrelated harmoniously.

Plurality of *Kami*

This harmony might have originated from a Japanese cosmogony in which there is no creator god but rather a plurality of *kami* coming into existence one after another generated by other *kami*. According to Japanese mythology as narrated in two important sources of Shinto theology, the *Kojiki* (*Records of Ancient Matters*, 712 CE) and the *Nihon shoki* (also known as *Nihongi*, *Chronicles of Japan*, 720 CE), natural phenomena are themselves the offspring of *kami*. This is apparent especially in the myth about the divine couple Izanagi and Izanami, who came together to give birth to the eight islands of Japan and the various other *kami*. It may be worth contrasting the procreation described in this ancient Japanese myth (the cosmogony of generation) to the Judeo-Christian cosmogony of creation. The cosmogony of generation, as expressed in the *Kojiki* and *Nihon shoki*, puts special emphasis on the notion of *musuhi* (the generative force), which is innate in all beings, while the cosmogony of creation is based on the notion of God as the single Creator, the transcendent origin of creation.

The Japanese myth also illustrates the proliferation of *kami* closely related to the people and the land. The fact that *kami* are collectively called *yaoyorozu no kami* (8 million *kami*) denotes a polytheistic world of *kami*. This polytheistic character of Shinto has never been lost, although the Shinto doctrine of the *kami's* oneness was developed through medieval and early modern times in conjunction with Buddhism and neo-Confucianism.

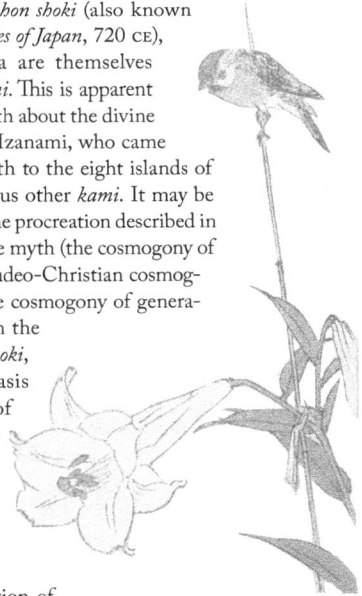

Shrine and Forest

Considering the intimacy between *kami* and nature (especially mountains and woods), it is not surprising that most Shinto shrines are built in forests. The ancient shrines (*jinja*) were often objects of nature such as a grove or a wooded hill (*moriyama*). The fact that the characters for *jinja* 神社 are also read as *mori* (grove) shows that Shinto shrines were originally sacred groves or forests inhabited by *kami*.

According to a myth recorded in the *Nihon shoki*, the wind god Susanowo, a violent and unpredictable deity but also a cultural hero, created trees (cedar, cypress, and camphor, for instance) from his own bodily hair and taught his children how best to use the various types of wood. In addition, he made his children sow the seeds that changed the Japanese islands into a land of green forests. This myth shows the special interest the ancient Japanese paid to the cultivation and preservation of forests. From the ancient to the early modern period, the authorities and local rulers treated Shinto shrines and their forests with respect and consequently protected them.

Shinto and Rice

Shinto has also been connected with rice. The deep ethnic significance that rice has for most Japanese makes it an indispensable element of Shinto. Rice and *sake* (rice wine) are typical offerings to a Shinto altar. The sacred rope (*shimenawa*) that marks the border of a shrine or signifies the presence of *kami* is commonly made from rice straw. Planting seedlings and eating the annual harvest are important formal rituals of the emperor. The origins of Shinto can be traced to the middle of the first millennium BCE, when hydraulic rice agriculture was first established in Japan.

The *Kojiki* and *Nihon shoki* recount myths about the killing of female Earth deities, whose dead bodies produced rice and other precious crops. These Hainuwele-type myths—referring to the Wemale (Indonesian) creation myth in which the sacrifice of the maiden Hainuwele, herself a "product" of mingling human blood and the sap of a coconut branch, resulted in the growth of tuberous plants that became a staple of the Wemale diet—indicate that agriculture allowed human beings to render their societies autonomous from the natural environment and produce new environments in which humans exercised some control. The rice rituals in Shinto show that Japanese society construes a religious cosmos through cultivating nature and transforming it into a living landscape, which symbolizes the inherent relationship between Shinto and the environments of the Japanese archipelago.

Japanese View of Nature

This inherent relationship also can be seen in the Shinto festivals (*matsuri*) such as the spring festival, in which the *yama no kami* (mountain *kami*), widely regarded as ancestral *kami*, descend to the village as the *ta no kami* (*kami* of the rice paddy) to assist people in rice cultivation and production, and the autumn festival, in which the *ta no kami* return to the mountain following the harvest and reassume the role of *yama no kami*. As seen in these examples, generation and rebirth are naturally linked with the annual cycle of planting and harvesting. This view of nature and soul easily leads to the concept of the immanent nature of human beings, who have been strengthened by their sensitivity to the transitory aspects of both nature and mortals. Thus, exorcism and purification rites to drive out "pollution (*kegare*)," which are essential to Shinto, can be considered to be the way of reestablishing order and balance among *kami*, human beings, and nature.

If an animistic view of nature can be implied in the expression "nature of life" (nature is full of life) and a pantheistic notion of nature can be implied in the expression "life of nature" (all nature can be seen as one holistic life), the worldview of Japanese people can be seen to be composed of two distinct dimensions, penetrating into each other from the ancient times to the present. The mythical and religious representations of nature in Japanese culture mentioned above have formed the Japanese concept of nature. The Japanese see nature as something that always contains harmony or order. Every natural thing—mountains and rivers, rocks and trees, thunders and flowers, winds and insects—can be seen as living *kami*, which altogether compose the harmonious cosmos.

Shinto, as well as other religious traditions in Japan, has traditionally seen nature as immanently divine and, as a result, has considered the correspondence between external beauty and internal equilibrium as self-evident. Regarding nature as divine and sacred, the Japanese people have not considered nature as inferior or in opposition to human beings. They have preferred to live embedded in nature by participating in modes of expression and ritual such as flower arrangement, the tea ceremony, literati art works, and Zen painting, all of which adapt or represent some element of the natural. Nature, then, as religiously and aesthetically signified in Japanese history, is a kind of abstraction of an idealized world including human beings as well as *kami*.

It is ironic that the Japanese people, who have long been known for their "love of nature," have had to witness (and some have been to one degree or another responsible for) the destruction of nature in modern times. After the fall of the Tokugawa shogunate (1600/1603–1868), a period in which Buddhism and neo-Confucianism were favored, the Meiji government (1868–1912) intended to use Shinto as a state-sponsored religion that would both unify the new nation-state and reestablish symbolic power of the emperor. Under the strict control of the government over a limited number of "government shrines," and many other local shrines were destroyed. More drastic were changes after the end of World War II in 1945, when the rapid industrialization and urbanization transformed the life of local communities. On the other hand, shrines were to become endangered as postwar land reform required that many shrine buildings be used for other purposes, such as schools.

After the severe environmental destruction during the rapid economic growth from the 1960s to 1980s, however, the religious cosmologies of shrine forests and *kami* mountains based on animistic world view came to be revaluated. As a result, more and more people in and out of Japan are focusing on the potentiality of Shinto as an "ecological religion."

Yotaro MIYAMOTO
Kansai University

FURTHER READING

Asquite, Pamela J., & Kalland, Arne. (Eds.). (1997). *Japanese images of nature: Cultural perspectives*. Richmond, U.K.: Curzon Press.
Breen, John, & Teeuwen, Mark. (Eds.). (2000). *Shinto in history: Ways of the kami*. Honolulu: University of Hawaii Press.
Brinkman, John T. (1996). *Simplicity: A distinctive quality of Japanese spirituality*. New York: Peter Lang.
Earhart, H. Byron. (2004). *Japanese religion: Unity and diversity*. (4th ed.). Belmont, CA: Thomson/Wadsworth.
Ellwood, Robert. (2008). *Introducing Japanese religion*. New York: Routledge.
Hartz, Paula R. (2004). *Shinto*. (Updated ed.). New York: Facts On File.
Havens, Norman, & Inoue Nobutaka. (Eds.). (2001–2006). *An encyclopedia of Shinto*. 3 Vols. Tokyo: Institute for Japanese Culture and Classics, Kokugakuin University.
Inoue Nobutaka. (Ed.). (2003). *Shinto: A short history*. New York: Routledge Curzon.
Kamata Toji. (2000). *Shinto towa nanika: Shizen no reisei wo kanjite ikiru*. [What is Shinto?: To live feeling the spirituality of nature.] Tokyo: PHP Kenkyusho.
Kasulis, Thomas. (2004). *Shinto: The way home*. Honolulu: University of Hawaii Press.
Miyake Hitoshi. (1995). Nihon no minzoku shukyo ni okeru sizen-kan. [The idea of nature in Japanese folk religion.] *Shukyo Kenkyu [Journal of Religious Studies]*, 69(1).
Motoori Norinaga. (1968). *Kojikiden, Vol 1*. [The complete works of Motoori Norinaga, (9 vols.)]. Tokyo: Chikuma-shobo.
Nelson, John K. (2000). *Enduring identities: The guise of Shinto in contemporary Japan*. Honolulu: University of Hawaii Press.
Sonoda Minoru. (1987). The religious situation in Japan in relation to Shinto. *Acta Asiatica, 51*.
Sonoda Minoru. (1995). Shizen fudo to shukyo bunka. [The religious nature of a social-ecological system.] *Shukyo Kenkyu [Journal of Religious Studies]*, 69(1).
Sonoda Minoru. (2000). Shinto and the natural environment. In John Breen & Mark Teeuwen (Eds.), *Shinto in History: Ways of the Kami*. Honolulu: University of Hawaii Press.
Sonoda Minoru. (2005). *Bunka to shiteno Shinto*. [Shinto as a culture.] Tokyo: Kobundo.
Sonoda Minoru. (Ed.). (1988). *Shinto: Nihon no minzoku shukyo*. [Shinto: Ethnic religion of Japan.] Tokyo: Kobundo.
Ueda Kenji. (1991). *Shinto shingaku ronko*. [Consideration on Shinto theology.] Tokyo: Daimeido.

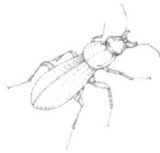

Sikhism

The beliefs of Sikhism lend themselves to ecological thinking: creation is a manifestation of the divine, and humanity must learn to live in harmony with it all. Ecological awareness has intensified since the 1990s; among other efforts, Sikh environmentalists and global organizations have collaborated on faith-based plans for a Sikh response to the environmental crisis.

The word *Sikh* means something like "learner of truth." Sikhism emerged in fifteenth century Punjab with the Sikh guru Nanak; ten other gurus have followed him. Guru Nanak considered himself neither Muslim nor Hindu—though influenced by both traditions—and often preached against religious intolerance. According to Guru Granth Sahib, the Sikh scripture that contains the sayings of Guru Nanak and the other ten Sikh gurus, all of creation is a manifestation of God. Because of this belief, there are many who argue that Sikhism is inherently ecosophical, that is, divine wisdom pervades all of creation and humans ought to live in harmony with creation. Humans are the "god-conscious" beings of the Earth, and human spiritual discipline should be aimed at living in harmony with the rest of God's creation, which means following God's *hukam* (or commandments). These commandments are collected together in the Rehat Maryada, or the Sikh Code of Conduct. One such commandment with environmental implications surrounds the *langar*, a community kitchen that serves a free meal, usually vegetarian, in the *gurdwara* (house of worship) every day. This meal sharing is an opportunity not only to recognize interdependence with all other humans—no one is turned away from the meal—but also one's nourishment from the rest of God's creation.

Contemporary Sikh environmentalism can be traced to Bhagat Puran Singh Ji (1904–1992), the "Mother Teresa" of Sikhism, who devoted his live to alleviating the suffering of humanity. In addition to his service to terminally ill and crippled peoples of Punjab, he also wrote and spoke about the dangers of soil erosion and environmental pollution, making connections between sick people and a "sick" environment.

More recently, in 1999, Sikh communities around the world gathered to celebrate the beginning of the current three-hundred-year cycle and named it the Cycle of Creation (Sikhism measures time in cycles of three hundred years). This cycle will focus upon Sikh relationships to the natural world.

As a result of this, there are now many groups of Sikhs coming together in organizations to address environmental issues. EcoSikh, one such organization, was developed through a collaboration of Sikh environmentalists, the Sikh Council on Religion and Education (SCORE), the Alliance of Religions and Conservation (ARC), and the United Nations Development Programme (UNDP) to address five key areas of Sikh environmentalism: assets, education, media and advocacy, eco-twinning, and celebration. The *Guide to Creating Your EcoSikh 5-Year Plan: Generational Changes for a Living Planet* (ARC, SCORE, & UNDP 2009), outlines actions Sikh communities can adopt to protect the environment. As well as encouraging awareness of resources and promoting environmental efforts such as the greening of the *langar*, they propose the concept of "eco-twinning." In its broadest sense, "twinning" refers to the affiliation of two groups

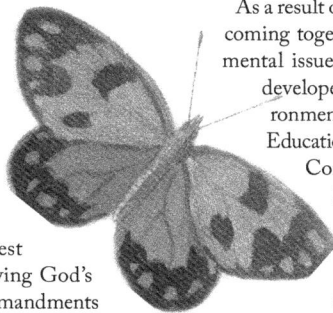

with shared characteristics to reach a common goal; eco-twinning provides pairings of *gurdwaras* in south Asia with others around the world, especially in first world countries, with the idea that these sister communities focus on environmental problems specific to their location and support one another through financial and educational means. Because many environmental issues are global in perspective, this will help groups uncover their planetary relations.

Though scholarship on Sikhism and ecology is sparse, some writing does exist. No doubt this scholarship will grow as the global Sikh community (some 23 million strong) continues to focus on the Cycle of Creation, and as the wider Earth community recognizes the beneficial implications of a Sikh ecospirituality.

Whitney A. BAUMAN
Florida International University

FURTHER READING

Alliance of Religions and Conservation (ARC). (n.d.) ARC and the faiths. Retrieved July 7, 2009, from http://www.arcworld.org/faiths.htm

Alliance of Religions and Conservation (ARC); Sikh Council on Religion and Education (SCORE); & United Nations Development Programme (UNDP). (2009, June 22). *Guide to creating your EcoSikh 5-year plan: Generational changes for a living planet.* Retrieved July 9, 2009, from http://ecosikh.org/wp-content/uploads/2009/06/EcoSikhPlansforGenerationalChangeGuidebook.pdf

Dwivedi, O. P. (1989). *World religions and the environment.* New Delhi: Gitanjali Publishing House.

EcoSikh. (2009). Retrieved July 7, 2009, from http://ecosikh.org

Lourdunathan, S. (2002, September). Ecosophical concerns in the Sikh tradition. Retrieved July 9, 2009, from http://www.sikhspectrum.com/092002/eco.htm

Narayan, Rajdeva, & Kumar, Janardan. (Eds.). (2003). *Ecology and religion: Ecological concepts in Hinduism, Buddhism, Jainism, Islam, Christianity, and Sikhism.* New Delhi: Deep & Deep Publishers.

Singh, David Emmanuel. (Ed.). (1998). *Spiritual traditions: Essential visions for living.* Bangalore, India: United Theological College.

A NEW BATTLE FOR SIKHISM: THE ENVIRONMENT

Since the fifteenth century, and throughout Sikhism's embattled history in India, concern for the environment has been an inherent part of the Sikh belief in creation as a manifestation of the divine. In the late 1990s, Sikhs began to address contemporary environmental concerns, mobilizing to fight for the restoration of Earth's resources. Martin Palmer, the current Secretary General of the Alliance of Religions and Conservation (ARC) describes how the Sikh tradition of measuring time helped shape this turn of events.

In Sikhism, time is measured in 300-year cycles. In 1999 Sikhs moved into their third such cycle. The first two cycles had been named as they began, and although the names were inspired by events just before each new cycle, they also shaped the spirit of that cycle. For example, the years between 1699 and 1999 were called the "Cycle of the Sword," because in the late seventeenth century the Sikhs were fighting for their lives against the Mughal Emperors who had invaded India; the Sikhs decided to fight back not just for themselves, but to protect all the weak and vulnerable. The Cycle of the Sword ended with a terrible civil war in the Punjab, when Sikh militants sought to create a separate state and the Indian government crushed them.

As they approached 1999, the Sikh leaders wanted a very different theme for the next 300 years. At the time ARC [Alliance of Religion and Conservation] was working very closely with the Sikhs on developing land management and alternative energy schemes. Through our discussions, the idea arose of naming the new cycle the "Cycle of the Environment" or the "Cycle of Creation." [The Cycle of Creation] was agreed [upon] by the whole community and now the Sikhs have made a 300-year commitment to focus on the environment. What does this really mean? Well, one early benefit is that many Sikh temples now hand out tree saplings as a sign of blessing to worshippers instead of a sticky sweet. It is estimated that 10 million saplings are being distributed every year, making up the woodlands and gardens of the future. Religions can make commitments like this because they think in the long, long term and have the experience of having done so for a long, long time.

Source: Martin Palmer with Victoria Finlay. (2003). *Faith in Conservation: New Approaches to Religions and the Environment*, pp. 30–31. Washington, DC: The World Bank.

Unitarianism and Unitarian Universalism

Founded in Hungary in the sixteenth century, Unitarianism focuses on reason, rational thought, science, and philosophy. Unitarian ecological theologies have begun to develop in Europe. In the United States, Unitarianism has mostly avoided environmentalism, but Unitarian Universalists have developed a theology of humans in relation to the environment, and promote respect for the "interdependent web of all existence" in their guiding principles.

Unitarianism, founded by Ferenc Dávid in Hungary during the Protestant Reformation of the sixteenth century, spread around the world and has a small following in the United States. Its theology differs from many mainstream Protestant Christian denominations in that Unitarianism does not believe in the idea of the Trinity or the divinity of Jesus. Unitarianism professes beliefs in reason, rational thought, science, and philosophy.

Unitarianism took hold in the northeastern United States in the eighteenth century. One of the most famous and revered Unitarians is Ralph Waldo Emerson, who wrote the book *Nature* in 1836. Emerson's work places him among the distinguished group of early environmental philosophers in the United States.

The American Unitarian Church merged with the Universalist Church of America in 1961 to form the Unitarian Universalist Church, with headquarters in Boston, Massachusetts. Unitarians and Unitarian Universalists consider themselves as belonging to two different denominations, although there is an overlap in membership. Within the United States, Unitarian Universalists are greater in number.

Unitarian Universalists have developed a theology of the human in relationship to the environment conveyed by the Seven Principles of Unitarian Universalists. The seventh principle, "respect for the interdependent web of all existence of which we are a part," embodies concern for the ecosystem; the principle has become the basis for the Unitarian Universalist (UU) environmental theology. UUs also developed a practical "green" certification program for their congregations in the United States in 2002. This accreditation process requires that congregations and sanctuaries provide ecology-based worship and religious education, and demonstrate a focus on environmental justice and sustainable living. More than fifty-nine Unitarian Universalist congregations have been accredited as "Green Sanctuaries" since the implementation of this program.

Unitarianism, on the other hand, has a lesser known environmental theology, despite Ralph Waldo Emerson's contribution. For example, ecology and the environment are not part of the American Unitarian Conference principles. In fact, in the 1990s, several Unitarian theologians expressed concern that the Unitarian Church not take on the environment as an issue for fear that it would dilute the theology into secularist beliefs.

Outside the United States, Unitarianism is a liberal religious movement with a significant presence. Members of the International Council of Unitarians and Universalists, a network of organizations joining Unitarians, Universalists, and Unitarian Universalists, can be found in many European countries including Ireland, United Kingdom, and Hungary, as well as in Australia, New Zealand, South Africa, and Canada. In Europe, Unitarians have begun to develop ecological theologies. Several theologians reflected on the human theological connection to nature

in "Unitarian Views of Earth and Nature," the 1994 publication of the Unitarian Headquarters in London. In the United Kingdom, Unitarians formed the Unitarian Earth Spirit Network in 1990 to address the need to support those who wanted to develop an ecological theology and practice. Beliefs of this network include: (1) revering the totality of the divine reality of nature that is revealed to us through the infinite multiplicity of forms and forces; (2) evolving creative ways of worship for body, mind, and spirit; (3) affirming a Pagan spiritual perspective as being fully compatible with the human quest for self-knowledge and ultimate meaning; and (4) encouraging ways of practical action on social issues which are directly related to a nature-centered faith and philosophy. Today, the Unitarian Earth Spirit Network is connected to the Unitarian Universalist Covenant of Unitarian Universalist Pagans based in the United States.

Future sustainability discussions will inevitably benefit by including the voices of Unitarians around the globe, who continue to call for development of ecological theology, and the Unitarian Universalists, whose guiding principle is to promote respect for the "interdependent web of all existence."

Eileen M. HARRINGTON
University of San Francisco

FURTHER READING

American Unitarian Conference. (2007). Retrieved May 8, 2009, from http://www.americanunitarian.org/

Dorris, Robert E. (2007). *A Unitarian perspective*. Frederick, MD: PublishAmerica.

Palmer, Joy A. (Ed.). (2001). *Fifty key thinkers on the environment*. London: Routledge.

Small, Fred. (2009). Ecology, justice, and compassion. Retrieved July 13, 2009, from http://www.uua.org/visitors/uuperspectives/59580. shtml?time010

Tomek, Vladimir. (2008). Environmental concerns: Unitarian responses. Retrieved May 8, 2009, from http://www.religioustolerance.org/ tomek12.htm

Unitarian Earth Spirit Network. (2009). Retrieved May 8, 2009, from http://www.unitariansocieties.org.uk/earthspirit/index

Unitarian Universalist Association of Congregations. (2009). Retrieved May 8, 2009, from http://www.uua.org/

Nature Spiritualities

Concepts of "nature" are critical to discussions about sustainability. The term's many meanings, images, and uses shape various senses of humanity's moral place in the world. Imagining sustainability may require new ways of looking at nature, including non-Western models that do not separate humanity from the rest of nature.

Nature is an encompassing, elusive, and malleable concept, bearing various meanings across and within cultures. Indeed, it bears so many linguistic uses and such interpretive complexity that defining nature seems impossible—certainly so within an encyclopedia article. But that very complexity makes "nature" an unavoidable dimension of the moral imagination and an important concept of analysis for understanding the discourses of sustainability.

Especially in Western cultures, nature often serves to identify and separate the categories of human, cultural, artificial, and technological. In Western religious worldviews, the natural may stand in contrast to the spiritual, supernatural, or transcendent. In ethics, nature has sometimes denoted a premoral realm of existence, which human agents then overlay with value or invest with purpose. In each of these cases, nature has often been defined or used as that which stands other to humanity and its projects.

Some critics have therefore argued that the concept of nature stands as an accomplice to dualisms that separate humanity from Earth, and cultural from ecological systems. When used as a contrastive concept, it allows persons and cultures to individuate themselves from the surrounding living world and often to hold themselves superior to it. So the very concept of nature, or at least the way it has been typically deployed

in the Western world, may create attitudes that allow the degradation of the Earth and the alienation of humanity.

Many critics have therefore argued that the path to sustainability must include different ways of perceiving nature, alternative metaphors of the natural, and more apt uses for its interpretive function. Some propose to re-enchant nature, finding value, authenticity, or sacredness in the living world. Others wish to subvert nature/culture binaries by including social and religious worlds within an ecological context or by tracing the pervasive presence of natural forces or ecological agencies though every human system. Still others would keep nature as a contrastive concept precisely in order to underscore human responsibility for natural systems and the nonhuman world. For insofar as it is a ward of human powers, societies have stewardship obligations for nature.

These alternative proposals have drawn increased attention to conceptual uses of nature that do not produce so sharp a contrast with the human, cultural, or spiritual. Nature might be, for example, the encompassing world within which humans and other animals or spirits appear. It might name the divine, or the generative ground of life, or the structure of existence. In some non-Western, indigenous, and traditional worldviews, nature concepts appear in stories that privilege a reflexive, inextricable relation among humans and the nonhuman, divine, or extrahuman.

Within ethics, some concept of nature often functions normatively to support a framework of moral agency. Nature might provide grounding principles and values, or, on the other hand, it might be that which moral agency must control, transform, and overcome. It is sometimes used synonymously with "human nature," and then alternatively referring to embodiment, rationality, or will. It may refer to conative goods of any living being, as well as

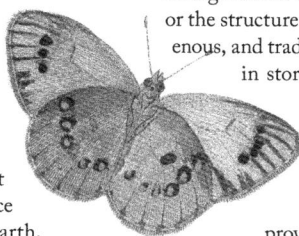

ambivalent desires and tendencies to evil. Despite the variety, in each case the concept of nature supports and helps regulate a moral framework that orients an agent's decisions and actions.

Nature's normative function within a system of ethics therefore corresponds to background worldviews, practical projects, and discursive systems. Those worldviews and the everyday uses of the concept define what nature means for humanity's self-understanding; they orient humanity to its own embodied existence and to Earth as a moral field. They also regulate the way nature matters for ethics by establishing nature's relative priority over other normative criteria (for example, reason, law, scriptures, tradition, and common good).

Views of sustainability usually include some implicit notion of nature and how it matters for moral agency. Describing and evaluating those notions presents a central interpretive task for cultural critics. Simply illuminating the many meanings, metaphors, and uses of nature at work in public discussion might do much for clarifying debates over sustainability.

Willis JENKINS
Yale Divinity School

FURTHER READING

Cronon, William. (Ed.). (1996). *Uncommon ground: Rethinking the human place in nature.* New York: W. W. Norton.

Evernden, Neil. (1992). *The social creation of nature.* Baltimore: Johns Hopkins University Press.

Rolston, Holmes, III. (1994). *Conserving natural value.* New York: Columbia University Press.

Worster, Donald. (1994). *Nature's economy: A history of ecological ideas.* Cambridge, U.K.: Cambridge University Press.

ON NEEDING NATURE

In the following passage from Conserving Natural Value, *philosopher and environmental ethicist Holmes Rolston III writes of the importance and meaning of nature in our modern lives.*

Americans sing "America the Beautiful," glad for purple mountains' majesties and the fruited plains stretching from sea to shining sea. People on the frontier found that they had no sooner conquered a wilderness than they had come to love the land on which they settled. As sung in the musical *Oklahoma[!]*, "We know we belong to the land, and the land we belong to is grand." Of those drawn to the city for livelihood or commodities, many really prefer to live in the "suburbs," so as to remain also near the country, in some place not consummately urban but where there is more green than anything else, where, with the neighbors, there are fencerows and cardinals, dogwoods and rabbits. We cherish our hills of home, our rivers, our bays, our country drives. Real estate agents term these "amenities" with our "commodities," but this is really nature mixed in with our culture. We want greenbelts in cities, mountains on the skyline, parks, seashores and lakeshores, spits, headlands, islands, forests, even wildernesses, including deserts, tundra, and swamps to visit. Most people identify with some countryside; indeed, our affections toward the city are often exceeded by those we have toward the landscapes on which we were reared.

Source: Holmes Rolston III. (1994). *Conserving Natural Value,* pp. 9–10. New York: Columbia University Press.

Nature Religions and Animism

Nature religions see the cosmos as a set of interrelationships among beings, human and other-than-human. The Ojibwa worldview, which accepts that even stones can enter into relationships and are thus beings, is an example of animism. Interpretations of nature religion, by observers and participants, lead to differing views of the extent to which humans must change if the world is to be sustained.

The term "nature religions" attempts to categorize an amorphous array of religious movements in which the core or focus is the celebration of nature or which consider nature sacred. Highlighting this concern with nature is useful only in the context of identifying other religions as deity-focused or self-focused. For example, the participants in monotheistic religions typically attempt to adjust their lifestyles, desires, hopes, and antipathies to those associated with their deity. Teachings derived from the deity are fundamental. What is important in self-religions, such as New Age, is the progressive enhancement of self-knowledge and personal well-being. Everything can be a tool to enable practitioners to realize their true potential. By contrast with these trends, the term "nature religions" identifies a shared perception that humans (groups or individuals) are bound up in the wider context of the living world or cosmos. This context is often defined as a communal or relational one: the world is alive with beings that call upon one another to live harmoniously. People are invited to adjust their lives to engage respectfully. Nature religions implicitly and sometimes explicitly challenge any notion that humans are separate from, let alone better than, any other beings. Some nature religions might encourage a reversal of the prevalent modern privileging of humanity over all other existences, suggesting and even insisting that the diminishment of human presence or activity would benefit the rest of life. Most commonly, nature religions are about participation and entail quests for locally meaningful forms of belonging, engagement, relationship, and harmony.

It is vital to note that "nature" in this term is a multivalent and resonant word. It can refer to a notion that authenticity, beauty, and truth are best, or only, found "out there" beyond the cities, in rural or even wilderness domains. This is usually romantic, even when it results in radical activism, because it requires a dualistic separation between human culture and other-than-human nature, and imagines "wilderness" as pristine ecosystems (unaffected by humanity) rather than as the result of human activities as diverse as hunter-gathering and genocidal clearance of previous human populations. "Nature" can also act as a reference to the entire larger living world or cosmos, usually stressing the value of all beings and communities. This "nature" is inclusive of humanity and its varied habitats, urban, rural, permanent, transient and so on. One element of the "religious" contribution to "nature religion," however, is indicated by a call to treat the world as sacred—as worthy of veneration, respect, care, responsible and sustainable relationality—in its own right. Nature religions' ethical imperative involves limiting human rights to treat the world as a resource or utility principally for human benefit. The sanctity of the world in nature religions is not best seen in the setting apart of some places, persons, or acts as being more-than or separable from others. Rather, sacrality is observable in the deliberate setting of limits on human acts, constructions, desires, and expansionism.

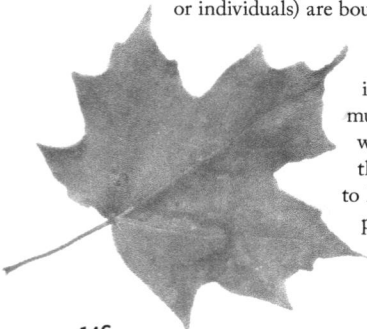

Some nature religionists may equally indicate that there are, or should be, limits on the activities and expansive presence of other species or individuals. But the recognition that humanity is almost uniquely capable and responsible for such massive changes in the dynamic ecosystems that together form the world reinforces the invitation to self-limitation in human ambitions or possibilities.

"Nature religions" is an umbrella term—expansive and deserving of considerable contest or debate. It can embrace the various new, self-identified Pagan traditions of Druidry, Wicca, and Heathenry; various "ethnic" reconstructions (Norse, Lithuanian, Hellenic and other traditions); and various other eclectic variations on the theme of developing contemporary Earth-respecting spiritual practices. It can also embrace many if not all indigenous religious traditions. The term is heuristically useful as it points to a difference from religions that privilege transcendent realities but should not be taken to mean that those so labeled have a Western-style notion of "nature" or a culture/nature dualism.

Should Human Behavior Change?

It is also noteworthy that both "nature" and "nature religion" have been valued in dramatically differing ways among observers and participants. In recent decades both terms have been increasingly positively evaluated, but they can be contrasted negatively both with divine and human authority and centrality. These shifting evaluations are admirably surveyed and discussed by the historian of religion Catherine Albanese and the environmental and social ethicist Bron Taylor. In brief, those committed to the (distinct) views that humans are the pinnacle of evolution or the stewards of God's creation often hold that removing humanity from the center of attention is naïve or wrong, and that the world will not benefit from radical changes in human usage. Nature religionists usually disagree and insist that there is an urgent need to alter human behaviors for the benefit both of humans and the world.

Exactly how much change is required, how change might be achieved, and whose benefit takes priority, are among the issues that divide nature religionists (and others) along allegedly "deep green" and "light (or shallow) green" lines. The darkest green elements (as Taylor discusses) evidence what some perceive to be a sinister, anti-human tendency and frequently insist that for life to flourish human well-being must be treated as irrelevant. For some (extreme) eco-activists, such as some Earth First!

activists, any thoughts about what should be sustained must focus on the nonhuman majority of the world. Self-identified "deep green" nature religion is manifest in ritual and meditative attempts by humans to "think like" and act on behalf of other-than-human beings. Usually this results in efforts to mitigate the worst effects of human separatism while seeking the well-being of other species whose lives might, after all, enrich those of humanity. Meanwhile, "light/shallow green" ecology (usually a label applied by others) involves environmentalism on behalf of species or ecosystems that are or may be necessary for human sustenance. Rainforests, for example, are to be saved in the hope that cancer cures will be found or because of their role as carbon sinks and oxygen producers. Dark, deep, and shallow green movements and individuals share similar religious acts, especially in ritual and meditation, even as they are differentiated along activist or putatively political lines.

Animism

Within these broader trends, the term "animism" has been gaining ground both among academic observers and among nature religion practitioners. It was once associated mainly with the theory of religion proposed by Edward Tylor (1832–1917), the first professor of anthropology at Oxford University. In his two-volume *Primitive Culture* (1871) he argued that religion is "a belief in souls and spirits," explaining that this was an ancient but still prevalent mistake that falsely appears to explain some common experiences. If someone dreams of meeting a deceased relative, or has a feverish vision of distant places, they may think that this means that people possess spirits that survive death and souls that can separate from bodies to gain knowledge unobtainable by the normal senses. Tylor was certain that religion—this mistaken animation of the world by souls and spirits—would fade away in the face of modern science as it demonstrated the superiority of human rationality and technology. This understanding of animism was rapidly challenged and is now largely cited only as an example of early anthropological theorizing. It can only contribute to nature religions and debates about sustainability by suggesting that some people value elements of the world for nonempirical or spiritual reasons rather than valuing physical existences (matter of any kind) for any intrinsic reason.

Animism is of far more importance when the term is used in a quite different way. Firstly, the word began to be used by those who wanted a term to encapsulate their sense that the world is a community of living beings, only some of

whom are human. The world is animated, hence "animism" might usefully label varieties of nature-centered worldviews and lifeways. Secondly, scholars studying among various indigenous peoples and among contemporary, self-identified eco-activist Pagans have also found the term to be valuable. They frequently cite the work of Irving Hallowell and what he learned among the Ojibwa of Berens River in southern central Canada.

Animism and the Ojibwa

Animism is intrinsic to Ojibwa grammar, casual and deliberate discourse, and relationality as people seek to learn and perform appropriate and sustainable ways of behaving in the larger-than-human community. In the Ojibwa language (and that of all Algonkian nations) a grammatical distinction is made between animate and inanimate genders but not among masculine, feminine, and neuter genders. A suffix is added to nouns that refer to animate persons rather than inanimate objects. Verbs indicating the actions of animate persons differ from those referring to acts done to inanimate objects. For example, the researchers John Nichols and Earl Nyholm report that in the Minnesota Ojibwa dialect the plural form of the word *asin* (stone) is *asiniig*, identifying stones as grammatically animate. The question arises, is this *just* a grammatical oddity (somewhat like the French reference to tables *as if* they were female)? Do the Ojibwa treat grammatically animate stones as animate persons? Do they speak with stones or act in other ways that reveal intentions to build or maintain relationships? Irving Hallowell asked an old Ojibwa man, "Are *all* the stones we see about us here alive?" The old man answered, "No! but *some* are" (1960, 24). He had witnessed a particular stone following the leader of a shamanic ceremony around a tent as he sang. Another powerful leader is said to have had a large stone that would open when he tapped it three times, allowing him to remove a small bag of herbs when he needed it in ceremonies. Hallowell was told that when a white trader was digging his potato patch he found a stone that looked like it might have been important. He called for the leader of another ceremony who knelt down to talk to the stone, asking if it had come from someone's ceremonial tent. The stone is said to have denied this. Movement, gift-giving, and conversation are three indicators of the animate nature of relational beings, or persons.

Hallowell makes it clear that the key point is not that stones do things of their own volition (however remarkable this claim might seem) but that they engage in relationships. For the Ojibwa the interesting question is not, in fact, "how do we know stones are alive?" but "what is the appropriate way for people (of whatever species) to relate?" This is as true for humans as it is for stones, trees, animals, birds, fish, and all other beings that might be recognized as persons. Persons are known to be persons when they relate to other persons in particular ways. They might act more or less intimately, willingly, or respectfully. Since enmity is also a relationship, they might act aggressively. The "person" category is only applicable when beings are relating with others. This is quite different from the understanding of ontology in most European-derived cultures, in which personhood is an interior quality, a fact about the self-consciousness of individual humans. It offers a challenge to dominant notions of humanity and the world in modernist thought and practice. If animists are people who seek to act respectfully as participants in the myriad relationships that form their local, regional, and global environments ("nature" in its several senses), then they are required to attend to the needs of human and other-than-human neighbors.

Animism embraces the notion that the world is constituted differently from that theorized by monotheistic religions. It might also contest the failure of modern science to take seriously its own insight and evidence of human interrelationship and interdependence with all other beings. In religious language, humans are co-creators of the world. In more scientific language, we are integral participants in the current stage of the world's evolution. In both domains, a far from cozy or romantic vision of the world is required. Humans and all other species are required to attend to the needs of others and cannot, without impunity or systemic penalty, commit the hubris of acting alone to be the sole beneficiary of any act. Kinship and co-evolution requires that we cease conducting experiments (in laboratories or in the wider world) that are only for the benefit of humans—let alone only for some humans. Just as it must be immoral to expect every person in the next half million years to perfectly protect the world from our radioactive waste, so it cannot be moral to harm individuals or communities for the negligible benefit of a generation seeking to continue to live by extreme patterns of consumption.

In many indigenous animist communities (which we must perceive to be formed of many mutual and competing, specific and diverse inter-species relationships of varying degrees of closeness), there are experts who deal with the difficulties that necessarily arise. Humans cannot survive,

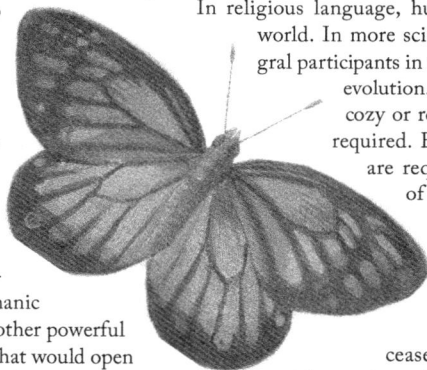

let alone thrive, without taking the lives of other animals or of plants. If such beings are treated as persons deserving of respect, the violence conducted towards them must be (a) treated personally and (b) mitigated carefully. The name applied to people who have the job of negotiating between humans and those beings that humans necessarily harm and sometimes insult (e.g., by treating such harm casually or carelessly) is "shamans." This term is derived from Siberian cultural groups and is applicable to many similar religious experts in mediation worldwide (though this too requires some care).

Nature Religion and Sustainability

Nature religionists, animists in particular, are likely to insist that present levels of human consumerism are unsustainable. They might go further and encourage a view that any form of consumption must take into account the value and needs of others, human and other-than-human, in this and future generations. Sustainability, for such people, is a matter of appropriate relationships conducted with respect and responsibility. Although some nature religionists believe that humans are expendable, indeed that the world might be better off without humans, the majority hold that humans are integral participants in the community of life. A post-human world is likely to be the result of a devastation badly affecting all other life rather than one that benefits from human extinction. A swift cessation of human hubris and pretended separation, and their consequent hyper-consumption and pollution, may just follow from a radical adjustment to the animistic perception that humans are full participants in a fully relational world. A

number of environmental educators and activists are finding the rituals and mediation strategies of shamans invaluable in redirecting people toward life in a sacred material world in which a gift economy (replete with everyday and extraordinary ritual acts of reciprocity, as invitingly incited by Ronald L. Grimes) may prove truly sustainable for all life.

Graham HARVEY
The Open University

FURTHER READING

Albanese, Catherine L. (1990). *Nature religion in America: From the Algonkian Indians to the New Age.* Chicago: University of Chicago Press.

Grimes, Ronald L. (2002). Performance as currency in the deep world's gift economy: An incantatory riff for a global medicine show. *ISLE: Interdisciplinary Studies in Literature and Environment,* 9(1), 149–64.

Hallowell, A. Irving. (1960). Ojibwa ontology, behavior, and world view. In S. Diamond (Ed.), *Culture in history: Essays in honor of Paul Radin* (pp. 19–52). New York: Columbia University Press. Reprinted in Harvey, Graham. (Ed.). (2002). *Readings in indigenous religions* (pp. 18–49). London: Continuum.

Harvey, Graham. (Ed.). (2003). *Shamanism: A reader.* London: Routledge.

Harvey, Graham. (2005). *Animism: Respecting the living world.* New York: Columbia University Press.

Nichols, John D., & Nyholm, Earl. (1995). *A concise dictionary of Minnesota Ojibwe.* Minneapolis: University of Minnesota Press.

Plumwood, Val. (2002). *Environmental culture: The ecological crisis of reason.* London: Routledge.

Taylor, Bron. (Forthcoming). *Dark green religion.* Berkeley: University of California Press.

Tylor, Edward B. (1871, 1913). *Primitive culture* (Vols. 1–2). London: John Murray.

WHAT IS RELIGIOUS NATURALISM?

Religious naturalism, unlike a nature religion, develops spirituality—as well as a core understanding of nature—out of modern scientific understandings of the world. Thus they are not reclaiming old traditions (like some neopagan traditions), but are new understandings of spirituality emerging from things like

cosmology, evolution, and even neuroscience. See, for example, Donald A. Crosby, *A Religion of Nature* (SUNY 2002) or Ursula Goodenough, *The Sacred Depths of Nature* (Oxford, 1998).

WHITNEY BAUMAN

New Age Spirituality

Although the New Age and sustainability movements are distinct, there is significant overlap between the two. Both are strongly oriented toward the future and have generally positive assessments of human nature and potential, but not all New Agers are concerned with environmental sustainability, and some of their beliefs may work against efforts towards social and economic sustainability.

The New Age movement is a loosely connected set of practices, values, and beliefs that began to coalesce in Great Britain and the United States in the 1960s and 1970s, and has continued to spread in subsequent decades. The term itself refers to many adherents' belief that a new age of human evolution is either approaching or has begun. Although there is little that is common to every practitioner, most share an interest in health, spirituality, and self-exploration, and many value knowledge and practices derived from "traditional" (usually non-Western) religions or personal intuition rather than from religious authorities. Certain strands have also developed a keen interest in science, particularly quantum mechanics. Many authors who have been influential in New Age circles—including especially Fritjof Capra, Ken Wilber, and David Bohm—write extensively on the relationship between science and spirituality.

Although the New Age and sustainability movements are distinct, there is significant overlap in both personnel and ideas. In addition to Capra, for example, notables such as David Suzuki, Eckhart Tolle, Brian Swimme, Paul Hawken, and Thomas Berry have all been influential to individuals in both circles. Still, given the broad range of behaviors, ideas, and practices designated "New Age," there is no simple, direct correlation with sustainability. Rather, there are points of both continuity and discontinuity, revealing a promising yet decidedly ambiguous legacy.

Regarding environmental sustainability, some strands of New Age encourage environmental activism, emphasizing holistic thinking, harmony with nature, and the spiritual importance of "power spots," such as Glastonbury in the United Kingdom or Sedona and Mt. Shasta in the United States. Along with the assertion that the Earth is a living organism (known as the Gaia Hypothesis), such interests have given certain segments of the movement a decidedly "earthy" tone. Indeed, New Age sentiments have motivated activist organizations such as Greenpeace and several overtly Earth-friendly farming or gardening communities, including The Farm in Tennessee, Findhorn in Scotland, and Perelandra in Virginia. But other less socially active strands are more interested in gurus, channeling, and healing than in environmental problems, and may not embrace environmental sustainability at all in their behaviors and ethics. Some strands of New Age thus take environmental sustainability quite seriously, whereas others choose to focus their spiritual energy elsewhere.

The New Age movement is ambivalent regarding social sustainability as well. The overall ethos tends to be individualistic, advocating the exploration of personal truths rather than communal values. Moreover, the movement, which is predominantly white and middle class, has focused little energy on addressing problems such as race and class inequality. Popular New Age ideas such as the "Law of Attraction," which asserts that people's thoughts control their reality, detract attention from systemic and structural forces contributing to inequitable circumstances,

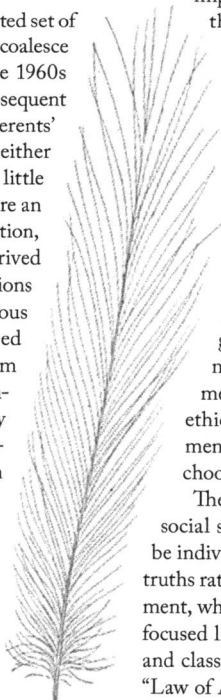

tending instead to blame troubles on the victims themselves. The movement's tendency to deny the reality of the negative (except to the extent that it is considered an opportunity for spiritual growth) would thus seem to make it ill equipped to deal seriously with the world's social problems. Despite these seeming weaknesses, a substantial portion of the movement's rhetoric has focused on promoting positive societal change. For example, a central message of *The Aquarian Conspiracy* (1980), a book often considered to be the quintessential statement of New Age beliefs, was that an expanded view of human potential could lead to a radical, beneficial transformation of society. The New Age focus on the power of positive thinking can thus contribute to efforts to move toward social sustainability, while also having the potential to be a significant stumbling block.

The New Age movement is equally ambivalent about economic sustainability. Many of its critics have condemned it as a superficial consumer phenomenon, arguing that its individualism and willingness to appropriate spiritual resources from other cultures make it an emissary (albeit karma-coated) of destructive capitalism. By contrast, the movement's marketability—it forms the core of the marketing segment known as "Lifestyles of Health and Sustainability"—gives it at least some economic clout. Considering that many New Agers prefer environmentally friendly products, they may be well positioned to promote sustainability through the power of the pocketbook.

A number of the New Age movement's ideas thus overlap with and contribute to ongoing conversations about sustainability. Given that both are strongly oriented toward the future and have generally positive assessments of human nature and potential, such affinity is not surprising. That the overlap is not complete is no less surprising: like most social movements, New Age is heterogeneous and moves in many different directions simultaneously, sometimes toward and sometimes away from the equally meandering path of sustainability.

Robin GLOBUS
University of Florida

FURTHER READING

Bloom, William. (Ed.). (2000). *Holistic revolution: The essential New Age reader*. London: Allen Lane.

Ferguson, Marilyn. (1980). *The Aquarian conspiracy: Personal and social transformation in our time*. New York: G. P. Putnam's Sons.

Heelas, Paul. (1996). *The New Age movement: The celebration of the self and the sacralization of modernity*. Oxford, U.K.: Blackwell.

Pike, Sarah M. (2004). *New Age and neopagan religions in America*. New York: Columbia University Press.

York, Michael. (2005). New Age. In B. R. Taylor (Ed.), *The encyclopedia of religion and nature* (pp. 1193–1197). London & New York: Thoemmes Continuum.

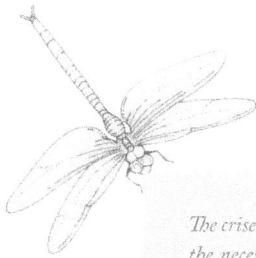

The crises of our time, it becomes increasingly clear, are the necessary impetus for the revolution now under way. And once we understand nature's transformative powers, we see that it is our powerful ally, not a force to be feared or subdued. Our pathology is our opportunity.

MARILYN FERGUSON

Source: Marilyn Ferguson. (1980). *The Aquarian Conspiracy: Personal and Social Transformation in Our Time*, p. 25. New York: G. P. Putnam's Sons.

Shamanism

Although an exact definition of shamanism and shamans is difficult to arrive at, there are consistencies across cultures. Generally, shamans represent mediators between the worlds of humans and nonhumans who, in their contact with the "spirits" of nature, attempt to maintain harmony, if not "sustainable management," with the natural world.

As an academic term *shamanism* both clarifies and occludes our understanding of certain indigenous and prehistoric practices that might be termed religious. Shamans may heal the sick, cause illness, speak to spirits, or become possessed by them, journey to other worlds, seek out game by supernatural means, and alter consciousness to enter a state of ecstasy. But this list should not be seen as finite or even representative, and definition is problematic. An approach to shamans and some of the terms used to define them intellectually—such as *healing, sorcery, spirits, altered states, journeying,* and *ecstasy*—are all loaded with meanings and often tell more about the observer and what the observer wants shamans to be than about shamans themselves. While an exact definition of shamanism and shamans is difficult to arrive at, there are cross-cultural consistencies in what shamans do. Generally, shamans represent mediators between the worlds of humans and nonhumans who, in their contact with the "spirits" of nature, attempt to maintain harmony, if not "sustainable management," with the natural world.

Origins of the Term

The term *shaman* (pronounced SHAYmuhn, SHARmuhn, or SHARmahn; there is no accepted pronunciation) derives from the Tungus language group spoken by a variety of Siberian peoples, including the Evenki. The anglicized *shaman* is rendered phonetically as šaman or sama:n. The Evenki did not use written language or use the term in a general sense to encompass everything that shamans did. The term came into Western use, normalized via the Russian, as Christian missionaries began to target Siberian tribes for conversion and so needed a pagan religion against which to define themselves. By the eighteenth century, the German term *shamanen* and British *shamanism* were in widespread use, as the practices of shamans, bizarre to Western minds, became fetishized as "other." As explorers encountered new peoples across the globe, so a variety of indigenous religious practices came to be associated with shamanism.

Shamans and Shamanisms

Shamanism is now in popular use to refer to medicine men, witch doctors, healers, sorcerers, and others who engage with spirits for certain socially sanctioned tasks. The term gives a sense of coherency and specificity, and has been applied across cultures and through time. But such application risks being misleading, that the "religion" of shamanism with a discrete shamanistic worldview exists. Rather, there are shamans, and these men and women work within animistic or "animic" ontologies (ways of being) and epistemologies (ways of knowing), acting as agents who negotiate harmony between human persons and nonhuman persons, sometimes called spirits. But the term *spirit* problematically draws a spirit/matter dualism that may not be recognized by the community at issue. In addition to approaching indigenous ontologies sensitively, it is important to foreground the diversity of shamans' practices in order to embrace cultural distinctiveness. It might be better to speak of the plural, shamans and shamanisms, rather than the singular, shamanism and the shaman.

Neoshamans and Green Shamans

Shamanism has significant currency among New Age practitioners, pagans, and other alternative interest groups, perhaps best described as "neoshamanisms." For many people interested in shamanisms, shamans represent indigenous healers who, in their contact with the spirits of nature, maintain sustainable management of the natural world. Indigenous communities more generally are perceived to be harmonious in their engagements with nature, and shamans are marked out as occupying the preeminent spiritual wing of this ethos. This Western view co-opts shamans, distorting their practices away from local animic contexts in which relations between human people and nonhuman people are negotiated, toward a globalized metanarrative (a simplistic and all-encompassing explanation) in which shamans are the spiritual caretakers of the environment. Small-scale societies have a much smaller impact on the Earth's resources than Western countries have. But traditional slash-and-burn agriculture, practiced in the Amazon for instance, and evidence indicating that prehistoric peoples may have hunted a number of large animals to extinction in various parts of the world, demonstrates that humans are capable of irreparable damage to nature. This is not to dismiss, however, the significance and relevance of indigenous engagements with nature to the modern world.

Shamans and Animists

Animists, in many indigenous communities, understand the world as filled with people, only some of whom are human. There are human people, and there are other-than-human people—such as stone people, tree people, and fish people—and it is the role of shamans to maintain harmonious relations between humans and nonhumans. Animism in the Amazon, for instance, is predatory. Just as the world is filled with persons, so killing other persons is necessary to survive. It might be said that everyone is eating everyone else all of the time, in a series of cannibalist relations. Animic ontologies attempt to do violence with impunity, with shamans brokering good relations, but all too often, human behavior offends nonhumans. It is then the task of shamans to engage with nonhumans via "adjusted styles of communication," which enables them to "see as others do," or meet the communicative level of others persons, to restore harmony.

Shamans and Sustainability

While indigenous and prehistoric lifeways may not necessarily be "green," their respectful, relational approach to the world, and understanding of community as not restricted to humanity, offers a practical guideline to Western people as to how living can attempt to be respectful, relational, and sustainable. Living sustainably requires humans to engage with the natural world respectfully, rather than regard it as a resource for exploitation. Humans are not "king of the hill", but simply one form of life in a diversely living world.

Robert J. WALLIS
Richmond the American International University in London

FURTHER READING

Atkinson, Jane Monnig. (1992). Shamanisms today. *Annual Review of Anthropology, 21*, 307–330.

Harvey, Graham. (2005). *Animism: Respecting the living world.* London: Hurst; New York: Columbia University Press; Adelaide, Australia: Wakefield Press.

Harvey, Graham. (Ed.). (2002). *Shamanism: A reader.* London: Routledge.

Harvey, Graham, & Wallis, Robert J. (2007). *Historical dictionary of shamanism.* Lanham, MD: Scarecrow Press.

Humphrey, Caroline, & Onon, Urgunge. (1996). *Shamans and elders: Experience, knowledge, and power among the Daur Mongols.* Oxford, U.K.: Oxford University Press.

Hutton, Ronald. (2002). *Shamans: Siberian spirituality and the Western imagination.* London: Hambledon.

Narby, Jeremy, & Huxley, Francis. (Eds.). (2004). *Shamans through time: 500 years on the path to knowledge.* London: Thames and Hudson.

Price, Neil S. (Ed.). (2001). *The archaeology of shamanism.* London: Routledge.

Taylor, Bron R., & Kaplan, Jeffrey. (Eds.). (2005). *The encyclopedia of religion and nature.* New York and London: Continuum.

Thomas, Nicholas, & Humphrey, Caroline. (Eds.). (1994). *Shamanism, history, and the state.* Ann Arbor: University of Michigan Press.

Wallis, Robert J. (2003). *Shamans/neo-shamans: Ecstasy, alternative archaeologies and contemporary pagans.* London: Routledge.

Paganism and Neopaganism

Paganism and Neopaganism include contemporary spiritual practices and religions that celebrate and revere nature. Pagans honor their sacred relationship with Earth and all that lives on Earth. The principles of their Earth-based spirituality foster sustainable lifestyles and provide the basis for the discussion and formulation of an ethics of sustainability.

Paganism or Neopaganism typically describes a collection of contemporary spiritual practices and religions that are grounded in this world and celebrate nature. Within the context of sustainability, two questions will be addressed: First, how does Paganism support sustainability? Second, to what extent do Pagans practice sustainable lifestyles?

Debate continues about how to define Paganism and the extent to which Paganism is a nature religion. This article will treat Paganism as a range of spiritual practices that celebrate nature, marking the processes of life and death, seasonal changes, and lunar cycles.

Contemporary Paganism takes many forms, the most common being witchcraft, initiatory Wiccan traditions, Druidry, and eclectic Paganism. Less prevalent forms include Goddess spirituality, Ásatrú (Norse Paganism), shamanism, and Reconstructionist traditions. Pagans are usually polytheists who honor immanent deities (deities that are inherent to or dwell within the material world), treat the Earth as sacred, and hold the animist belief that "all that exists lives."

An Ethics of Sustainability

In as much as Paganism celebrates nature, it offers an excellent grounding for an ethics of sustainability. Theoretical discussion has only begun quite recently, perhaps because Paganism is rooted in practice, not belief. However, several Pagans have offered an ethics, and while the influences and details vary, all discussions are rooted in the theme of *relationship*.

The idea that the Earth is a single organism, scientifically formalized in British scientist James Lovelock's Gaia hypothesis, was an early influence on Pagan ethics, initially through Oberon Zell-Ravenheart (1971), and later, via influential British Wiccans like Doreen Valiente and Stuart and Janet Farrar. Zell-Ravenheart co-founded the Pagan Church of All Worlds in 1962. Doreen Valiente had an early and enduring influence on British Traditional Wicca while Stuart and Janet Farrar wrote several widely read books about that same tradition. More recently, animist beliefs which require a respectful relationship with other-than-human beings have been brought to the foreground: Emma Restall-Orr's Druid ethics of connection, Douglas Ezzy's "intimate relationship" with place, Thom Van Dooren's "sacred community" (de Angeles, Restall-Orr, and Van Dooren 2005), and Starhawk's systems-based model all emphasize this principle.

While deep ecology and ecofeminism are influential, other approaches have been fruitful: the feminist theologian Carol Christ applies process philosophy, which recognizes that "all beings are connected in the web of life" (Christ 2003); Sylvie Shaw (2004) uses ecopsychology to understand the spiritual power of nature; and Starhawk increasingly draws on permaculture principles to learn how to design human systems that mimic natural systems. Bioregionalism is another significant influence: Chas Clifton emphasizes that a Pagan must "learn where you are on the earth" (1998), while bioregional animism—relating to the land or bioregion as the source of one's religion and culture—has grown from Cascadia, a bioregion in the northwestern United States and Canada, in 2000 into a global movement.

There is a coherent and commonly held Pagan ethic of sustainability grounded in sacred relationship, but the question of how that relationship can be maintained remains less clear.

Sustainable in Practice?

Research into Pagans' lifestyles is inconclusive: although Regina Smith Oboler's 2004 study found above average levels of sustainable behavior amongst U.S. Pagans, other factors made conclusions difficult. Barbara Davy suggests that only a minority of Pagans are environmentally active, but this is to be expected: Pagans, like most people, strive to live up to their ethical principles and often fall short. But certain aspects of the cultural history of Paganism may be inimical to an ethics of sustainability. Some claim that the influence of esotericism can create inconsistencies by encouraging Pagans to "understand 'nature' as a symbol" rather than the actual living environment (Davy 2007). Starhawk concludes that Paganism's potential to encourage sustainable lifestyles depends on rooting it "in the real earth, and not just in our abstract ideas" (Starhawk 2005).

Such a grounded spirituality emerges from practical embodied knowing. Genuine relationships take time and require careful observation, so Starhawk's Earth Activist Training combines a permaculture design course with Earth-based spirituality. Adrian Harris' Sacred Ecology emphasizes the embodied knowing of gut feelings, while Susan Greenwood notes that a "connected wholeness" (2005) can emerge through dancing or drumming. Harris subsequently identified more of these "processes of connection" including trance, ritual, and the wilderness effect theorized by ecopsychology (2008).

Although Paganism principles strongly support sustainable lifestyles, the rich potential inherent in those principles is not always realized in practice. Pagans are increasingly engaged in developing an ethic of sustainability, however, and exploring how their spiritual practices can best encourage sustainable behavior.

Adrian HARRIS
Faith, Spirituality and Social Change Project

FURTHER READING

Christ, Carol P. (2003). *She who changes: Re-imagining the divine in the world*. New York: Palgrave.

Clifton, Chas S. (1998). Nature religion for real. Retrieved August 5, 2008, from http://www.chasclifton.com/papers/forreal.html

Davy, Barbara J. (2007). *Introduction to Pagan studies*. Lanham, MD: AltaMira Press.

de Angeles, Ly; Restall-Orr, Emma; & Van Dooren, Thom (Eds.). (2005). *Pagan visions for a sustainable future*. Woodbury, MN: Llewellyn Publications.

Ezzy, Douglas. (2005). I am the mountain walking: wombats in the greenwood. In, Ly de Angeles, Emma Restall-Orr, and Thom Van Dooren, *Pagan visions for a sustainable future*. Woodbury, MN: Llewellyn Publications.

Greenwood, Susan. (2005). *The nature of magic: An anthropology of consciousness*. Oxford, U.K.: Berg Publishers.

Harris, Adrian P. (2008). *The wisdom of the body: Embodied knowing in eco-Paganism*. (PhD thesis). University of Winchester, U.K.

Oboler, Regina Smith. (2004). Nature religion as a cultural system? Sources of environmentalist action and rhetoric in a contemporary Pagan community. *The Pomegranate: The International Journal of Pagan Studies*, 6(1), 86–106.

Restall-Orr, Emma. (2005). The ethics of Paganism: The value and power of sacred relationship. In, Ly de Angeles, Emma Restall-Orr, and Thom Van Dooren, *Pagan visions for a sustainable future*. Woodbury, MN: Llewellyn Publications.

Shaw, Sylvie. (2004). At the water's edge. In Jenny Blain; Douglas Ezzy; & Graham Harvey (Eds.), *Researching Paganisms*. Walnut Creek, CA: AltaMira.

Starhawk. (2004). *The Earth path*. New York: HarperCollins.

Starhawk. (2005). Pagan politics, Pagan stories: An interview. In Ly de Angeles, Emma Restall-Orr, & Thom Van Dooren, *Pagan visions for a sustainable future*. Woodbury, MN: Llewellyn Publications.

Van Dooren, Thom. (2005). Dwelling in sacred community. In, Ly de Angeles, Emma Restall-Orr, and Thom Van Dooren, *Pagan visions for a sustainable future*. Woodbury, MN: Llewellyn Publications.

Zell-Ravenheart, Oberon (under the name of Otter G'Zell). (1971, July 1). Theagenesis: The birth of the goddess. *Green Egg*, 4, 40.

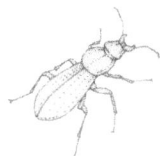

Wisdom Traditions

Wisdom was one of Plato's four cardinal virtues; the original concept involved knowledge about the interconnectedness of life, a subject inherent in discussions about sustainability. Since Plato, wisdom has developed a religious significance that is found in many diverse traditions. Wisdom, therefore, has become a virtue of sustainability that could serve as a basis for a global religious ethic.

The notion of wisdom is connected with philosophy (from the Greek *philos-sophia*, which itself means "love of wisdom"). Yet the gradual detachment of this classical understanding of philosophy from its original sense means that philosophy today is more often than not associated with a much narrower pursuit of knowledge. In its ancient meaning, philosophy was about life and the relationship of everything with everything else. In religious terms, that relationship is necessarily inclusive of religious commitment, including (in many cases) acknowledgment of the divine. Since sustainability is about maintaining relationships between humans, other creatures, and the planet, wisdom is most properly linked with, and some might say integral to, the pursuit of sustainability.

Abrahamic Faiths

Judaism, Christianity, and Islam all draw on traditions adhered to by the biblical patriarch Abraham and, in this sense, share many of the same resources, though different emphases come to bear in the three different religions. The Hebrew tradition of wisdom develops most profoundly that corpus of books in the Hebrew Bible known as the wisdom literature: Proverbs, Job, Ecclesiastes, Psalms, Song of Songs, and the books of Wisdom and Sirach in Apocrypha, though examples of writing that show some affinity with the wisdom genre may be found throughout the

Hebrew Bible. In the Jewish tradition, wisdom was learned in the context of family life, through education, and, to a lesser extent, through observation of the natural world. Much wisdom literature seemed to support the status quo in that it affirmed royal traditions and hierarchical social arrangements. In this sense it identifies with those elements of the tradition that many believe are inimical to ecologically sensitive practice. This is particularly evident among ecofeminist interpreters of wisdom, where wisdom is portrayed as necessarily being in antithetical relationships to all hierarchical structures.

There is, however, a more subversive tradition of wisdom that points away from hierarchical arrangements. Those proverbs that encourage the reader to pay attention to non-human life encourage the kind of careful attention with which naturalists are familiar, though the writers were clearly ignorant of much of the science. An example here is Proverbs 6:6–9, where humans are exhorted to notice the "way of the ant." This seems to be more than just an implicit natural science; rather it is a promotion of a different kind of social order as epitomized in the life of ants. By recognizing wisdom in creatures that lack rulers, and even in the smallest and most insignificant of creatures—namely ants, badgers, locusts, and lizards—the royal, hierarchical wisdom tradition is challenged.

In Proverbs (Chapters 1–9) there are also references to "woman wisdom," where wisdom is celebrated not so much as the means of success in human society but as present at the primordial Creation of the world. This links Hebrew wisdom with Creation, so much so that some scholars believe that wisdom always carries an implicit theology of Creation. In Proverbs 8, wisdom is even described as a co-Creator, playfully engaged in Creation, but one who also acts as the voice of the Earth, seeing that she is aware of how the interconnectedness of the universe comes together. Such an idealized vision of wisdom, which is also associated

with the Torah or "Law" in Hebrew thought, finds a counterpoint in the book of Job, which deals explicitly with the issue of unjust suffering. It is important that this strand is given due attention, as otherwise wisdom could be thought of as presenting a vision that fails to recognize sufficiently the suffering embedded in life's experiences. In such a context God is portrayed as one who speaks of the care of all creatures, not just humankind, and there are also hints that God discovers wisdom in the Earth, but this is acquired through creating, rather than akin to human searching. Such wisdom is then established and confirmed by God, and would seem to challenge more Platonic notions of wisdom being present as ideas on the divine mind. Wisdom is also associated with the spirit of God in the book of Wisdom (which was included in an ancient Greek version of the Hebrew Bible—the Septuagint—and remains in the Roman Catholic and Eastern Orthodox Old Testament); it fills the whole Earth (Wisdom 1:6) and emanates from God's glory as the breath of God (Wisdom 7:25).

Christian and Muslim Interpretations

The association of wisdom with the Torah and eventually the divine in Hebrew thought is radicalized still further in Christianity, where divine wisdom comes to be associated with the person of Christ. The earliest understanding of Christ was arguably a Wisdom Christology. Those poems associated with wisdom in the Hebrew tradition are deliberately aligned with the Christ figure. The Gospel of John mediated such a transition through a more hierarchical Logos imagery (having to do with the word in John's gospel, as in, "in the beginning was the word"), and eventually the background in *sophia*, or wisdom, traditions became suppressed. Many of the epistles associate Christ and the cross with wisdom, as in Colossians 1 or Corinthians 1. Such an understanding overturns a simple correlation between a human search for wisdom and Christian discipleship, for now more ascetic traditions come into view, where identification with Christ's cross becomes (in a paradoxical way) the mark of true wisdom. Such identification is not related to an inappropriate masochism but rather presented as a willingness to suffer for the sake of the good. In other words, it carries a sacrificial element. In addition, virtues such as wisdom are understood as not simply learned in human communities; they are also perceived as gifts given from God, through the grace of the Holy Spirit.

In Islam, wisdom in an environmental context is equated with the practice of stewardship (*khalifa*), understood as engendering a right sense of responsibility for the Earth. This is linked with two other key ideas in Islam, namely, *tawhid* (unity) and *akhirah* (accountability). The word for Earth, *arn*, occurs 485 times in the Quran. The term

masakin describes the dwelling of all creatures, including human beings. The Earth is named as the beginning and end of human life, and the intimate relationship between humankind and the Earth sets up an appropriate response of respect and care, based on the ultimate divine ownership of the Earth. The emphasis on *taqwa* (or best provision for the Earth stemming from fear of its divine owner) during the festivals that mark the end of hajj—the annual pilgrimage to Mecca—also speaks of careful responsibility for the Earth. There are specific instructions not to be wasteful at harvest time (Quran 6:41), reminiscent of the Hebrew proverbial traditions. Some Islamic scholars are strongly critical of the global domination of the Western view of science and its materialistic forms of knowledge; they call for an Islamic science that retains a sense of nature as sacred while also insisting on a strong sense of the transcendence of God as Creator. Yet, according to the Quran, the main purpose of humankind is to act as a vicegerent on Earth (Quran 2:30), so that the way humans are related to the natural world is bound up with this primary sense of stewardship.

Practical Wisdom in Other Traditions

The development of practical wisdom represents another lens through which it is possible to consider the wisdom traditions. In those traditions encompassing Western values, practical wisdom can be distinguished from more theoretical wisdom that is concerned with how to think appropriately about the relationships between God, humanity, and creation, even though, as indicated above, there are strong practical implications. Practical wisdom, or *prudence* in classic traditions, is concerned with deliberation, judgment, and action, and in this sense cannot be separated from ethics. In the Aristotelian tradition, prudence or practical wisdom is the correct discernment of a particular course of action, a way of expressing a particular virtue. Practical wisdom can also be named as a virtue, or habit of mind that is oriented toward excellence. That excellence is not simply about what is good for the individual, but about the common public good or what is good for the community as a whole.

It is here that the Western traditions can find common ground with Asian traditions. For Confucius, for example, the cultivation of a moral sense has a high priority, and those that sought to acquire morality had to fit into the patterns found in the universe, leading to a peaceful, flourishing society. Confucian thinkers also affirm the role of the "heart and mind" in making decisions. The term they use for this (*in*) contained the cognitive and the emotional faculties as well as the moral sense. Christian theology has tended to separate these two functions. For example, Thomas Aquinas (c. 1225–1274) distinguished the intellectual virtues of understanding (*scientia*) and wisdom from the theological virtues of faith, hope, and charity. He strongly believed in the unity of virtues, however, so that wisdom was necessarily rooted in charity; the close connection between wisdom and compassion also resonates strongly with Buddhist wisdom.

Confucian wisdom, like that in the Abrahamic traditions, is oriented toward the good, not just of the individual but also of society as a whole. All traditions argue for a purgation of forms of selfish behavior or self-seeking as being the antithesis of wisdom. Neo-Confucian traditions also stress the importance of practice, so that knowledge without action fails to lead to progress in the moral life, including a particular emphasis on daily practice. This is an important ingredient of sustainability, for without due attention to patient implementation of good practice, all more theoretical calls for sustainability will fail to become concrete. For neo-Confucian thinkers, there was a grand design for individuals, families, and society: moral self-cultivation was the way to bring human needs into harmony with the natural world and nature's capacity for producing goods. Traditional Abrahamic faiths also adhere to belief in an ordered universe, but it was one that more often than not placed humanity as ruler of the natural world, hence the strong tradition of stewardship in Islam. There is rather less sense of finding harmony with nature than of becoming masters of it for human benefit.

Wisdom as a Virtue for Sustainable Living

The wisdom traditions remind us of the paramount importance of looking to our own human attitudes and dispositions. While for Abrahamic wisdom, the source of such insight ultimately comes from God, neo-Confucian wisdom reinforces the holistic nature of such a task. In other words, it is not just about the individual journey, but about our relationship to others and to the natural world. For those following the neo-Confucian tradition, this amounts to an expression of "the Way." For Jewish writers, such an orientation is impossible without reference to the Torah. For Christian writers, such an orientation is impossible

without reference to Christ, who is also the Way, the Truth, and the Life—and one might also say Wisdom incarnate. For Muslim writers, Muhammad provides the pattern for right human living according to wisdom.

A rather different way of perceiving wisdom takes its cues from practices that may be found in African proverbial wisdom traditions. These traditions also share some common ground with indigenous religious traditions. Arguably, those who have pressed for an ecological wisdom more often than not mean that which is, by its very nature, against any form of hierarchy or elitism that seems to persist in the Abrahamic faiths, even though there are strands within it that subvert such tendencies. The African proverbial tradition of wisdom is intuitive, relies on oral transmission, is focused on benefits for the group, and is shared in common with others through daily practices.

Wisdom may therefore be thought of as being grounded both in an understanding of the divine (for those traditions that adhere to belief in God) and as emerging from consideration of the natural world, or an ecological wisdom. In as much as wisdom connects very disparate religious traditions, it can be fruitful as a basis for discussion leading to a global religious ethic of sustainability.

Celia DEANE-DRUMMOND
University of Chester

Further Reading

Barton, Stephen C. (Ed.). (1999). *Where shall wisdom be found? Wisdom in the Bible, the church and the contemporary world*. Edinburgh, U.K.: T & T Clark.

Brown, Warren S. (Ed.). (2000). *Understanding wisdom: Sources, science and society*. Philadelphia: Templeton Foundation Press.

Chryssavgis, John. (2001). Sophia: The wisdom of God: Sophiology, theology and ecology. *Diakonia, 34*(1), 5–19.

Deane-Drummond, Celia. (2000). *Creation through wisdom: Theology and the new biology*. Edinburgh, U.K.: T & T Clark.

Deane-Drummond, Celia. (2006). *Wonder and wisdom: Conversations in science, spirituality and theology*. London: Darton Longman and Todd.

Deane-Drummond, Celia. (2008). *Eco-theology*. London: Darton Longman and Todd.

Habel, Norman C., & Wurst, Shirley. (Eds.). (2001). *The Earth story in wisdom traditions: The Earth Bible, Vol. 3*. Sheffield, U.K.: Sheffield Academic Press.

Editors and Editorial Advisory Board

Editors

Author Credits

"A Note on Writing about the Divine with Gendered Language" by **Willis Jenkins,** Editor of *The Spirit of Sustainability*
University of Virginia

Introduction: World Religions and Ecology
by **Mary Evelyn Tucker**
Yale University

African Diasporan Religions
by **Cheryl A. Kirk-Duggan**
Shaw University Divinity School

Bahá'í
by **Michael Karlberg**
Western Washington University

Buddhism
by **Christopher Ives**
Stonehill College

Christianity—Anabaptist
by **Kathryn S. Eisenbise**
Manchester College

Christianity—Eastern Orthodox
by **John Chryssavgis**
Greek Orthodox Archdiocese of America

Christianity—Evangelical and Pentecostal
by **Richard R. Bohannon II**
College of St. Benedict and St. John's University

Christianity—Mainline Protestant
by **Ernst M. Conradie**
University of the Western Cape

Christianity—Roman Catholic
by **John Hart**
Boston University

Christianity—Society of Friends / Quakers
by **Laurel D. Kearns**
Drew Theological School and University

Confucianism
by **Mary Evelyn Tucker**
Yale University

Daoism
by **James D. Sellmann**
University of Guam

Ecology, Deep
by **David Landis Barnhill**
University of Wisconsin, Oshkosh

Eschatology
by **Antonia Gorman**
Humane Society of the United States

Fundamentalism
by **Laurel D. Kearns**
Drew Theological School and University

God
by **Charles Mathewes** and **Chad Wayner**
University of Virginia

Hinduism
by **Christopher Key Chapple**
Loyola Marymount University

Indigenous Traditions—Africa
by **Ibigbolade S. Aderibigbe**
University of Georgia

Indigenous Traditions—Asia
by **E. N. Anderson**
University of California, Riverside

Indigenous Traditions—Australia
by **Deborah Bird Rose**
Macquarie University

Indigenous Traditions—North America
by **Melissa K. Nelson**
San Francisco State University

Indigenous Traditions—Oceania
by **Mary N. MacDonald**
Le Moyne College

Indigenous Traditions—South America
by **Tirso Gonzales**
University of British Columbia Okanagan
and **Maria E. Gonzalez**
University of Michigan

Indigenous Traditions—The Arctic
by **Fikret Berkes**
University of Manitoba

Islam
by **Frederick Mathewson Denny**
University of Colorado at Boulder, Emeritus

Jainism
by **Christopher Key Chapple**
Loyola Marymount University

Judaism
by **Lawrence Troster**
GreenFaith

Meditation and Prayer
by **Jay McDaniel**
Hendrix College

Mormonism
by **George B. Handley**
Brigham Young University

*National Religious Partnership for the
   Environment*
by **Laurel D. Kearns**
Drew Theological School and University

Nature Religions and Animism
by **Graham Harvey**
The Open University

New Age Spirituality
by **Robin Globus**
University of Florida

Paganism and Neopaganism
by **Adrian Harris**
Faith, Spirituality and Social Change Project

Peace
by **Terrence Jantzi**
Eastern Mennonite University and **Aaron Kishbaugh**
Independent scholar, Singers Glen, Virginia

Pilgrimage
by **Sigridur Gudmarsdottir**
Reykjavik Academy

Sacrament
by **John Hart**
Boston University

Sacred Texts
by **Forrest Clingerman**
Ohio Northern University

Sacrifice
by **Christopher Key Chapple**
Loyola Marymount University

Science, Religion, and Ecology
by **Holmes Rolston III**
Colorado State University

Shamanism
by **Robert J. Wallis**
Richmond the American International University
  in London

Shinto
by **Yotaro Miyamoto**
Kansai University

Sikhism
by **Whitney A. Bauman,** Assistant Editor of *The Spirit
  of Sustainability*
Florida International University

Sin and Evil
by **Frederick Simmons**
Yale Divinity School

Stewardship
by **Susan Power Bratton** and **Austin
  Cook-Lindsay**
Baylor University

Theocentrism
by **Forrest Clingerman**
Ohio Northern University

*Unitarianism and Unitarian
  Universalism*
by **Eileen M. Harrington**
University of San Francisco

Virtues and Vices
by **Louke van Wensveen**
Academia Vitae

Wisdom Traditions
by **Celia Deane-Drummond**
University of Chester

Image Credits

The illustrations used in this book come from many sources. There are photographs provided by Berkshire Publishing's staff and friends, by authors, and from archival sources. All known sources and copyright holders have been credited.

Bottom front cover photo is of fireflies (*Pyractomena borealis*) on an Iowa prairie, by Carl Kurtz.

Engraving illustrations of plants and insects by Maria Sibylla Merian (1647–1717).

Beetle, dragonfly, moth, and ladybug illustrations by Lydia Umney.

Front cover images, left-to-right:

1. *Grass-roofed church, Iceland.* Photo by Amy Siever.
2. *Shinto shrine, Japan.* Photo by Amanda Prigge.
3. *Prayer tags, Taiwan.* Photo by Karen Christensen.

Pages VIII, 159, 160, 164, *Design in Nature.* Photo by Carl Kurtz.

Pages IX, X, 156, *Yellowthroat female.* Photo by Carl Kurtz.

Page 2, 25, *White pelicans feeding.* Photo by Carl Kurtz.

Pages 4, 7, 35, 38, 40, 44, 48, 136, 140, 152, *Great Barrington nestled in the Berkshires.* Photo by Berkshire Publishing staff.

Page 9, 82, *Rock cairn.* Photo by Shuke Yixuan.

Pages 11, 18, 21, *Great blue herons.* Photo by Carl Kurtz.

Page 13, *Mountains in northern New Mexico.* Photo courtesy of the Library of Congress.

Page 14, *Prairie fire.* Photo by Carl Kurtz.

Page 27, *Praekestolen, Geiranger Fjord, Norway.* Photo courtesy of the Library of Congress.

Pages 31, 154, *Distant Berkshire hills.* Photo by Berkshire Publishing staff.

Pages 46, 134, *Prune orchard near Santa Clara, California.* Photo courtesy of Oregon State University.

Pages 54, 58, 64, 67, 71, 75, 78, 122, *Bobolink.* Photo by Carl Kurtz.

Pages 86, 91, *Rose mallow.* Photo by Carl Kurtz.

Pages 96, 98, 100, 102, 105, 108, 110, *False white indigo.* Photo by Carl Kurtz.

Page 114, *Common blue violet.* Photo by Carl Kurtz.

Page 117, *Sweet coneflowers.* Photo by Carl Kurtz.

Pages 127, 130, *Reflected light.* Photo by Carl Kurtz.

Page 142, *Mount Everett.* Photo by Berkshire Publishing staff.

Pages 144, 146, 150, *Kildeer.* Photo by Carl Kurtz.

Index

Bold entries and page numbers denote articles in this volume.

Bold entries and page numbers denote articles in this volume.

eligion-and-Sustainability.indd Page 167 9/9/15 4:08 AM f-479 /209/BER00056_R1/berxxxxx_disk1of1/xxxxxxxxxx/berxxxxx_pagefiles/Black_Files/Berk ...

INDEX • **167**

Bold entries and page numbers denote articles in this volume.

Religion-and-Sustainability.indd Page 169 9/9/15 4:08 AM f-479 /209/BER00056_R1/berxxxxx_disk1of1/xxxxxxxxxx/berxxxxx_pagefiles/Black_Files/Berk ...

INDEX • **169**

Bold entries and page numbers denote articles in this volume.

Bold entries and page numbers denote articles in this volume.

Proverbs
  African tradition, 55, 158
  Hebrew Bible, 156
psycho-ecology. *See* ecopsychology.
Puebla Conference, 105
Pueblo Corn Dances, 69
Purusa Sukta, of the Rig-Veda, 118

Q

Quaker Earthcare Witness (QEW), 109
Quakers. *See* **Christianity, Society of Friends /**
  Quakers
Quechua Andean / Amazonian natural order, 76–77
Quran (Koran), 7, 122–124, 126, 157
  See also **Islam**; **Sacred Texts**

R

racism, 83–84
rainforests, 147
  See also Amazonia; tropical rainforests
Rastafarianism, 82
reciprocity, 19, 31, 68–69, 71, 73–74, 80, 121, 149
reconstructionist traditions, 154
reductionism, 114
Reed Dance, 56
Reflections on Things at Hand (Jinsilu), 112
Rehat Maryada, 140
relativism, 34
religion
  and ecology, xv, 85
  of the market, 117
  See also other specific religions
Religious and Scientific Committee, 99
religious environmentalism, 15–16, 120–121
Religious fundamentalism. *See* **Fundamentalism**
religious Naturalism, 149
Renewing the Earth, 5, 105
restoration, 129
Reuben tribes, 132
Rig Veda, 7, 117–118
  See also **Sacred Texts**
right relationship, 7, 84–85, 108, 109
Ring of Bone Zendo, 94
Rio Earth Summit, 86
Robertson, George Scott, 62
Robertson, Pat, 15
Robinson, Tri, 15
Rolston, Holmes, 10, 12, 36
Roman Catholicism. *See* **Christianity,**
  Roman Catholic

Ruether, Rosemary Radford, 106
Ruhi Institute, 88
rural communities, 72
  and farming. *See* agriculture
Russia, 78, 79
  and shamanism, 59

S

Saami, 80
Sabbath, 8, 42, 130, 133
Sabbatical Year, 130–131
Sacrament, 4–6
  creation as, 5
  definitions, 4–5
Sacramental Commons: Christian Ecological Ethics,
  5, 106
sacred ecology, 155
Sacred Texts, 7–8
  challenges, 8
  interpretations, 7
  sustainability in, 7–8
Sacrifice, 33–37
  horse, 117–119
  future considerations, 37
  and sustainability, 36, 117–120
  traditional models, 33–35
St. Elias Mountains, 79
Salmon, Enrique, 68
Salt marches (in India), 120
salvation, 15, 28, 39, 96
Salvation Army, 15
Sametshirkhar, Bihar, 129
San Francisco Zen Center, 93
Sarvodaya movement, 93
Saudi Arabia. *See* **Islam**; Mecca
Schaeffer, Francis, 15, 100
Schumacher, E. F., 92
science, Bahá'ís' view of, 89
Science (journal), 130
  See also White's Thesis; "The Historical Roots of Our
    Ecological Crisis"
Science, Religion, and Ecology, 48–51
scientific ecology, 79
Second Coming. *See* Parousia
Sect Shinto (*kyoha-shinto*), 136
Seed, John, 22
Seven Principles of Unitarian Universalists, 142
"shallow ecology," 21
  "The Shallow and the Deep, Long-Range Ecology
    Movement." *See* Naess, Arne
  See also ecology, deep

Bold entries and page numbers denote articles in this volume.

Bold entries and page numbers denote articles in this volume.

This **BERKSHIRE** *Essentials* book was distilled from the

Berkshire Encyclopedia of Sustainability VOLUMES 1–10

Knowledge to Transform Our Common Future

In the 10-volume *Berkshire Encyclopedia of Sustainability*, experts around the world provide authoritative coverage of the growing body of knowledge about ways to restore the planet. Focused on solutions, this interdisciplinary print and online publication draws from the natural, physical, and social sciences—geophysics, engineering, and resource management, to name a few—and from philosophy and religion. The result is a unified, organized, and peer-reviewed resource on sustainability that connects academic research to real world challenges and provides a balanced, trustworthy perspective on global environmental challenges in the 21st century.

Ray C. Anderson

General Editor

Sara G. Beavis, Klaus Bosselmann,
Lisa M. Butler Harrington, Robin Kundis Craig,
Michael L. Dougherty, Daniel S. Fogel,
Sarah E. Fredericks, Tirso Gonzales,
Willis Jenkins, Louis Kotzé, Chris Laszlo,
Jingjing Liu, Stephen Morse,
John Copeland Nagle, Bruce Pardy,
Sony Pellissery, J.B. Ruhl, Oswald J. Schmitz,
Lei Shen, William K. Smith, Ian Spellerberg,
Shirley Thompson, Daniel E. Vasey,
Gernot Wagner, Peter J. Whitehouse

Editors

10 VOLUMES • 978-1-933782-01-0
Price: US$1800 • 6,084 pages • 8½ × 11"

"This is undoubtedly the most important and readable reference on sustainability of our time"

—Jim MacNeill, Secretary-General of the Brundtland Commission and chief architect and lead author of *Our Common Future* (1984–1987)

"The call we made in *Our Common Future*, back in 1987, is even more relevant today. Having a coherent resource like the *Encyclopedia of Sustainability*, written by experts yet addressed to students and general readers, is a vital step, because it will support education, enable productive debate, and encourage informed public participation as we join, again and again, in the effort to transform our common future."

—Gro Harlem Brundtland, chair of the World Commission on Environment and Development and three-time prime minister of Norway

Praise for Berkshire's "This World Of Ours" series

This Is America: A Short History of the United States is the latest in Berkshire's "This World Of Ours" series, acclaimed by some of the world's leading scholars. *This Fleeting World: A Short History of Humanity*, the first in the series, was praised by Bill Gates, founder of Microsoft and author of *The Road Ahead*. The books tackle big subjects such as China, America, Islam, sports, environmental history, and Africa—even the universe—in about a hundred pages. Each book is designed to be read in one or two sittings.

This Is China

"It is hard to imagine that such a short book can cover such a vast span of time and space. *This Is China: The First 5,000 Years* will help teachers, students, and general readers alike, as they seek for a preliminary guide to the contexts and complexities of Chinese culture."

> Jonathan Spence, professor of history,
> Yale University; author of
> *The Search for Modern China*

This Fleeting World

"I first became an avid student of David Christian by watching his course on DVD, and so I am very happy to see his enlightening presentation of the world's history captured in *This Fleeting World*. I hope it will introduce a wider audience to this gifted scientist and teacher."

> Bill Gates, founder of Microsoft

This Is Islam

"*This Is Islam* provides interested general readers and students with a concise but remarkably comprehensive introduction to Islam. It is a clearly presented guide that provides both a broad overview and important specifics in a way that is easy for both experts and non-specialists to use."

> John Voll, professor of Islamic history,
> Georgetown University

Forthcoming titles in the series include *This Good Earth: A Short History of Human Impact on the Natural World*, *This Sporting World*, and *This Is Africa*.

www.ingramcontent.com/pod-product-compliance
Lightning Source LLC
Chambersburg PA
CBHW080423270326
41929CB00018B/3135